QUEEN VICTORIA, 1857

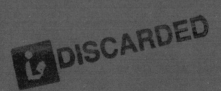

THE QUEEN'S CHOICE

The National Capital Commission

Issued under the authority of
The Honourable David J. Walker, P.C., Q.C., M.P.
Minister of Public Works

A STORY OF CANADA'S CAPITAL BY WILFRID EGGLESTON

THE QUEEN'S CHOICE

OTTAWA, 1961

Roger Duhamel, F.R.S.C.
Queen's Printer and Controller of Stationery
Ottawa, 1961

Price $6.00   *Cat. No. W 93–261F*

Contents

CHAPTER ONE

From the Highest Tower

The soul of a city—where is it to be sought? A Chancellor of Manchester University, a nobleman who had been an active traveller in his youth, once attempted an answer to this question, illustrating his theme by the great cities of the world he had known. He said that he had made a practice of climbing the highest tower in every foreign town when he visited it for the first time, in order to see its pattern and sense its character.

"Much can be learned from these high places," he wrote, "though only physical aspects present themselves to the eye. Roofs are eloquent and do not always withhold a glimpse of an interior; but broadly speaking the guidance one receives from these high-level surveys is general in nature—the scale of the city, the sweep of its river, the pulse of its arteries—those ruling features, be they symbols of religion, warfare, commerce, or seafaring, which control the destiny or govern the sentiment of a community."

The Earl of Crawford and Balcarres, who wrote those lines, would have found in the Canadian capital a tower eminently suitable for his purpose. From the balconies near the summit of Ottawa's soaring Peace Tower he could have learned much—"the scale of the city, the sweep of its river, the pulse of its arteries." The anatomy of the Canadian capital would have been exposed on all sides, and at his feet, all around the Tower, he would have found its symbolic core.

The spectator of today makes his way to the high balconies of the Peace Tower by a devious but fascinating route. He enters the Parliament Building through the great Gothic arch of the main entrance, climbs marble steps to Confederation Hall, turns right or left to another set of stairs, comes to the impressive ironwork grill leading to the Memorial Chamber, takes a leisurely elevator half way up the tower, and makes a short detour to a second elevator. This in turn gives access to the four balconies of the tower, at a point two hundred feet above the base, and three hundred and sixty feet above the Ottawa River. In his ascent, he has left behind him the high vaulted ceiling of the Memorial Chamber, the carillonneur's private studio, the carillonneur's console, and the fifty-three bells of the carillon. He stands at the lower rim of the great clock faces: still above him soars the clock, the framework of carved stone above the clock, the steep copper roof, the four posts at the very summit, and the stout flagstaff which supports the flapping Red Ensign, as high above him still as a ten-storey office building. From the four balconies just below the clock he can survey in turn the whole breath-taking panorama of the National Capital Region, which in any season presents one of the finest views in the world.

The dominant feature of this view is the great river from which the capital of Canada takes its name. The Ottawa River flows toward the city out of the far west and the north-west, from the Precambrian Shield, from a lonely land of ancient rock and jagged pine, from the haunt of the loon and the whip-poorwill, the elk and the moose, the wild goose and the bluejay. By the time it reaches Canada's capital city, the Ottawa has tumbled six hundred miles from the height of land, collecting the waters of noble tributaries from north and south; it is still a hundred miles away from its junction with the St. Lawrence, still three hundred miles short of tidewater, and the storied Gulf. As it approaches Parliament Hill it pours over the Chaudière Falls in restrained fury and then winds more tranquilly around the limestone cliffs on which Parliament Hill is based.

The capital region is a network of waterways, as we can well see from our vantage point. It is a grand "meeting place of the waters". We can look down on the eight entrance locks of the Rideau Canal, the northern terminus of a 125 mile waterway which enters the city limits below Black Rapids and bisects the heart of the capital region. On a clear day in winter we can trace the separate flow of the Rideau River, as it parts from the Canal at Hog's Back and meanders lazily along to the limestone cliffs a mile or so to the east, where it shimmers down in a 40 foot double curtain. The Rideau Falls excited the admiration of Samuel de Champlain in 1613, and can be admired today from a charming little park between the French Embassy and the National Research Council's headquarters building.

The north shore of the Ottawa, on the Quebec side of the river, is also broken by a network of streams. Brewery Creek is really a tiny arm of the river itself, which meanders through the city of Hull and makes an island of its downtown section. It rejoins the parent river a mile or two further along, directly across from the Rideau Falls. The downstream junction of Brewery Creek and the Ottawa River has been immortalized as a naturalist's paradise by Malcolm MacDonald, son of a British Prime Minister, who once wrote a delightful book about it, *The Birds of Brewery Creek*. From his wartime home at Earnscliffe, as High Commissioner for the United Kingdom, Malcolm MacDonald studied it as lovingly as Thoreau ever did Walden Pond, paddling across the Ottawa at daybreak all through the year while the river was open, crossing on skis and snowshoes during the winter months, compiling his charming calendar of the seasons. He could have said, with Thoreau, "How many mornings, summer and winter, before yet any neighbour was stirring about his business, have I been about mine." "I wonder," he wrote, "how many inhabitants of Ottawa realize that more than 170 species of birds can be found during the year in a small area on the edge of the city. It is charming to know that so near the East Block, where civil servants prepare Acts of Parliament, the love life of Spotted Sandpipers is also being enacted; that within spitting distance of diplomatic cocktail parties in Rockcliffe Park many kinds of Warblers, Vireos and Finches also hold their social gatherings; and that not far from the mumble of legislators' oratory on Parliament Hill can be heard too the querulous scream of the Yellow-bellied Sapsucker."

A little further east of the exit of Brewery Creek, still within easy glimpse of our observation post in the Peace Tower, another great tributary, the Gatineau, joins the Ottawa. This historic gateway into the Laurentian Mountains, for a century and a half a busy timber chute, now the site of hydro-electric plants generating over half a million horse power, likewise flows out of the mysterious north, and still links Ottawa with the unspoiled wilderness which is woven so intimately into Canada's early history.

2

What is this land which calls Ottawa its capital? "Canada is the water and the wood," sings James Wreford, that rare combination of poet and geographer, "it is the melting of winter snows down innumerable freshets, the sound of cataracts on turbulent streams, the gleam of countless lakes; the mantle of forest that reaches from coast to coast; a freshness and a wildness that occurs in every province and to which Canadians go back as a perennial source of inspiration." It is a happy circumstance that Ottawa, the national heart and symbol, was located in a part of Canada where these fine images are all highly appropriate.

Canada is a transcontinental country of such sweep and variety that no single region can offer a complete microcosm representing the whole. Yet the view of the topography, the revelation of the geology, visible from the Peace Tower gives a surprisingly rich sample of the land which is Canada. The view to the southward, east and west, is of a rich alluvial plain, still tree-canopied, the wide soil-mantled region which in post-glacial days was a great marine estuary. The Ottawa River Valley blends south-eastward into the St. Lawrence Lowlands, the wealthiest and most populous region in the whole of Canada. Across the Ottawa River to the north and west looms the solemn Precambrian Shield—containing some of the oldest rocks in the world—approaching almost to the doorstep of the city of Hull. The national capital region contains a rich sampling of its rocks, lakes, brilliant hardwoods, gloomy conifers. Only the Maritime tidewater, the high plains, the great peaks of the far west, are missing. From the Peace Tower we can see the Laurentian Mountains in rosy granite and variegated gneiss, similar geological formations to those which contain much of Canada's mineral wealth. The fine farms of the Ottawa Valley represent Canada's agricultural resources. The forests which at one time clothed the whole area still supply the rafts which float down streams piercing the capital region. Most of the varieties of native trees which constitute the large part of Canada's forest resources are still to be found within an easy drive of Ottawa. And the hydro-electric power which compensates for the lack of buried carboniferous fuels in the central region of Canada is abundantly developed on the Ottawa and the Gatineau.

Ottawa's climate, too, is typical of much of continental Canada. It lies in the path of "the everlasting sweep of circumpolar storm". Prevailing winds are north-west and south-west: fronts advancing from these quarters supply the dynamic surges of our weather systems. At times Ottawa steams in moist superheated air from the Gulf of Mexico: at others it shivers from polar currents sweeping down beneath hard sapphire skies. Spring is a swift sudden season and autumn a blaze of crimson and gold. Ottawa knows the humid languors of August and the sub-zero thrusts of January; and in between there are temperate and golden spells of weather with sufficient variety to be salubrious and interesting.

There is no better clue to a city's essential character than in the testimony of those who have loved it in times past. Archibald Lampman was one of these. He had the skill, too, to record his affection. In one of his newspaper columns, *At the Mermaid Inn*, contributed to the Toronto Globe in February, 1893, he confessed his sentiments:

"I have often been tempted to sing the praises of Ottawa—this city from which I write—not as a commercial city or as the seat of government, but as a site, as a most picturesque and wholesome foundation for the dwelling of men . . . I venture to say that Ottawa will become in the course of ages the Florence of Canada, if not of America, and the plain of the Ottawa its Val D'Arno. Old Vasari said that there was a certain 'air' in Florence which possessed a magical potency in exciting intellectual and imaginative energy. The great Florentine artists found that they could only produce their best at Florence. In other cities—even in Rome—they experienced a decline of power, which they could only attribute to the inferior quality of the atmosphere.

"I have noticed the same thing about Ottawa," Lampman reported. "Perched upon its crown of rock, a certain atmosphere flows about its walls, borne upon the breath of the prevailing north-west wind, an intellectual elixir, an oxygenic essence thrown off by immeasurable tracts of pine-clad mountain and crystal lake. In this air the mind becomes conscious of a vital energy and buoyant swiftness of movement rarely experienced in a like degree elsewhere."

3

Architects say that the cluster of Gothic buildings on Parliament Hill can be regarded as a fine flowering of the 'Romantic Revival' of Gothic architecture in the 19th century. It is the finest such group on the North American continent, and is irreproducible today.

The original buildings were constructed in the years 1859-76. The central Parliament Building itself was destroyed by fire in February, 1916; the present Centre Block or Parliament Building was built in the years 1916-27.

The original Parliament Building and the present Library of Parliament were designed by Thomas Fuller. The East and West Blocks were designed by Frederick Warburton Stent and Augustus Laver. The present Parliament Building and Peace Tower are the creation of John A. Pearson and J. O. Marchand. A study of the styles of the present buildings and of plans and drawings of the Block destroyed by fire brings out some interesting differences in current taste and in the genius of individual designers.

Gothic Architecture has no native roots, of course, in North America. It is a revival of a medieval European tradition. Its appropriateness for a new country, and the nature of its symbolic significance for Canada, are partly matters of individual opinion. The reason why Gothic was chosen is discussed later on in this book. A quick answer might be that the government buildings are Gothic because that was the fashion of the time; because a picturesque site called for a picturesque style; because the Canadian parliament was a daughter of the Mother of Parliaments, and because its architecture inevitably drew inspiration from The Palace of Westminster erected a decade earlier.

Are there deeper reasons why Gothic was chosen? Some commentators have thought so. William Wilfred Campbell, the Canadian poet, thought that Gothic was 'the highest expression of man's aspirations', that the buildings served to reveal to descendants of French and British peoples their common ancestry, their common artistic sense, and their common Christianity.

Why Gothic rather than Classical or Italian? Was it because the Canadians are a northern people, descendants of Norsemen and Normans? Does Gothic better express a national temperament with serious and even austere overtones? The lines of Gothic architecture point skyward. An American tourist paused at the main gate to Parliament Hill and asked a bystander: "What is the name of that cathedral?" The *original* Centre Block reflected a more playful, more jocund mood perhaps. A comparison suggests a sterner, grander, aspect in John Pearson's 1916 creation. Perhaps it is necessary to recall the grim and sacrificial years of the First World War. Something precious was lost, certainly, when the original building burned down, but there were gains of another sort.

Dr. R. H. Hubbard writes that the original Centre Block shows "the influence of the Oxford Museum, begun in 1855 by Deane and Woodward with a prayer from Ruskin. Both designs had chapter houses—at Ottawa this became a Library; both had 'chromatic' or 'Venetic' stonework from Italy. Fuller's building also had towers from Germany and roofs from France; and its front was dignified by rows of very pointed windows and a tower which reflected his study of the Cloth Hall at Ypres." Jacques Gréber (Ottawa's venerable planner) feels that the original building was more consistent with the genius of Gothic. The present Centre Block, he feels, is somewhat severe. Certainly a deep affection developed for the old building, and there was a sense of desolation when it was destroyed by fire. In a letter to Pelham Edgar a few days after its destruction the poet Duncan Campbell Scott wrote:

"I hope that the building may be restored without the practice of any vandalism, but I have my doubts. I hear talk of 'a larger, more imposing, up-to-date building.' The very phrases make one shudder. We had a building that was beautiful and harmonized with the site, and there will be some people who will want to destroy it because they can put up some thing more beautiful. If they can put up a more beautiful building, let them put it up somewhere else. Let us preserve the beauty that we have."

But tastes differ. Alan Gowans praises the architectural purity of the present Centre Block, with its detail drawn more consistently from one period: "Few buildings, surely, exemplify the spirit of Gothic architecture as impressively as this soaring Peace Tower." It has inspired a memorable tribute from the author of *The Unknown Country*. "No Canadian can stand and look at this cluster of buildings, and let his eye follow the stern shaft of the Victory Tower upward to its ultimate spire," wrote Bruce Hutchison in 1944, "without feeling that somewhere on this Hill, perhaps by a happy accident, architects, masons and stone carvers have managed to grasp and materialize the beauty of Canada, the vastness of its land, its loneliness, its youth, and its hope."

4

The basic plan of the Parliament Building is simple. The central stem extends northward from the richly-carved Main Entrance to Confederation Hall, along the Court of Honour to the Parliamentary Library, in a straight line several hundred feet long. In general, the West half of the Building, divided by this grand corridor, is the House of Commons part; the East half is the Senate part. The division is not exact: for example the largest Commons committee room is in the East half of the building. But to a considerable extent there are dual offices and facilities: one wing contains the suite of the Speaker of the Commons, the other the suite of the Speaker of the Senate; so with the Clerks; the Sergeant-at-Arms has his office in the West wing; the Gentleman Usher of the Black Rod, his opposite number in the Senate, in the East wing, and so on. There are two Reading rooms, there are Commons Committee rooms, and Senate Committee rooms; and in the main the members' offices of the Commons are in the West wing and those of the Senate in the East wing.

The term 'House of Commons' was taken over from Westminster and is so rich in connotative associations that any change is inconceivable. It is not, however, strictly applicable to the Canadian chamber. There are no Estates of the 'Lords Spiritual and Temporal' in Canada, therefore, no 'Commoners' in that sense. Our House of Commons is the body of *elected* representatives of the people: the Senate is the body of *appointed* representatives. With universal suffrage and triumph of the democratic system in the 19th century our 'House of Commons' has become the supreme, though certainly not the exclusive, symbol of national sovereignty. In constitutional theory the Senate, the House of Commons, and the Queen together form the federal government of Canada.

The House of Commons occupies the largest Chamber in the Parliament Building: its floor space is 72 feet by 54 feet, and the ceiling is 50 feet high. The Galleries accommodate 600 persons. The floor of the Chamber comfortably seats the present representation of 265 members. The Press Gallery is at the North end of the Chamber. The doors are of Canadian white oak finished in gold colour, and trimmed with hand-wrought steel. The ceiling of the Chamber is of Irish linen, hand painted after it was put into place. The cornice is of gold leaf.

The Speaker's Chair is an exact replica of the chair in the British House of Commons at Westminster, as designed by Augustus Pugin (1812-52) and as installed in that building in 1844. Above the Chair the Royal Coat of Arms is carved, the oak being of great antiquity, having been at one time a part of the roof of Westminster Hall, erected in 1397 in the reign of Richard II. This Chair was a gift of the United Kingdom Branch of the Empire Parliamentary Association. It was accepted in a ceremony on May 20th, 1921, the presentation being made by a former Speaker of the British House, Rt. Hon. James W. Lowther. It is an interesting historical fact that at Westminster, from the original of this Chair, the fateful motion was put in March, 1867 which enacted the British North America Act and thus brought into being the Dominion of Canada.

When the House of Commons is in session, when the Speaker is in The Chair, the spectators in the Gallery will see the Mace resting on the Clerk's Table in front. The Mace has an interesting background. The fire of 1916 broke out so suddenly and fiercely that the Chamber was cleared at once, and the original Mace was abandoned to the flames. The old Mace was a facsimile of that used in the British House of Commons, and was obtained in 1845, when Sir Allan MacNab was Speaker of the Legislature of the United Province of Canada, while Montreal was the provincial capital. When rioters burned down the Buildings in 1849, the Mace was seized by a leader of the assault, who struck down the Sergeant-At-Arms with an axe-handle. When the riot leader sought to make off with the symbol of power, intending to destroy it in a public place, two young citizens of Montreal thwarted his attempt, taking it from him by force, and carrying it to Sir Allan MacNab. It was in its proper place when the Legislature assembled again in Toronto: it 'ambulated' from 1849 to 1865 as the capital of Canada moved back and forth between Toronto and Quebec City, and it was resting on the Clerk's table at Ottawa on that November day in 1867 when the first Parliament of the Dominion convened.

In the fire of February 3rd, 1916, this historic Mace was lost. When the ruins had cooled down, and could be probed, all that was found was a ball of gold and silver and other ingredients melted down into a lump of alloy. The Senate Mace was borrowed for the resumed sittings of the House of Commons in temporary quarters in the Victoria Museum. When word of the loss reached the other side of the Atlantic, the Sheriffs of the City of London, joined by Sir George Perley, High Commissioner for Canada in London, cabled an offer to replace it, and the Lord Mayor of London presented the new Mace to Sir Robert Borden later on in the year.

The House of Commons is a spectacle of endless interest. Granted that there are long periods of routine and even tedium, over the years no theatre addict has ever occupied so choice a seat as a reporter in the Press Gallery. This Chamber, and its predecessor before the fire of 1916, have seen and heard the reflection at least of almost every consequential Canadian event since 1866. All the great federal politicians and statesmen have played their parts in it. They have orated, debated, triumphed, been laughed down, been thwarted, been vindicated.

Here Sir John A. Macdonald wove his spell of colloquial magic on his followers; here Alexander Mackenzie displayed the intellectual integrity of a master craftsman; here Sir Wilfrid Laurier held the House in thrall with his Gallic grace; here Sir Robert Borden grew in gruff majesty of character; here Arthur Meighen dazzled the House with analytical brilliance; here the enigmatic roly-poly personality of Mackenzie King confounded in time all his critics and belittlers; here R. B. Bennett (later Viscount Bennett) raked his opponents fore and aft with devastating fluency; here Louis St. Laurent introduced a courtly nobility and a sweet reasonableness; here John Diefenbaker skilfully brought down a regime which seemed destined to go on forever, and moved across to the supreme triumph of the government benches.

It was here, too, as the historians tell, in the Chamber which fire destroyed, that D'Arcy McGee made what some thought his finest speech and then stepped out into the April night to a fateful rendezvous with an assassin's bullet; here that Lucius Seth Huntingdon arose to demand the inquiry out of which the "Pacific Scandal" emerged; here Louis Riel's execution was debated; here Tilley as Minister of Finance introduced the famous 'National Policy' budget; here Mackenzie Bowell found himself trapped in a "Nest of Traitors"; here the House of Commons abruptly adjourned a 1916 debate on the Fisheries estimates at the frantic call of "Fire" from the Commons entrance; here the constitutional crisis of 1926 arose, after the vote of a disregarded 'pair' had brought down the brief Meighen-Drayton regime; here Mackenzie King's famous 'five cent' speech virtually guaranteed his party's defeat at the next election; here the Liberals entered the 'Valley of Humiliation'; here in lonely and obstinate adherence to his pacifist convictions J. S. Woodsworth voted against a declaration of war in 1939; here the mild and constitutional statesman M. J. Coldwell ran across the floor of the House and shook his fist at the Speaker during the Pipeline Debate.

The Senate Chamber is smaller, richer, more exquisitely appointed than the dignified legislative hall of the Commons. Its crimson carpet, red leather chairs, gold-leaf outlines of the glass ceiling, its wealth of symbolic devices and emblems, its haunting murals of the First World War, its embroidered canopy over the Throne chair, combine to make it the most sumptuous ceremonial hall in Canada. Its seating capacity is about half that of the Green Chamber. It is a jewel-like setting for the great ceremonial and social gatherings of the Canadian capital. The reigning Queen has opened Parliament here; the Drawing Room of Their Excellencies was held in it; here the solemn ritual of the confederation of Newfoundland was consummated; in it the premiers of all the provinces have sat with the federal government in historic parley. Its entrance hall is devoted to royal portraits. At the bar, when Parliament is summoned, the members of the House of Commons, led by their Speaker, assemble to hear the Governor General read the Speech from the Throne.

The Senate as legislative body is short on histrionics and long on experience and political sagacity. No administrations are created or destroyed in the Red Chamber, no governments rise and fall there; no division can end a regime; no votes are courted or converts won. The Senate is not a drawing card for the public and the press, and some observers mistake quiet dignity for inaction. Everyone discusses Senate Reform and no one would pretend that the institution could not be improved. But talk of abolition is inadequately informed: the Senate is solidly imbedded in the Constitution, and it has a valuable role to play in federal government. The average level of law-making capacity in the Senate is high; its years of experience many; its scrutiny of legislation invaluable; and its independent investigations a useful supplement to the work of the Commons.

5

The Parliamentary Library is unique in its architecture and, "for all its wedding-cake ornateness," Dr. R. H. Hubbard thinks, "is probably the most graceful building of its period." Treating the Centre Block in the spirit of a medieval cathedral, Thomas Fuller attached to it the kind of Chapter House as is found beside a number of the great English cathedrals and collegiate churches. The Chapter House was commonly polygonal in form and linked to the cathedral proper by a connecting covered passage: it was the council house for the chapter of canons associated with it. Fuller was familiar with the octagonal chapter houses of Westminster, Wells and Salisbury Cathedral: he seems also to have drawn inspiration from the recently built University Museum of Oxford and the Reading Room of the British Museum. It was a happy decision, and gave Canada a building whose silhouette adds immeasurably to the view of the Parliament Building from Nepean Point and other vantage spots to the north. The dimensions of the Library and the mode of construction called for a high degree of engineering skill, and the use of such picturesque Gothic devices as the flying buttress. The diameter of the interior is about 140 feet, and the summit of the lantern rises almost as high, making it nearly forty feet higher than the venerable ceiling of Westminster Hall.

Fuller's decision to make the Library a separate building, connected by a corridor, is a detail that saved it in the fire of 1916. The metal doors between the two were closed just in time by M. C. MacCormac, one of the librarians, and the Ottawa firemen concentrated on saving the Library, once it became apparent that the Centre Block was doomed to be gutted. Loss in the Library itself was thus confined to water damage, though hundreds of volumes of periodicals and some other books stored in the Centre Block were lost.

Many celebrities of Canadian history have been nurtured in the Parliamentary Library. Obscure young men have browsed at the stacks unconscious of their high destiny. John Wesley Dafoe was one of these. Sixty years later he recalled that he often saw Charles Tupper the younger dipping into its treasures. The alcove devoted to French literature, he recalled, was frequented by a "youngish, kindly companionable man," who "was generally regarded as one whose career had not fulfilled its earlier promise." But appearances are often deceptive, for the year was 1884, and the "kindly companionable man" was Wilfrid Laurier.

A second fire, on August 4th, 1952, broke out in the library roof. Again it was water which caused the bulk of the damage. The 1952 fire led to a decision to take no further chances with this cherished landmark. The whole interior was reconstructed from the sub-basement upwards. All its original beauty was carefully restored. Over two million dollars was spent in the process, and it was four years after the fire before the library was re-opened.

6

The silhouette of Ottawa, approached from any direction, is dominated by the shaft of the Peace Tower, which rises 292 feet from the base, and whose flagstaff soars well above the 300 foot mark. As the base is 160 feet above the Ottawa River, this is the highest point in the entire capital region. The Peace Tower, as Jacques Gréber has pointed out, crowns the whole composition of the buildings on Parliament Hill, and "has the same meaning to Canadians that the dome of the Capitol in Washington has to Americans, or Big Ben to English people."

In the original building, before the fire of 1916, the central tower was not so prominent. Indeed, the old Tower of the Parliament Building itself was surpassed in height by the Mackenzie Tower of the West Block. The silhouette of the original cluster of buildings had been planned with great artistry, and some critics feared that the proposed new Peace Tower would impair the long cherished harmony of the Hill.

A first examination of the Parliament Building after the fire led to the proposal that it should be completely restored but not rebuilt. The exterior walls appeared to be in fair condition. The first report of John A. Pearson and J. O. Marchand, chosen as chief architects, recommended such a step. But further examination disclosed serious structural damage. There was the additional consideration that the old building had been seriously over-crowded. (The Holt Capital Planning Commission in 1915 had recommended an enlargement by extending wings from the east and west walls.) By September 1916 a contract had been entered into for the reconstruction of the building, one storey higher, in such a way as to add 50% to its original floor space.

The visitor to Ottawa today can read in the architecture of the Centre Block, especially in the severe proportions of the great tower, and in the Memorial Chamber, a reflection of the years of agony and national sacrifice during which this reconstruction took place. It was decided to make the new building a monument to the service and sacrifice of Canadians in the World War then indecisively raging. The tower was to be a symbol of Victory, or of Peace: there was to be a Memorial Chamber to commemorate the fallen. The tower was to be a campanile as well as a clock tower. The visitor today can trace these sentiments as they evolved. In Confederation Hall he will read an inscription dated July 1st, 1917, fifty years after Confederation, recording the dedication of the building, then in course of construction:

AS A MEMORIAL OF
THE DEEDS OF THEIR FOREFATHERS
AND OF THE VALOUR OF THOSE
CANADIANS
WHO IN THE GREAT WAR FOUGHT FOR THE
LIBERTIES OF CANADA
OF THE EMPIRE
AND OF
HUMANITY

The corner stone of the tower itself was laid by the Prince of Wales on September 1st, 1919. The tower was completed for dedication at the Diamond Jubilee ceremonies on July 1st, 1927.

7

Many famous monuments and memorials are impressive from their sheer size. The location of Canada's Memorial Chamber within the Tower limited its floor dimensions to twenty-four feet square. How to create within this narrow space a worthy arcanum for its high purpose was a great challenge to the architects and designers. That they succeeded so well is itself a miracle. "Infinite riches in a little room"—was Christopher Marlowe's phrase ever more apt? The inspired prose and poetry of English literature were rifled for its inscriptions; the whole story of Canada's participation in the First World War is carved on its walls. The very stones embedded in the floor come from the French and Belgian battlefields, whose names are so redolent of glory and agony for an earlier generation. The chapel walls rise to the fan tracery of the vaulted dome forty-seven feet above the base of the great stone that is the Altar of Remembrance. On the altars rest the two Books of Remembrance —the golden books in which in illuminated script is the name of every Canadian who fell in those dreadful days, of 1914-18 and 1939-45. Throughout the year, in calculated sequence, a new page is turned, so that every name in it is open to the eye of the observer once every year.

It is little better than a travesty to condense a description of this exquisite and storied Chamber into a few lines. There is no adequate substitute for the pilgrim—he must see it for himself. It has been called "the holiest spot on Canadian soil". On the walls, sharing place of honor with noble lines from Pericles' Funeral Oration, from the New Testament, from Bunyan and Binyon and McCrae, this text serves as a solemn invitation:

READ HOW FREE MEN THROUGHOUT THIS LAND
KEPT FAITH IN THE HOUR OF TRIAL, AND
IN THE DAY OF BATTLE, REMEMBERING THE
TRADITIONS THEY HAD BEEN TAUGHT, COUNTING
LIFE NOTHING WITHOUT LIBERTY

8

The Peace Tower was designed to be the crowning feature of the newly constructed Houses of Parliament, when it was completed in 1927. In Mackenzie King's words at the inauguration of the Carillon, on July 1st, 1927, "the idea was one alike of beauty and vision." Its flagstaff was the highest point in the national capital. Ever since then a powerful light has radiated out to the world from the top of the bronze flagpole whenever the House was sitting. And the light is extinguished every night when the session adjourns. Just below the summit of the tower, four clock faces nearly sixteen feet in diameter are visible day and night for great distances around. The hour and the quarters are struck upon great bells of the tower. So it is at once a clock tower, and a bell tower, and a carillon tower, as well as a memorial, and the sacred setting of the Chapel of Remembrance.

The story of the tower was recalled in eloquent and poetic terms by the Prime Minister of the day, W. L. Mackenzie King, during the Diamond Jubilee celebrations, when for the first time through the magic of radio broadcasting the people of Canada could share in the ceremonial, and hear the message of the bells.

Reconstruction after the great fire of 1916 was well under way when the Armistice of 1918 was signed, Mackenzie King recalled on that occasion. The main tower was dedicated as a memorial to the Peace. As the Tower of Victory, it was to crown the work of the builders. "Having decided to reproduce at Ottawa the chimes at Westminster," Mr. Mackenzie King said, "the government next gave careful consideration to the larger project of installing a carillon."

"Mr. Frederick C. Mayer, the greatest living authority on carillons, who had just completed a survey of the carillons of the world, was invited to come to Ottawa to advise on the project. When Mr. Mayer saw the Peace Tower, viewed its commanding position, and the wide open spaces by which it is surrounded, he grew enthusiastic over its possibilities, and became emphatic, in such a setting, the Government had it within its power to secure for the people of Canada what would prove to be the finest carillon in the world."

By a happy coincidence, a native of Toronto, and the first Canadian in history to graduate from the Mechlin Carillon School in Belgium, was available for appointment as the first Dominion Carillonneur. Percival Price was succeeded by the present carillonneur, Robert Donnell, in 1939.

There are 53 bells in the carillon, with a range of 4½ octaves. The largest bell, the Bourdon, weighs 22,400 lbs., and the smallest weighs ten lbs. The Bourdon conveys the spirit of the Tower in the inscription carried on its rim: Glory to God in the Highest and on Earth Peace, Goodwill Toward Men.

"Such is the message of the carillon," said the Prime Minister at the dedication in 1927. "A message of rejoicing and thanksgiving known in Biblical lore as 'The Angel's Song'. It was heard from the skies nearly twenty centuries ago by a few shepherds who watched their flocks by night.

"Back to the skies it returns at noon today, not the echo of a mystical strain heard on a Judean moor, but the voice of a nation in thanksgiving and praise which will sound over land and sea to the uttermost parts of the earth, and which, in the course of time, from the place where we are now assembled, may yet be borne down the centuries to come."

9

The statues erected on Parliament Hill provide a brief rollcall of the Canadian statesmen whom succeeding governments have most desired to honor in bronze and stone. A tourist may welcome a few words of identification and background. During the Second World War an eminent London lawyer came back from a stroll around the Buildings and put this question to several Canadians in turn: "You have a statue up there bearing the simple name BROWN: nothing more; who was he?" No one could help him! And a friend of mine once heard a French-speaking Canadian and an immigrant Italian arguing with spirit before the statue of CARTIER, the ironical point at issue being,—was it a Frenchman or an Italian who first discovered Canada?!

There are two pre-confederation figures on Parliament Hill,—Robert Baldwin and Sir Louis H. Lafontaine, who are honored as the architects of responsible government—really popular government—in the 1840's.

There are also four Fathers of Confederation; and three Prime Ministers who have held office since Confederation.

Sir John A. Macdonald, self-styled 'cabinet-maker', the 'Wizard of the North', 'Old Tomorrow', was a relatively late convert to Confederation, but he was our first Prime Minister, a great nation-builder, and no one will now dispute his right to pride of place.

Sir George Etienne Cartier was the opposite number of Macdonald in French-speaking Canada. "But for him Confederation could not have been carried," as Macdonald testified.

Hon. George Brown, "Big George", Reform leader of Canada West, eminent editor, broke a political *impasse* in 1864 by a statesmanlike gesture which led directly to the Charlottetown and Quebec Conferences, and thus to federal union.

Hon. Thomas D'Arcy McGee, poet and prophet of Confederation, was doomed to be its martyr also.

The three prime ministers since 1867, singled out for political immortality (and chosen from the twelve who followed Macdonald), are these:

Hon. Alexander Mackenzie, the honest stone-mason.

Sir Wilfrid Laurier, the Plumed Knight with the silver tongue.

Sir Robert Borden. ("His stature rises as the perspective lengthens").

There will be others erected some day. Any one who reads the story of federation with an acute eye must wonder why Sir Alexander Galt has so far been passed over: he was the master-craftsman of fiscal ways and means, he blue-printed the terms of union, and perhaps he saw earlier than any one else exactly how such a union could be consummated.

The statue of one imperial monarch towers a few feet above the memorials to all these Canadian statesman. Queen Victoria, with crown and sceptre, guarded by a watchful lion, is there to remind us who sat on the throne when Canada was united into a Dominion "with a constitution similar in principle to that of the United Kingdom."

Just east of the Main Entrance on Wellington Street, not on the Hill but of it in spirit, stands a statue of Sir Galahad, commemorating the gallant act of Henry Harper, a civil servant who gave his life on December 6th, 1901, in a vain attempt to save a fellow-skater, Miss Bessie Blair, from drowning in the icy waters of the Ottawa.

10

The entrances and exits of Parliament Hill abut on Wellington Street. This public avenue, which Jacques Gréber calls a "monumental artery", is exactly as old as Bytown, dating from October 1826. Considering that it forms a sort of esplanade for the symbolic core of parliamentary Canada, it is a pity it was not made much wider. Still, we should be grateful that Colonel John By, who could not be expected to foresee the Parliament Buildings, insisted that it be made 99 feet wide instead of 66. Wellington Street begins at Confederation Square, and its straight sweep westward extends only eight blocks. It is pinched off at the western extremity by a bay of the Ottawa River, and is forced to curve off to the southwest, where it is joined by Sparks Street in an acute angle. This monumental portion of Wellington Street being so short, the utmost advantage needs to be taken of it. When the government buildings began to overflow Parliament Hill, Wellington Street was an obvious site for additional offices. The Langevin Block, which occupies the south side of Wellington between Elgin and Metcalfe, was originally thought of as an integral part of the cluster on the Hill. It was called the Southern Departmental Block, to round out the group otherwise composed of the Eastern Departmental Block, the Western Departmental Block, and the Centre Block or Parliament Building.

The Holt Commission in 1915 foresaw a great expansion of government buildings, and strongly urged that they be located along two main routes, each of them overlooking the Ottawa River. One was Wellington Street, west of Parliament Hill, the other was Sussex Street, especially the west side of it, looking toward the limestone cliffs.

As we walk along Wellington Street westward from the Parliament Buildings, we can see how one of these old plans is being impressively realized, with much yet to be done. Beginning about 1929 a series of departmental blocks and government buildings were erected on the cliffs and plateaus west of the Parliament Buildings, adjacent to Wellington Street and between it and the River. On the right or north side of Wellington, as we walk westward, we come first to the Confederation Building, then to the Justice Building. The Supreme Court Building is set back impressively above the Ottawa River. Three large "temporary" buildings, constructed during the war, still occupy most of the available space up to the point where Wellington is bent southwestward by the angle of cliffs above the Ottawa. When they are demolished the site will be available for the National Library, for two or three smaller buildings, and for a monumental Mall running parallel to Wellington and striking Bank Street at about the axis of the Mackenzie Tower on the East Block.

On the south side of Wellington, west from the Langevin Block, there is the historic Rideau Club, the United States Embassy, some office buildings, the Bank of Canada, and then two more massive government buildings, erected since the end of the Second World War, housing the Department of Trade and Commerce and the Department of Veterans Affairs. The triangle created by the merging of Wellington Street and Sparks Street is currently being converted into a public park. Those who remember the ignoble scatter of commercial buildings in the Wellington-Sparks-Cliff Street area before the reconstruction began are aware what a great improvement has been made there in thirty years.

Another principal axis is still in the making along what is now called Sussex Drive.

Sussex Street was only a few yards long when Wellington Street was established in 1826-7 as the principal thoroughfare of Upper Town. Rideau Hall began as a private home in the heart of "MacKay's Bush", and at first little more than a bush trail connected it with Bytown. The lease and then the purchase of Rideau Hall for a viceregal residence in the 1860's focused public attention on the route between it and Parliament Hill. At Confederation the track or trail between the two was in an execrable state most of the time. Viscount Monck found it expedient at times to proceed by boat from the foot of Governor's Bay on the Ottawa, to the landing below Parliament Hill. The desirability of a grand ceremonial boulevard between Government House and the Parliament Building was obvious enough, but for forty years it remained only an idea, and successive incumbents of Rideau Hall grumbled in private if not in public at the state of the roads and bridges. The first serious proposal to make Sussex Street part of an attractive driveway for the Viceregal processionals was advanced at about the turn of the century. The Ottawa Improvement Commission (created in 1899) built King Edward Avenue as one of its first projects, and some planners thought King Edward Avenue should be made part of a formal route beween Rideau Hall and Parliament Hill. But Frederick G. Todd, the landscape architect, rejected this proposal, on the ground that such a route involved the use for half a mile of busy Rideau Street, with its street cars and heavy commercial traffic. Todd saw the dazzling possibility of using an alternative route along the Ottawa river bank, and thus making a drive "grandly characteristic of the city." "I believe," he added, "that if properly carried out such a boulevard would become famous the world over for its picturesque beauty and the magnificence and extent of its views." The only immediate consequence of Todd's recommendation was the half-hearted and faulty construction of Lady Grey Drive. In the past decade, however, considerable progress has been made in realizing the dream first conceived and promoted by Frederick Todd.

A visitor who explores the present Sussex Drive, and the parks and buildings between it and the Ottawa River will find many historic and attractive scenes. The route for a pedestrian might begin at the East Entrance to the Parliament Buildings, turn east to the corner of the Chateau Laurier, north along Mackenzie Avenue, across Major's Hill Park, to Nepean Point, and then along Sussex Drive over the Rideau River bridges and as far as Rideau Gate and the entrance to Rockcliffe Park.

On the right, as we proceed east on Wellington Street, lies Confederation Square or Place, dominated by the impressive War Memorial which commemorates those Canadians who served and fell in the First World War.

A few yards further east we cross over the Rideau Canal, and can look down over the parapet on the 'staircase' of locks. This is a flight of eight, which lifts boats from the level of the Ottawa River to the elevation of the city plateau, and permits them to navigate without further barrier as far as Hartwell's Locks, opposite Carleton University, nearly four miles away. The parapet of this bridge draws many spectators, to watch vessels being 'locked through', or to admire on the northern horizon the blue-grey line of the Laurentian Hills. Down to the left, half way up the flight of locks, is the oldest building in Ottawa, the engineers' storehouse in which the Historical Society of Ottawa now houses its rich collection.

The spires and towers of the Chateau Laurier capture some of the glamour of a child's book of fairy tales: they are best seen from a distance, from the broad walk in front of the Peace Tower, or from Elgin Street beside the National Gallery. The Chateau Laurier was designed in 1910 by D. H. Mac-Farlane. The south end of Major's Hill Park, which originally extended right up to the Rideau Canal Bridge, was conveyed to the Grand Trunk Railway company to provide its site, amid much public criticism. The construction of the Chateau Laurier provided Ottawa with attractive architecture as well as a fine hostelry, but it did tend to cut off Major's Hill Park from the centre of the city. Colonel By's residence once stood near the centre of this park, affording from its verandah what Joseph Bouchette, Surveyor General of Lower Canada, called the finest view in the province. The ceremony of 'firing the noon-day gun' takes place in Major's Hill Park. This is an event of some antiquity, in North American scales of time. An order-in-council of March 6th, 1869, reported that "it would be a great convenience to every one connected with the Public Service, and to the citizens of Ottawa generally, if the true time were made known to the public by the firing of a 12 o'clock gun." A nine-pounder iron gun was obtained from the Imperial Military Forces, and the first shot was fired on April 26th, 1869, on a signal conveyed by 'magnetic telegraph' from the McGill College Observatory at Montreal. For over 90 years the firing of the cannon has echoed across Entrance Bay and has startled casual strollers on Parliament Hill.

Hamilton MacCarthy's fine monument to Samuel de Champlain occupies a prominent site on Nepean Point. The famous explorer is seen facing toward Parliament Hill across the bay he first explored in June, 1613, his right hand holding a replica of the astrolabe which was lost a few days later sixty miles upstream, and found again in 1867 by a farm boy helping his father to clear land.

North-east of the Champlain monument, between Lady Grey Drive and Sussex Drive, there are two stone buildings of uncommon interest. The first houses the Public Archives of Canada, an indispensible treasure house of

Canadian history, dedicated to Joseph Howe's noble injunction: "A wise nation preserves its records, gathers up its muniments, decorates the tombs of its illustrious dead, repairs its great public structures, and fosters national pride and love of country, by perpetual reference to the sacrifices and glories of the past." Adjoining it to the north is the castellated almost prison-like stone structure housing the Royal Canadian Mint.

Half a mile beyond the Royal Canadian Mint, Lady Grey Drive rejoins Sussex Drive, and just north of the junction, on the banks of the Ottawa, we see one of Ottawa's historic residences, Earnscliffe, now the home of the High Commissioner for the United Kingdom, once the residence of Canada's first prime minister, Sir John A. Macdonald. In one of its bedrooms the great Canadian statesman died on June 6th, 1891.

Across Earnscliffe Avenue, also on the commanding cliffs above the River, we see the neo-classic columns and pediments of the National Research Council's head office. This is the 'mother house' of scores of laboratories and research centres scattered about the city and across Canada.

North-east of the NRC building the Rideau River's two branches, separated by Green Island, make their picturesque leap into the Ottawa. Not so many years ago this area was a bleak confusion of lumber mills and factory yards, completely obscuring or destroying the effect of the scenic cascades which once caught Champlain's eye, and delighted generations of voyageurs along the Ottawa into the great North-West. Its restoration into a public park is one of the striking achievements of recent years. Adding greatly to the architectural distinction of the area is the new Ottawa City Hall, on Green Island, which illustrates the passion of the modern architect for "free-flowing space and flooding light."

In a young capital where architectural distinction is still rare the elegance and grace of the French Embassy, across the street from the Rideau Falls Park, make an indelible impression. It was the first Embassy building built for that express purpose in Ottawa, and it set a noble example for other countries to follow.

A few hundred feet further along the cliff above the Ottawa River the official residence of the Prime Minister of Canada also enjoys a breath-taking view to the north and west. This was the home of one of Ottawa's prominent lumber 'kings'; then undistinguished for its architecture, but since remodelled by the Canadian government in closer harmony with its magnificent setting and its official purpose.

Sussex Drive comes to an end a few feet further on in a sort of dual gateway. To the right is the Lodge leading into Government House Grounds; to the left the driveway enters Rockcliffe Park, which even a half century ago possessed — as Frederick Todd saw it — "such picturesqueness, such magnificent views, such variety of landscape and waterscape as to make a park of very unusual beauty."

12

In the Ottawa Valley scale of time, Rideau Hall is a residence of respectable age. It dates back to the middle 1830's, and was originally built by Thomas MacKay, the Scottish stone mason and contractor who became a leading citizen of Bytown and New Edinburgh. When MacKay died in 1855, it was an interesting well-built family home of eleven rooms, locally known as "MacKay's Castle", and situated in the heart of "MacKay's Bush". Ten years later the provincial government leased the house and over eighty acres of land around it in preparation for the arrival of the Governor General, Viscount Monck, and his entourage. Shortly after Confederation the new Dominion Government purchased house and land from the MacKay estate, and made extensive alterations and improvements.

Some vice-regal history can be traced in the series of expansions. In 1868, in preparation for Lord and Lady Lisgar, a new wing was added, a conservatory and the entrance lodge were built. In the winter of 1872-3, the beautifully-proportioned ballroom was added. Three hundred guests were present when Lord and Lady Dufferin entertained in it for the first time, with a play staged by the Vice-Regal family and household staff, followed by music and supper. In 1878, very extensive additions and improvements were made to prepare for the arrival of a royal chatelaine, the Princess Louise, daughter of Queen Victoria, and wife of the Marquis of Lorne. In 1910, for a second royal tenant, the Duke of Connaught, son of Queen Victoria, further extensions were made. The whole facade was rebuilt and an entrance of classical style was crowned with the royal coat of arms, sculptured in stone.

A chapel was built and an organ installed during the tenure of the Earl of Aberdeen (1893-98). A panelled study was added by Earl Grey. Lord and Lady Byng (1921-26) supervised the building of a rock garden. A beautiful Chinese room was furnished by Lord and Lady Willingdon (1926-31).

There have been nineteen Governors-General since Confederation. The first native-born Canadian to be named to the high office was the Rt. Hon. Vincent Massey, on February 28, 1952. The break with the older tradition was confirmed by the appointment of Major General Georges Vanier, a native of Montreal, who assumed office on September 15, 1959.

In contrast with the eleven rooms of MacKay's original "Castle", the present Rideau Hall contains sixty rooms. Fifty guests can be seated in the dining room, and at State dinners the ballroom will seat 150 persons.

The grounds surrounding Rideau Hall are laid out in the style of an English park. There is history also in the spacious vice-regal estate, once part of Thomas MacKay's 1100 acre holdings on both sides of the Rideau River. Ceremonial tree-plantings in the park began in 1906, when Prince Arthur of Connaught planted a red oak tree, which now stands over sixty feet high. The reigning Queen Elizabeth planted a ten-foot sugar maple on the grounds when she came to Ottawa as Princess Elizabeth in 1951; and in 1957, as reigning sovereign, she planted a red maple. Her father and mother planted a tree there in 1939. Famous names perpetuated in the tree-planting ceremonies have included Stanley Baldwin, President Truman, President Eisenhower, and Emperor Haile Selassie of Ethiopia.

13

Something of Canada's capital can thus be learned from the balconies of the Peace Tower, and from a promenade along two of its principal arteries, Wellington Street and Sussex Drive. The symbolic core gives hints of the larger reality. A comprehensive guide to the national capital region is another matter. So is an investigation of the civic life and character of urban Ottawa. A student of the subject will not soon exhaust the available materials. What is attempted in the following pages is essentially a record of Ottawa as the Capital City of Canada, from the decisive moment when Queen Victoria chose it from among six competitors, to the eventful period of growth after the Second World War, still in full spate as this account is being completed.

CHAPTER TWO

The Dynamics of Government

Anyone who writes about "Ottawa" discovers that the same word is in use to denote several quite distinct entities; and so it is useful to distinguish between them. Ottawa is the seat of the federal government of Canada: it was so designated in the British North America Act. Ottawa is also an urban area situated within the province of Ontario and subject to its jurisdiction. The corporation of the city of Ottawa embraces a sharply defined urban municipality in Ontario. But the word "Ottawa", by extension, has also come to mean the whole National Capital area, as described in a Federal Act: in this sense it occupies 1,800 square miles, and is situated partly in Ontario province and partly in Quebec. Again, by a familiar device of rhetoric, as in the headline OTTAWA WAGES WAR ON UNEMPLOYMENT, it is understood that "Ottawa" can mean the federal cabinet, supported by parliament, the 'government of the day'.

Ottawa as federal capital is similar in civic government to several world capitals and quite unlike most others. A broad division of world capitals would reveal three types: those which have grown up as a matter of history in the most important city within the state: such is London, Paris, Rome. A second type is wholly artificial or synthetic in the sense that it is created *de novo*, from scratch, by decree, in virgin and hitherto uninhabited territory. Such are Canberra and Brasilia. A third type — and Ottawa fits into it — embraces those capitals created by decree but located in an existing urban centre which was not the historic, industrial, commercial or cultural centre of the country. Ottawa was a thriving saw-mill town, a market town for farmers and lumbermen, a site of important water powers, a communication centre of some promise, an urban community of about ten thousand people, when it was first chosen to be a seat of government. It was not, in 1857, and is not now, *the* metropolis, — the industrial, financial, cultural or intellectual capital of the country.

A federal capital created by legislation is almost certain to take on characteristics different from an ancient seat of power and population which has been built up by a dynasty of kings or emperors. As the British town planner, Sir William Holford, said in commenting on the future of Brasilia:

"Federal capitals are political acts of faith and do not have their roots implanted deep in the facts of economic geography as other cities do."

Commercial and industrial Ottawa existed for a quarter of a century before the seat of government was transferred to it; and the location of the Canadian capital did not, to say the least, impair the prospects of Ottawa the Ontario town. It may be idle to speculate on what Ottawa would be like today had the choice of capital gone to one of the other rival cities. It seems to be reasonable to suppose that Ottawa and Hull would be twin industrial and commercial areas, modest in size, clustered about the water power site of the Chaudière, and on each side of the three rivers which meet here. Major General Howard Kennedy, in testimony before a parliamentary committee in 1956, suggested that such an Ottawa would have been "another Pembroke".

It may be pertinent to recall that the actual Ottawa in 1960 ranked as the 22nd city in Canada in order of manufacturing importance. In the same year there were about 11,000 employees in industry located in the city of Ottawa. The E. B. Eddy Co. employed 2,300 of these. It is sometimes contended that the presence of the national capital has discouraged the location of new industry in Ottawa. However, to offset any such influence there are substantial industries which would probably not have been located here if Ottawa were not the capital. Included among the 11,000 employees mentioned above were 245 in Atomic Energy of Canada, Ltd., 260 in the British American Bank Note Company, 385 in the Canadian Bank Note Company, Ltd., 620 in R. L. Crain Ltd., and 950 in publishing plants whose business was largely supported by the presence of the 50,000 employees of the federal government and the crown corporations connected with it. The 1960 population of Ottawa as national capital was 260,000: is it unrealistic to guess that without the seat of government it would have been a city of not more than 50,000 people today?

Ottawa as federal capital is unusual in its relationships with the provincial municipality in which it is principally situated. In those capitals of the world which grew up in conjunction with the growth of the principal city of the state, the state government has normally retained extensive and inclusive powers over the city government. In those capitals located by decree in a 'federal district' the state government is in an even more commanding position: in general it may be asserted that adjacent provincial governments have no authority over such federal districts. Moreover, when a new municipal organization is created within such a federal district it is likely to possess very little autonomy. According to Charles J. Woodsworth, for some years Editor of the Ottawa *Citizen*, "Ottawa is the only world capital where the city as such is entirely self-governing."

2

There are no labels on the different structures and precincts of Ottawa saying: "This is here as a part of the national capital" or "This is an element of

Ottawa the Ontario industrial community and would have been here in any event." Nevertheless the city of Ottawa today is an amalgam of these two elements. As one moves from street to street the 'federal capital' parts and the 'provincial manufacturing city' parts can be to some extent distinguished: but there are whole areas of shops and warehouses and residences in which any such distinction is quite blurred and undiscoverable.

Something has been said in the first chapter of the symbolic core of the national capital, and of two principal arteries profoundly affected in their architecture and general appearance by the fact of the national capital. It is not, however, principally buildings and thoroughfares that make a national capital: it is what goes on in and between the buildings; and something will be attempted here to describe that kind of activity.

Ottawa the federal capital is profoundly and continuously influenced by the kind of state Canada is; by its relations with the rest of the world; by the political philosophy of its people; by the rate of technological progress; by its political faith; by its political traditions; by its constitution; by its ethnic composition; and by its religious creeds. Even its architecture is slowly moulded by such considerations; and all the processes and activities and rituals of the federal capital are affected much more sensitively and profoundly. It may be useful to look at some of the attributes of the Canada of today, as reflected in its national capital; and to comment upon some of the effects and implications in modern Ottawa, considered as a "going concern", in terms of dynamics, rather than as a picturesque grouping of government buildings.

In form, to begin with, Canada is a constitutional monarchy: in effect, it is a parliamentary democracy.

In form, Canada is a monarchy, and Her Majesty Queen Elizabeth II is the head of the state. Though the Queen resides in another country, this of itself does not in any way signify subordination on Canada's part. Canada is a member of the Commonwealth, fully autonomous, equal in status to all other members, and not subordinate to any other. The fact that Canada's Queen is usually not resident here makes necessary the appointment of a Vice Regal personage, to reside in Canada. Canada's Governor General is the personal Viceroy of the Queen, appointed on the advice of the Canadian cabinet, and acts on her behalf when she is not in this country.

The relationship between the Canadian federal government and the Queen's Viceroy is similar to that between the government of the United Kingdom and Queen Elizabeth.

Though our ritualistic forms still trace the flow of authority from the Queen down to the people, the Queen and her personal representative have come to possess, in practice and in reality, only the 'right to be consulted, the right to encourage, and the right to warn,' as Bagehot phrased it.

However, the Governor General still possesses *title* to important prerogative powers, which he may exercise at his own discretion or on the instructions
of his sovereign. In practice these are now employed only in circumstances
which cannot be taken as thwarting the will of the Canadian people. He
has the right to refuse to dissolve parliament if he believes an alternative
government can be formed within the existing parliament. He has the right
to choose a prime minister in the event of the death of the incumbent, or
when no political leader clearly commands a majority in the House of
Commons. He has the power also to dismiss a Government and order a general election if he believes there has been a gross violation of the constitution
threatening parliamentary government. These powers exist but would be used
only in extraordinary circumstances.

His functions are valuable in other fields. As titular head of the government
he is Canada's official host to visiting heads of state and other distinguished
visitors. He presides at the official opening of Parliament, reads the Speech
from the Throne, gives Royal Assent to bills, signs Orders in Council, holds
investitures, acts as honorary patron for worthy organizations, serves as a
symbol of unity and continuity for the Canadian nation from coast to coast.

3

Canada is in substance a parliamentary democracy. It is, therefore, right and
fitting that in the symbolic pattern of the capital the Parliament Building
should have high place of honor, and that its tower should have been the
outstanding, most commanding, most impressive edifice in the whole region.
Whatever the constitutional forms or theories, the underlying principle is that
the will of the people decides government policy. The Canadian voter on
election day freely chooses his own member to make laws on his behalf.
Collectively, the Canadian voters choose the government of the day. Subject
only to the important observation that Canada is a federal union, and that
there are *eleven* legislative centres in Canada, the heart of political Canada
is to be found on Parliament Hill, and especially in the House of Commons,
when the Speaker is in the chair and the Mace on the table.

Subject only to the constitution, Parliament is in theory supreme. To be
exact, it is supreme within those areas of legislative competence allocated to
it under Section 91 of the British North America Act. These are in any circumstances very great, and include all of the truly national responsibilities.
In time of war the peacetime powers are substantially enlarged. (Within the
allocated sphere of the provincial legislatures, however, they too are supreme
and autonomous.)

The theory that — subject to these reservations — the Canadian parliament possesses unlimited sovereignty refers to the position in which it has been placed by the constitution, but it will not fully satisfy the observer of things as they are. Developments of the past century have somewhat shifted the locus of "working" power. On one hand it is increasingly contended that — in the words of *The Economist* some years ago — "the unfettered sovereignty of the Cabinet has almost become, in the phrase that Hobbes used of the Crown, 'as great as men can possibly make it' ". On another hand it is increasingly argued that with the growing complexity of modern administration the senior civil service is accepting, and is using, some of the legislative and executive powers formerly exercised by the Cabinet Ministers.

This is not the place for a critique of trends in modern parliamentary government, but no one familiar with it will cavil at the statement of R. MacGregor Dawson, that "the federal government occupies a central and most indispensible position among all government agencies. The prime minister and the cabinet form the active executive that drives the entire mechanism."

Thus if a visitor is curious about the cardinal seats of power in the national capital, he will consider not only the Houses of Parliament (with, of course, especial reference to the House of Commons) but will look with respect on the Privy Council office in the East Block, on the Prime Minister's office in the same building, on the Prime Minister's residence (which in that sense is a more significant place than Rideau Hall), on the offices of the Cabinet Ministers, scattered about the environs of Parliament Hill, and on the senior civil service.

In one sense political power is diffused, in that it depends on public opinion, and on party organizations from coast to coast, and on the national political headquarters. But once a political party has come to power with a majority of the Commons seats, once the leader of it has been summoned to form a government, once that government has been sworn in — then very great power, *supreme* power within certain suggested limitations, resides in the Prime Minister and his colleagues. The Prime Minister is, indeed, as he should be under our constitution, the most powerful man in Canada.

How long is he so? To retain power, the Prime Minister must carry his colleagues with him, he must win a majority of the vote in the House of Commons on every substantive government motion. If he ever loses that majority — and every member of the House of Commons is free to vote as he chooses if he is willing to pay the price of disloyalty to his party — then the Prime Minister must offer his resignation to the Governor General. Why such governments almost never fall by Commons division is a fascinating theme which however cannot be pursued here.

The reporters who sit in the Gallery, and constitute in Carlyle's coinage (or in his echo from Burke) "the Fourth Estate", have no delusions as to who makes the news. They concentrate on the Prime Minister, the Cabinet, the government benches of the House of Commons. They do not neglect the Opposition, either, because one lesson of history is that the Opposition of today is the Government of tomorrow. They pay suitable attention to the senior 'bureaucrats'.

The dynamics of parliamentary government operate in and from the powerhouse of Parliament Hill. But to see the legislative and executive functions and services, as transmitted to the Canadian people, it will be necessary, a bit later, to shift our gaze to the departmental buildings and the civil and military service.

4

Canada is a federal state. This point baffles some visitors, and is neglected even by some Canadians. The fact has not much affected the architecture of Ottawa, but it can never be ignored by the people who govern Canada. A federal union is one in which the sum total of legislative power is divided. There are eleven seats of legislative authority in Canada. Ottawa as the seat of the federal government is unquestionably the most important, but there are many areas of jurisdiction into which Ottawa may not constitutionally trespass.

The federal nature of Canada finds some symbolic expression on Parliament Hill. Moreover, there are effects of federalism on the machinery of government which can be readily detected. Because the constitution of Canada allocates certain important powers to the ten provincial governments, there are unexpected gaps in the portfolios of federal government. There is no Department of Education at Ottawa. There is no Department of Municipal Affairs. There is no Department of Highways. The demarcation between federal and provincial responsibilities is not so sharp that the national government entirely escapes duties under these headings. Besides, Ottawa still administers the vast Territories. But in the main, schools, roads, local government and other local affairs are the business of the ten provincial capitals, not primarily of Ottawa.

Canada is a federal state because the Fathers of Confederation were led to adopt that kind of government, and this in turn because a unitary state was politically impossible as well as undesirable. The geography and the history of Canada ruled out a legislative union in 1867. "Canada presents a paradox of unity and diversity and the necessary political counterpart of this paradox is Federalism. Economic diversity, difference of race and culture, and sheer size insist upon regional self-government. Common allegiance and an underlying unity demand a national government." These words, contained in a brief of the province of Ontario to the Royal Commission on Dominion Provincial Relations in 1938, are as true now as when they were written.

The seat of the federal union thus maintains relations with internal, as well as external governments. The first cabinet chosen after Federal Union included a Secretary of State for the Provinces. A formal office for Dominion-Provincial relations was found to be expendable: but *ad hoc* relations of varying degrees of harmony have always existed. Within the Department of Finance today there is a Division entitled: "Federal-Provincial Relations". Federal-Provincial Conferences are frequent: they normally meet in Ottawa; and the extent of continuing federal-provincial co-operation at the non-political administrative level would surprise all but the best informed political scientists. (A rough census in 1957 found sixty-four federal-provincial committees actively engaged in coordination).

The symbolism of the federal union is seen at its most eloquent in the great entrance hall to the Parliament Buildings. Arthur Beauchesne, illustrious Clerk of the House of Commons for many years, described it in memorable language:

He saw it as "a high circular chamber with corridors branching off in three directions. It is approached by a flight of steps with marble risers. In the centre of the Hall is a great column of stone rising from the inlaid marble floor in which are represented the 16 points of the mariner's compass. At the base of the column is a skilfully carved Father Neptune and his dogs of the sea. The inlaid foam-flecked marble represents the waves. From the cap of the column spring the graceful ribs which sustain the stone-groined ceiling and unite at their apex in a circular sweep with the ribs that rise from the surrounding walls, representing the provinces of the Dominion each giving and receiving support."

The crests of the provinces are etched in limestone in the framework of Confederation Hall. The provincial coats of arms border the great Gothic Arch which forms the central entrance to the Parliament Building: provincial emblems enrich the Altar of Remembrance in the Memorial Chamber.

The necessities of the federal state find reflection, too, in the Supreme Court housed in the fine building overlooking the Ottawa River. Like all Supreme Courts in all lands, it is the final court of appeal for disputes carried up to it: but in a federal state like Canada it has additional and momentous duties. Now that appeals to the Judicial Committee of the Privy Council at Westminster have been abolished, the Supreme Court of Canada is the learned body to which the federal cabinet refers when seeking an interpretation of the British North America Act as it relates to the division of authority and the validity of federal or provincial legislation.

5

Canada is an autonomous nation within the Commonwealth. It ranks as one of the leading 'middle powers' of the world. It is a North Atlantic power by virtue of function, and a North Pacific power by geographical definition. In recent years Canada has participated in two global wars, and in numerous international negotiations aimed at a peaceful world society. Canada's world status has begun to make its distinctive mark on the nature of the Canadian capital. This appears most palpably in the tremendous expansion of the work of the Department of External Affairs, and the Department of Trade and Commerce. It is to be seen in the three score of Canadian embassies, ministries, consulates and other missions scattered about the earth; and in the diplomatic offices and residences within the city of Ottawa, representing almost all of the leading nations. The presence of the growing diplomatic corps begins to alter Ottawa society: it opens windows on an exciting and disturbing new world.

The power and pace of Canada's present participation in world affairs is all the more remarkable because it is so recent. Thirteen years after Confederation, on the ground that "Canada has ceased to occupy the position of an ordinary possession of the Crown" (Galt), London agreed to the location of a Canadian "high commissioner" there, but ruled out any idea that he should have even 'quasi-diplomatic' powers: the British Foreign Office would continue to handle Canada's external relations. It was 42 years after Confederation (1909) before the incipient nation found it necessary to create a high-sounding 'Department of External Affairs'. For years this was in practice little more than a 'post office' for routine correspondence to and from Westminster through the Governor General. The first supervisor of it, Sir Joseph Pope, was able to run the new office with six clerks. Canada was 60 years old (1927) before it established its first minister in a foreign country. As late as the outbreak of the Second World War, Canada had only eleven foreign service officers on duty in Ottawa and seven missions abroad.

The Second World War and the accelerating impact of international events since have transformed a once sluggish growth into a hive of activity. By 1960 the modest department inaugurated by Sir Joseph Pope in 1909 was costing $18 million a year to operate, with over 500 foreign service officers at work in 65 different countries, and at the headquarters of the United Nations and NATO.

The first diplomatic missions began to appear in Ottawa in the 1920's. France, the United States and Japan led the way among the foreign powers. A new polyglot and cosmopolitan atmosphere began to permeate the social and political life of the Canadian capital, as 'diplomatic row' extended.

Foreign Embassies and Legations began to appear, on Wellington Street, on Sussex Street, on the Driveway, on Wurtemburg Street, and in Rockcliffe Park.

Since the 1920's hundreds of talented young Canadians have been attracted into the Department of External Affairs, to serve in Ottawa or in distant lands. The cumulative effect of this concentration of *expertise* and capacity on the social fabric of the capital has never been measured but it has surely been influential. In the rest of the world the reputation of the Canadian public service has climbed to levels not inferior to that of any other country.

6

Canada has moved a long way toward the 'positive' social welfare state in the past fifty years, and this factor is also having profound and far-reaching effects on the size and nature of the national capital. Indeed I would guess that of the various developments being considered here this bulks the largest by any physical yardstick. The whole philosophy of the purpose and usefulness of the state has been re-written since Confederation, and this is the main reason why the 280 persons engaged in the Dominion civil service at Ottawa in 1867 have grown (with auxiliary services) to 50,000 in 1960 (about 330,000 in the whole of Canada); and why a federal budget of $14 million in 1867-8 has grown to over $6 billion.

To trace and document this revolutionary change in the role of government in Canada would be a lengthy task. In essence it has arisen out of the discovery that greater government intervention into what had hitherto been private fields of activity was inescapable, or profitable, or both. It is not only that the *laissez-faire* attitude of the mid-nineteenth century has been largely replaced by such collectivist doctrines as those of Lord Beveridge and J. M. Keynes. It would have been found in any event that as Canada evolved from a scattered group of relatively self-sufficient settlements into a homogeneous interdependent society, from rural to urban life, from the predominance of the extractive staples to a highly industrialized society, that the role and service of governments would have to be greatly amplified. Much more intervention would have been inevitable. For example, social insurance on a state-wide basis would be bound to replace the carrying of all social risks by the family or by small private groups.

Social insurance alone has required since the end of the Second World War the creation of an administrative organization of great magnitude. The Department of National Health and Welfare has become the largest peacetime spending department. It disburses not far short of a billion dollars a year. An army of civil servants is required to keep records and distribute vast sums in the form of family allowances, old age pensions, unemployment insurance, veterans' pensions, civil service and military service pensions; and a second army is needed to staff the tax collection machinery necessary to find the money for such distributions.

At Confederation the federal government was not in these fields at all. Today the evidences of a 'social welfare' state and the modern idea that the government is responsible for maintaining economic and financial health, minima of welfare standards, a high level of employment and national income, have written their consequences right across the face of the capital. The evidence is to be seen in such tangible form as the monumental office building being planned for Tunney's Pasture, the Veterans' Hospitals, the façade of the Bank of Canada, the great expansion of the Department of National Revenue, the hundreds of civil servants employed by the Department of National Health and Welfare, and the Department of Veterans' Affairs. A very substantial part of the life and activity of the Canadian capital is thus engaged in new state activities which would have staggered and alarmed the Fathers of Confederation, and which still send a shudder down the spine of the "bow and arrow" Liberals, vestigial disciples of Adam Smith and John Stuart Mill!

The extent and the degree to which governments now concern themselves with matters which only a generation or two ago were either exclusively in private hands or were not yet in existence at all almost defies description. Not that Canada exhibits extremes of socialist or statist doctrine; and indeed the Constitution allocates to the Canadian provinces many matters which in a unitary state would be directed from the national capital. But even so Ottawa has recently become the headquarters for a great range of new activities; and the departmental buildings, the offices, the personnel resident at Ottawa all reflect the fact.

Through government departments or crown corporations the federal government at Ottawa, for example, makes films, prints pamphlets, runs transportation companies, makes radioactive isotopes, operates a gigantic broadcasting system, manufactures explosives, runs a design centre, supervises pipeline corporations, controls atomic energy, mines uranium, plans parkways, acts as a patron for the arts, maintains historic buildings, administers the northwest territories, runs airlines, publishes magazines and operates bookstores.

Some of the government's activities are so specialized and so sophisticated that it is possible to live in Ottawa for many years and never even hear about them: and yet they are a lively part of modern Canada and they contribute to the mosaic of the national capital.

As the decades roll by Ottawa becomes a richer and more varied repository of Canadian archives, records, books, expertise, museum exhibits, paintings, designs, maps, and memoirs in which the life and history of Canada are embedded and preserved. This already makes Ottawa the Mecca for many students and researchers, and its appeal will grow with the years.

The presence of the federal government in Ottawa has attracted scores of national institutions and associations: many of these are, in effect, the head-quarters of 'pressure groups'; in any event these too color and enrich the professional, educational and intellectual life of the city.

The institutions of higher learning in Ottawa draw upon the wealth of Canadiana, and in turn contribute valuable elements to the intellectual and cultural complex of the city.

7

A relatively new government activity is in the field of scientific and technolog-ical research: this too has changed parts of Ottawa in a dramatic fashion: it accounts for the spacious headquarters building of the National Research Council on Sussex Drive, the impressive campus of modern laboratories on the Montreal Road, many of the utilitarian buildings of the Booth Street Mines complex, the Defence Research laboratories at Shirley's Bay, the Atomic Energy buildings at Tunney's Pasture, scientific field stations in the suburbs, radar towers and displays, and unadvertized laboratories engaged in classified research.

Most of this is of very recent origin. The Fathers of Confederation were completely innocent of such matters. The first modest research activity by the government dates back to the 1880's, and was largely confined to the Central Experimental Farm. The first organized federal government activity in scientific research as such came out of the first World War. Urged to do so by London, the Canadian Government in 1916 appointed an advisory com-mittee on scientific and industrial research. This was the parent body of the present National Research Council.

In 1920 it was estimated that $100,000 would cover the total annual expenditure on *all* research in all of Canada. Between the two wars substantial strides were made. Temporary accommodation for the National Research Council at Ottawa was found in 1929 in an old mill building near the Rideau Falls. The massive headquarters building on the banks of the Ottawa river was completed and partly equipped in 1932. By the outbreak of war in 1939, important fields of research were being pioneered.

But the great leap forward was still to come. It was partly triggered by the outbreak of the Second World War. In the opinion of Dr. C. J. Mackenzie, wartime president of the National Research Council, and later President of the Atomic Energy Control Board, the time was ripe for it in any event. Dr. Mackenzie singles out 1940 as the beginning of what he calls the World

Technological Revolution. All the leading countries in the world are being affected by it. Canada has been spectacularly changed, and much of the effect can be read in the lineaments of Ottawa today.

In Canada as a whole, Dr. Mackenzie reports, the growth has been about *25 times* in the period 1940-60. "During the same period," he told a gathering of newspapermen in Toronto on May 4, 1960, "the population increased only 60%, the Gross National Product about three times. In 1939 the National Research Council had a total staff of 300 and its budget was less than $1 million. Today the staffs of the National Research Council and its emanations (i.e. Defence Research Board and Atomic Energy of Canada Limited) number perhaps 8,000 and the expenditures in 1939 Constant Dollars are close to $45 millions." Canada was spending in 1960 in civil and military research about double what the United States was spending in 1935.

While important parts of the research are being carried on in other parts of Canada, the direction and administration of all the national activities in this field are concentrated in the national capital. The exponential curve of research activity since 1940 suggests that in the years to come this phase of Ottawa's life will continue to rise steeply in importance and consequence.

8

If the *anatomy* of the federal capital is seen to best advantage from the four balconies of the lofty Peace Tower, its physiology—the dynamics and mechanism of federal government—is most apparent from the galleries of the House of Commons. There, at any rate, the observer can see the end-products of the legislative process, he can watch the ebb and flow of party fortunes, and he can guess something of the complexity of modern bureaucratic administration. The reporter of the press gallery supplements, of course, what may be seen in the House in a dozen important ways. The Senate, the parliamentary committees, the East Block, the offices of the cabinet ministers, the Supreme Court, the chief diplomatic news sources, the regulative boards and commissions,—all these help to provide a reasonably complete and vivid picture of what goes on in a modern capital. Some important centres of policy making are closed even to the legislative reporter, whose card gives access to the lobbies, who can see any member in his room or lunch with him in the parliamentary restaurant, but who is barred from the party caucus, from cabinet council, from private departmental consultations, from parliamentary committees preparing their reports, from some secret laboratories...

In this sense it is true that even in a parliamentary democracy much of the public business is carried out in secrecy. This paradox is only partly eased by the fact that in one way or another a determined Opposition and a courageous

Press can in due course by persistent effort bring to light many things which originally occurred without benefit of public scrutiny. Inquisitorial machinery exists for the purpose, ranging from the question period in the House of Commons to the formal parliamentary committee of inquiry, the judicial investigation, and the Royal Commission.

Parliament reigns supreme by virtue of its final power to make and break governments, but its intervention is decisive only at long intervals. Great as is the interest of the legislative chambers, especially the House of Commons, it must be recognized that as the years go by a smaller proportion of significant detail becomes apparent in them. It is difficult to believe that any intelligent and industrious member of parliament in 1867 was very much in the dark about the activities of the 280 civil servants who made up the entire headquarters staff of that day. The latter were for the most part engaged in everyday tasks which the member thoroughly understood. The press of the day was in a similarly happy position. One fifth of the entire civil service was in the post office department, another fifth was busy supervising the collection of customs and excise revenues and in keeping the government books, another fifth looking after the building of public works or supplying modest services then provided to farming and fishing. Militia and defence required an Ottawa staff of 15! The Governor General's office required nine, the Privy Council 12, the Justice Department seven, and the Secretary of State 25. Since the entire Ottawa civil service was housed on Parliament Hill, any industrious member or reporter could make a complete tour of the key offices in a few hours, and find nothing going on in them that would require more than some native intelligence and political experience to fathom.

The situation today is such a transformation that it is hard to grasp the fact that less than a hundred years have gone by. Today there are close to 50,000 persons in the civil and military service stationed at Ottawa or employed by crown corporations and other emanations of the federal government. That is one dimension of difficulty, its sheer size. But an even more serious obstacle is the growing sophistication of some government services. It is a sobering fact that in government laboratories today much work is being done that the average member of parliament — or member of the press gallery — could not hope to understand in detail without years of specialized study.

Parliament is a venerable institution which has found it difficult to adjust itself rapidly enough to the recent revolution in the size, variety and complexity of modern government. As Principal J. A. Corry of Queen's aptly put it years ago: "Parliament had always been able to discuss the rules of fair play intelligently. But when it attempted to prescribe the detailed steps to be taken to achieve a desired result in a complex and ill-understood environment, it floundered."

The current realities as well as the ancient rituals and modern forms need to be kept in mind by anyone who seeks a clue to the maze of modern government as illustrated in Ottawa. A student of the British Constitution, on which Canada's is modelled, has argued that "for the best part of three hundred years, the Executive has been gaining ground over both legislature and judiciary." He adds that "The executive's power to say what the law should be has grown with the people's power to say who should constitute the executive." As a consequence, Parliament "has become an electoral college, a sounding board for grievances and a ministerial training ground, rather than a legislature. At most, it is today a law-appraising body, in no real sense a law-making body."

A similarly pessimistic view of bureaucratic growth led the same observer to complain that "though by legal convention it is Ministers who issue the Orders and administer the law, it is, in fact, civil servants who do both."

Without conceding that the Canadian evolution has gone so far in shifting power from parliament to the executive and to the civil service, the trend is just as evident here as at Westminster. The growing iceberg sinks further and further down into the water and less and less of government is seen on the surface. It is necessary to peer into more obscure depths to see its mass and power.

There is an endless fascination about modern government activity in such a capital as Ottawa because it is always changing, growing, developing. A whole book could be devoted to the subject without much more than scratching the surface. Some hint of its nature can, perhaps, be suggested by assembling a few typical snapshots.

9

Ottawa, in this sense, is a million separate events which are yet all connected into a meaningful pattern. It may be . . . a prime minister debating with himself the strategic gains and losses of a major decision . . . or merely a new courier with official documents exploring Tunney's Pasture or Confederation Heights. It may be an architect drawing plans for a Canadian embassy in Brasilia . . . or an auditor looking for a suspected violation of a tax law . . . a physiologist conducting experiments on reduction of radiation hazard . . . a veterinarian tracking down some exotic new disease in poultry . . . a justice of the Supreme Court deciding that in interpreting one section of the British North America Act an Eskimo must be considered as an Indian . . . a town planner rejecting on aesthetic grounds some proposed extension of a government building . . . an investigator sniffing out a combine in restraint of trade . . . a home economist trying out a new recipe for dried cod . . . a mapmaker filling in one more blank in the Arctic Archipelago . . . a curator deciding which of two paintings he ought to add to the national collection . . . a private M.P. urging a Minister to start some new public works in his riding to offset unemployment . . . a royal commissioner assessing mountains of statistics on freight rates . . . a paleontologist gloating over a new dinosaur fossil . . . an R.C.M.P. security officer debating whether an imported pamphlet is seditious . . . a technician testing a new guidance system for supersonic aircraft . . . an old age pensions officer examining a Family Bible submitted as proof of eligibility . . . an External Affairs officer reading the latest reports from Vietnam or Southern Rhodesia . . . a patent examiner puzzling over a Rube Goldberg contraption sent in by an inventor . . . a new M.P. gathering jewels of ornate prose to embellish his maiden speech . . . a chief of protocol planning the ceremonies for the arrival of a foreign dignitary . . . a chemist testing the toxicity of a new preservative for meats.

Perhaps such a list is inadequate if it leaves out sentiment and color and human foible and human splendor. Everyone has his own unique impressions and recollections of the national capital. Anyone who has lived long in Ottawa and has thought about its history might come up at any time with a more whimsical and unpredictable stream of memories and recollections.

So it might be for them that Ottawa was . . . an aged senator recalling wistfully his days in the saddle under the big sky . . . a table in the Rideau Club around which ministers gloat or worry . . . a bearded explorer from the Arctic reporting to his chief in the Victoria Museum . . . a congenial group sitting in the darkness in the carilloneur's studio high up in the Peace Tower stirred by great music . . . restive members lustily singing Allouette and Home on the Range as they wait for the division to begin . . . grave problems of Asia or Africa being settled in the cafeteria of the Chateau Laurier . . . a bereaved stone-mason carving the single word VIMY on a stone of the Parliament Buildings as he remembers his only son . . . a House of Commons page dreaming of the day when he will be escorted down the aisle as a new M.P. . . . a prime minister calling in rapid succession on the long distance telephone Fredericton, N.B., Cardston, Alta., and Biggar, Sask., to discuss with party leaders a declaration of war . . . a great civil servant, thoroughly spent, dying at the wheel of his automobile as he crosses a busy intersection . . . the jocund skirl of the bells in the Peace Tower to welcome the reigning sovereign . . . a lyric poet composing immortal lines on scraps of post office stationery . . . a scientist excitedly watching on a display tube for the first faint blips of Canada's first radar . . . a shocked ministry listening incredulously to the Clerk summarize the Yeas and Nays that foretell a general election . . . a famous French townplanner with his creative "green eye" perceiving through slum and smoke the noble capital city that is yet to be . . .

Aspect

*"The Senate Chamber is a jewel-like setting for
the great ceremonial and social gatherings of
the Canadian Capital. The reigning Queen has
opened Parliament here . . ."*

"*Canada's Governor General is the personal viceroy of the Queen, appointed on the advice of the Canadian cabinet, and acts on her behalf when she is not in this country.*"

The Changing of the Guard on Parliament Hill.

General Charles de Gaulle, President of the French Republic, amid an Ottawa throng.

A solemn moment in a ceremony at the Cenotaph, memorial to Canadians who gave their lives in two World Wars.

◄ *David Ben Gurion, Prime Minister of Israel, on a state visit to Ottawa.*

The Musical Ride of the Royal Canadian Mounted Police.

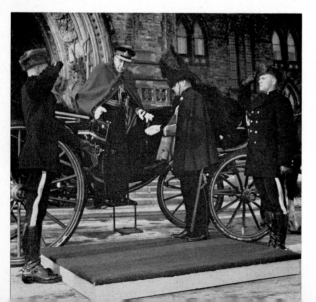

"The Governor General serves as a symbol of unity and continuity for the Canadian nation from coast to coast."

"*It is not principally buildings and thoroughfares
that make a national capital; it is what goes on
in and between the buildings . . .*"

"The Ottawa River winds tranquilly around the limestone cliffs on which Parliament Hill is based."

"*At times Ottawa shivers from polar currents
sweeping in beneath hard sapphire skies.*"

"The symbolism of the federal union is seen at
its most eloquent in the great entrance hall to the
Parliament Buildings."

"The House of Commons occupies the largest chamber in the Parliament Buildings: this Chamber and its predecessor before the fire of 1916, has seen and heard the reflection of almost every consequential Canadian event since 1866."

"*We can look down on the eight entrance locks of the Rideau Canal, the northern terminus of a 125-mile waterway . . . which enters the city below Black Rapids and bisects the heart of the Capital Region.*"

"*Some of the Government's activities are so sophisticated that it is possible to live in Ottawa for many years and never even hear about them: and yet they are a lively part of the modern Canada and they contribute to the mosaic of the national capital.*" *The Dominion Observatory, one of the 125 Government buildings in Ottawa, where scientists peer billions of miles into space.*

The Sparks Street Mall, while the City sleeps.

*"From the balconies near the summit of
Ottawa's soaring Peace Tower he could have
learned much . . . the scale of the City, the sweep
of the river, the pulse of its arteries."*

"*Architects say that the cluster of Gothic buildings on Parliament Hill can be regarded as a fine flowering of the Romantic Revival of Gothic architecture in the 19th century. It is the finest such group on the North American continent, and is irreproducible today.*"

"*Spring is a swift sudden season and autumn a blaze of crimson and gold.*" *The Ruins at Kingsmere constructed by the late William Lyon Mackenzie King.*

The Embassy of the United States of America on Wellington Street.

*"Canada's world status has begun to make
its distinctive mark on the nature of the
Canadian capital. It is to be seen in the
diplomatic offices and residences within the
city representing almost all the leading nations."*

Left

*"... on the cliff above the Ottawa River the
official residence of the Prime Minister of
Canada enjoys a breathtaking view to the north
and west."*

Below

*"In a young capital where architectural
distinction is still rare, the elegance and grace of
the French Embassy across the street from the
Rideau Falls Park, make an indelible
impression."*

The Hog's Back on the Rideau River.

Ottawa is a fine place to live.
The special charm and attraction
of its beautiful setting have been
assured by the National
Capital Commission. Thousands
of acres of sylvan parkland
and many miles of refreshing
riverfront have been developed
for public enjoyment.

The Commission co-operates
with nature in providing millions
of delightful spring blooms,
annuals and perennials
throughout the Capital.

"... *the beauty of Canada, the vastness of its land, its loneliness, its youth, its hope.*"

CHAPTER THREE

Algonquin Canoe to Steamboat

The story of Ottawa as a seat of government goes back only a little over a century. It was in the late autumn of 1857 that Queen Victoria chose it to be the capital of the United Province of Canada. At that time Ottawa (Bytown) was only three decades old. No settlement in the whole area was much older. The first settlers on the north shore of the river had arrived in 1800. When Philemon Wright and his Massachusetts colonists reached the junction of the Ottawa, the Rideau and the Gatineau, there was still not a single settlement above the mouth of the Lièvre River.

Yet, in a sense, it was already historic territory. The Ottawa River had first been ascended by a white man in the year 1610. For a hundred and seventy years afterwards a succession of discoverers, explorers, fur traders, missionaries, soldiers, *coureurs de bois*, had used the river as a highway. Nicolas de Vignau had passed by in 1611. Samuel de Champlain had portaged at the Chaudière in 1613. The river had seen such famous figures as Radisson and Perrot, Du Lhut and La Verendrye, the Jesuits Jogues and Brébeuf, the French officers de Troyes, d'Iberville and Lamothe-Cadillac. After the fall of New France the furtrader Alexander Henry had led a procession of British adventurers and colonizers, furtraders and discoverers — Joseph Frobisher, Simon McTavish, Alexander Mackenzie on his way to the Pacific and the Arctic, Lord Selkirk, enroute to the Red River, and scores of less famous voyageurs.

These came and returned and left no permanent mark on the meeting of the great waters. At last, in 1783, the first settlement surveyors arrived. The first civil land explorer drove his pegs on the south shore in 1793. The first private prospector for settlement lands reached the region at about the same time. Events moved faster after that. Wright's settlement was established in 1800. Colonel By came in the autumn of 1826, laying out Upper Town in the same year.

So, in one sense, the history of the Ottawa region goes back to the earliest years of North American exploration. The route of the Ottawa River is studded with some of the most famous names in North American history. The story of the Ottawa River, if adequately researched and imaginatively told, would become a glittering thread in the romantic story of the continent. An attempt to condense such a story into a dozen pages is an exercise in futility. Yet something must be attempted here, as a foundation for the later account of Bytown and Ottawa as a seat of government.

Communities grow up where they do for a variety of reasons. As technology advances, the reasons change too. (The air age created Gander and Frobisher Bay.) The meeting of the waters on the Grand River of the Ottawas was a natural site for a permanent settlement. The aborigines had used these waterways for thousands of years before the white man came. The Chaudière and Rideau Falls were natural barriers which no early traveller could ignore. There had to be unloadings, carryings, climbings, stoppings, overnight campings. In time of Indian warfare it was a natural site for ambushes: the voyageur—Indian or Frenchman—was most vulnerable at that moment when he struggled along a portage under his heavy burden of possessions, or with a canoe canopied over his shoulders.

The Chaudière Falls in their majesty long formed a sort of natural shrine for the awestruck Algonquins, if we can believe early records. The junction of the waterways may well have been the site of ancient Indian market places or the scene of annual trade fairs. There are no written records earlier than 1613, and so far the archaeologist has not been able to amplify the meager accounts of visitors very much. The first white man of all, Étienne Brûlé, seems to have come up the Ottawa river as far as the Rideau Falls in 1610, but he left no records. Only with the first-hand written reports of Samuel de Champlain are we on firm ground.

2

The first Europeans found the valley of the Ottawa River a densely forested wilderness, thinly occupied by nomadic peoples of the New Stone Age. A few forest trails wound through the dense woods, but the rivers and lakes were the only highways. The technology of the Algonquin was primitive, but his birch bark canoe was a marvellous means of travel and conveyance in his circumstances and way of life. The Algonquins' native land was a network of waterways. These were interrupted everywhere by rapids, waterfalls and land gaps between bodies of water, but such a craft of bark could be easily carried, and the Indians became experts at toting great loads of personal belongings, using tump lines and other harness. Among the natural waterways of the north eastern quadrant of North America the Ottawa River was a key route. The St. Lawrence River opens up the heart of the continent, and at the junction of the St. Lawrence and the Ottawa a branch waterway points directly west to Lake Nipissing, Lake Huron, Lake Michigan and Lake Superior. As later explorers and furtraders demonstrated, the canoe provided a convenient means of travelling all the way from tidewater at Quebec City to the base of the Rocky Mountains.

The Ottawa River is broken up by many rapids and waterfalls—there are more than a score of them between Ste. Anne and Lake Temiscaming—but the grandest and most impressive of them all was the Chaudière. Two and a half miles below the Chaudière another great stream, the Gatineau, flows into the Ottawa from the north, and a lesser but still mainly navigable water, the Rideau, joins it from the south. The Indian with his canoe could ascend the Rideau (once above the Hog's Back Falls) with relatively short and easy portages to the headwaters of the river in the Rideau Lakes country. And after that there was a navigable route down to Lake Ontario and the St. Lawrence.

Upstream from Montreal there were some long difficult rapids in the Carillon and Grenville sectors, but once past them there was unimpeded navigation westward on the Ottawa for another sixty miles. The Chaudière Falls, and the rapids immediately upstream formed another serious barrier. The flat river banks just below the Chaudière Falls, on both north and south shores, constituted natural canoe landings at the head of sixty miles of easy navigation. One of them became Wright's Landing, and the post of Wright's Village; the other, some years later, became Caleb Bellows' Landing and then Richmond Landing, a tiny settlement which predated Bytown by several years.

A logical site for a pioneer settlement in colonial days was a spot where the power of falling water could be harnessed for grinding grain and sawing wood. There was no lack of such power either at the Chaudière or where the Rideau River leaped forty feet over the cliff to join the Ottawa River on its way to the sea.

Added to such advantages were the endless forest wealth on every hand, and a broad alluvial plain mainly composed of rich deep soil. It was plainly to be seen that when the wave of occupation of North America reached the fringes of the Ottawa Valley, settlements would inevitably grow up around the Falls and the mouths of the two important tributaries.

When Samuel de Champlain first set eyes on the region, however, this stage in North American history was still a very long way off. Champlain came to the Ottawa River as discoverer, explorer and royal cartographer to the King of France. By 1613 he already had behind him an eventful decade of North American experience.

3

Champlain came to the junction of the rivers on a wild goose chase, as every scholar knows, but he was not aware of that when he first arrived off the mouth of the Gatineau River on the 4th of June 1613. His party was a modest one, borne in two birch bark canoes, carrying Champlain, three other

white men, and two Indians. The party had left St. Helen's Island, a league
from Mount Royal, on the 27th of May. Champlain had caught his first
glimpse of the Gulf of St. Lawrence a decade before; he had founded Quebec
five years earlier. He was now on a search for the de Vignau's fabled short
route to the Western Sea, which he hoped would lead Frenchmen westward
around the world to the riches of the East.

Visitors today can stand on Nepean Point or at the Lookout in Rockcliffe
Park and watch the great river as it flows past and see in their mind's eye
Champlain's two bark canoes as they were paddled westward toward the
Chaudière Falls. He was not the first European to come that way. In 1610,
that honor had fallen to Etienne Brûlé, who with a chief of the Hurons had
come upstream at least as far as the mouth of the Rideau. And in the following
year Nicolas de Vignau in the company of Indians had made his way up the
Ottawa as far as an Algonquin Camp on an island in Allumette Lake. De
Vignau, the most famous liar in Canadian history, was crouched in one of
Champlain's canoes as they made their way toward the Chaudière on the 4th
of June, 1613. It was de Vignau's exciting story of his discovery of an inland
lake which discharged into salt water, with its circumstantial detail of a
wrecked English ship on the ocean shore, which had lured Champlain away
from the St. Lawrence on this voyage of breathless anticipation.

No voyageur of those days could ascend the Ottawa without a thrill at the
sight of the Rideau River leaping in its twin falls over the limestone escarpment, much as the present sightseer on the river tour sees them, although in
greater and steadier volume. Champlain described them thus in the narrative
of his voyages: "There is an island in the centre, all covered with trees, like
the rest of the land on both sides, and the water slips down with such
impetuosity that it makes an arch of four hundred paces, the Indians passing
underneath it without getting wet, except from the spray produced from the
fall."

After he passed by the foot of the Rideau Falls Champlain would begin to
see fleck of foam and hear the thunder of the still more famous Chaudière
Falls upstream.

All witnesses agree that the Chaudière Falls in their primeval and pristine
majesty were among the great spectacles of North America. Early engravings
give more than a hint of the original magnificence. Many visitors since
Champlain have tried in prose to convey something of their grandeur.

"The scenery of Chaudière before its wild beauty was defaced by the axe
or its sparkling waters were utilized in slides and mill races was truly picturesque, almost indescribably grand," wrote J. L. Gourlay, author of an early
history of the Ottawa Valley. "The rocky cliffs, green with the cedars and
pine to the river's brink, its volume of water tossed, broken, dashed into

foam, that foam floating down like islands of pearls on the bosom of the dashing current, the whole surveyed from the brow of the hills on the east in the evening sun, to be comprehended, to be esteemed, to be rapturously admired, must be dwelt upon. Thus Samuel Champlain saw it, Mirrick and Stevens saw it, thus Philemon Wright saw it before a tree was removed or an arch had spanned it except the rainbow in its natural grandeur, in its virgin beauty, in its pristine sublimity. This is much the finest fall on the river."

The French name 'Chaudière' which is perhaps best translated into English as 'Cauldron', and which in turn represents the translation of an Algonquin name 'Asticou', was suggested by the whirling steaming waters of the Ottawa River tumbling into a rounded rock basin below. Champlain was quite explicit on this point in his narrative:

"The water falls at one point with such impetuosity upon the rock that it has, in the course of time, worn out a wide and deep basin. Into this the water rushes with a whirling motion, boiling up tumultuously in the midst, so that the Indians call it *Asticou*, which means 'Chaudière'" [as Champlain wrote it in French]. The Indians expressed their awe at this natural wonder by worshipping the Manitou of the Falls. Champlain described the ritual. A chief would collect pieces of smoking tobacco from each member of the assemblage, and these would be placed together in the centre of the group, who would dance and sing around them. An oration would follow, in which the praises of the Manitou would be extolled for protecting them against their mortal enemies. Then in a solemn parade to the edge of the waterfall the orator would fling the tobacco into the whirling flood.

4

When Champlain ascended the Ottawa, the northern half of North America was still a pathless wilderness, unknown to the white man, except in the Gulf region and the Lower St. Lawrence. But already Europeans were beginning to probe the Atlantic coastlines. Three years earlier, Henry Hudson had sailed on his last tragic voyage into the Bay that was to bear his name. Six years earlier, the first permanent English settlement had been located on the coast of Virginia. Seven years after Champlain's ascent of the Ottawa, the Pilgrim Fathers landed at Plymouth Rock. The settlement of North America proceeded inexorably through the years. Yet the junction of the rivers where the national capital of Canada was some day to stand remained unchanged, unaffected, for nearly two centuries more. Many romantic figures passed by. Whoever they were, eminent or lowly, the Chaudière Falls compelled them all to disembark, to portage, to resume their voyage in quieter waters upstream or down. There were endless scenes of violence along the river, as

Iroquois ambushed Algonquin, and as the forces of Frontenac and his successors sought to keep this vital fur trade route open to the west. Many books have been written about the days of the Jesuit martyrs and the coming of the fur traders, the explorers who passed up the Ottawa still dreaming of a western sea or a northwest passage. The names of those who have portaged at the Chaudière is, indeed, a roll call of most of the illustrious names of early Canadian history.

Yet the physical appearance of the region where the Rideau and the Gatineau came down into the Ottawa was unaltered by all these comings and goings. Alexander Henry the fur trader is said to have been the first English-speaking voyageur (he was born in New Jersey) to scan these scenes. That was in 1761, by which time a century and a half of French rule in North America had been terminated at Louisburg and on the Plains of Abraham. Yet nothing had changed around the Chaudière, there was still not a single settler on the banks of the Ottawa from Carillon Falls to Lake Temiscaming. Events in the outside world, however, were about to challenge and destroy the old isolation. Two decades after the fall of Quebec, the Thirteen Colonies were busy setting up an independent Republic. Loyalists and displaced persons were streaming into that part of British North America which had remained loyal to King George. There began to be a new interest in the virgin lands of Canada. In 1783, at the peak of the Loyalist migration into British North America, an economic survey was begun of the lands adjacent to the Rideau River. A Lieutenant G. French, under government instructions, left Carillon on the Ottawa River with a party not very different in size or means of locomotion from that used by Champlain 170 years earlier. French's party also travelled in two birch bark canoes. There were seven members of the Provincial Corps, two Canadians and an Indian guide. They reached the future site of Ottawa on October 2nd, and a week later had ascended the Rideau to its source.

French's report on the lands and other resources adjacent to the Rideau River upstream to its source is still extant: on the whole it reports very favorably on the land and timber on both sides. "It may all be cultivated except a few swamps and stony ridges," he wrote. French thought the soil suitable for hemp, flax and hops. "The timber is in general tall and straight without any underbrush, and I should suppose a man would be able to clear in the American Method an acre fit for seeding in eight days."

Ten years later the government of Upper Canada instructed its Deputy Surveyor, John Stegmann, to survey four townships in the northern portion of the Counties of Leeds and Grenville. These subsequently became the modern townships of Osgoode, Gloucester, North Gower and Nepean. "There is a legend to the effect that John Stegmann planted his last stake near Dow's Great Swamp, and was drowned in the Rideau River in the spring of 1794," writes A. H. D. Ross in his history of Ottawa.

5

The settlement of the Ottawa Valley takes on additional dimensions if we see it as an incident in the westward stream of American colonization which began on the Atlantic seaboard early in the 1600's, — an expansion which continued for over 250 years.

The origins of the communities which in due course became Ottawa and Hull, Aylmer and Richmond, the townships of March and Nepean and Gloucester, reflected in turn events as miscellaneous as the Fall of New France, the American Revolutionary War, the coming of the Loyalists, the Napoleonic Wars, and the War of 1812-14 between Canada and the United States.

The wilderness at the junction of the Ottawa and its two tributaries was potentially rich and theoretically available for settlers at any time after the menace of Indian raids had been ended. There were almost endless forests to be felled, and large areas of fine agricultural soil waiting to be cleared and tilled. But so long as the St. Lawrence-Ottawa region was under French rule there was no pressure on the area from potential settlers of French origin, and all others were forcibly restrained. The population of New France at the time of the fall of Quebec was still only about 60,000 and the St. Lawrence Lowlands still provided them with space for considerable expansion.

With the New Englanders the situation was different. The original settlements on the New England coast had long ago expanded to occupy all of the desirable lands on the east slopes of the Appalachians. The U.S. interior was opening up, and by 1800, American frontier families were occupying western New York State, western Pennsylvania, and eastern Ohio. There were known to be almost endless expanses of virgin land still further west in the heart of the continent. But for residents of the New England states, especially those living in the northern part, the unexploited land resources of British North America had the appeal of being virtually next door. Why plunge into the distant wilderness of the American west if there was room for profitable expansion near at hand? As a result, in addition to the migration of the Loyalists, there was a steady and growing stream of American settlers into both Lower and Upper Canada, from the end of the Revolutionary War until the outbreak of the War of 1812.

6

Philemon Wright, destined to win the title of "the Father of the Ottawa" was but one of the thousands of New Englanders who chose to pioneer in nearby

Canada rather than travel a thousand miles west to Ohio, Indiana or Illinois, in search of virgin land, timber and other natural resources.

The exact manner in which Philemon Wright first became interested in the Hull-Chaudière region (which had been divided up into townships in 1792, but was not yet surveyed) makes an interesting footnote to colonial history. Wright in the 1790's was a successful farmer and stock breeder of Woburn, Massachusetts, just outside Boston. He came of Kentish stock. There is a vague report that he had fought at Bunker Hill, but if so he was only 15 at the time.

In 1796, when Wright was 36, a promoter and land speculator of Bennington, Vermont, by the name of Jonathan Fassett, visited Boston looking for a farmer of substance prepared to go into partnership with him in acquiring rights for settling a large tract of virgin lands on the Lower Canada side of the Ottawa River, above the Carillon Falls. Fassett found in Philemon Wright of Woburn a good prospect for partnership, since Wright had already visited Lower Canada, seeking in vain for an extensive tract of virgin land, and was still eager to pioneer. Fassett represented himself to Wright as being in possession of warrants of survey of a number of Lower Canada townships, principally on the Ottawa River. What he did not tell Wright was that because of his own earlier participation in the American Revolution, fighting against King George, he was having trouble satisfying the Canadian authorities as to his prospective loyalty as an immigrant settler. Wright was soon deeply interested in Fassett's proposition, and on August 11, 1796, he entered into an agreement to purchase half rights from Fassett in four townships, paying Fassett £800 in New England currency. One of the four townships named in the agreement of sale was Hull. The others were Rippon, Harrington and Grandisson.

The following March, 1797, Wright rode to Montreal with three Woburn associates with the intention of looking over his recent purchase. At Montreal he learned to his dismay that Fassett had not been frank with him, that Fassett's warrant rights of survey in Hull, Harrington and Grandison had lapsed because of failure to satisfy the conditions, and that Fassett had probably never held rights in Rippon. Moreover, he discovered that three of these townships were situated so far back from the shoreline that they were worthless for settlement until roads should be built. Only Hull actually fronted on the Ottawa River.

There was a chance, however, that Wright was not too late to petition for a warrant of survey of a desirable township in his own name. He proceeded to Quebec City, where he filed a petition on April 17, 1797. His petition was laid aside, pending an inquiry, and for the next two years Wright pursued his claim, paid David Lovering to complete the survey, doing essential clearing, and erecting buildings, probably store houses.

The government of Lower Canada was keen to attract desirable immigrants, whether American or not. But every petitioner for land grants was required to satisfy the authorities that he was a person of character and principle, and a bona fide settler. Americans were required also to subscribe to a declaration that they would maintain and defend to the utmost of their power the authority "of the King in his Parliament as the Supreme Legislature of the Province."

Wright continued to receive assurances at Quebec City that his petition for land would be favorably heard, and he was able to obtain sureties and recommendations respecting his intentions and his character. In the meantime he was busy interesting a group of his Woburn neighbors to join him in a colonizing venture on the Ottawa River. In the autumn of 1799, he persuaded two Woburn farmers to accompany him on a more thorough survey of the resources of the region than he had been able to make in 1797. These Massachusetts pioneers spent several weeks on the scene, climbing numerous tall trees in order to get a better idea of the topography and resources of Hull township.

On his way back, Wright visited Quebec City again and presented a formal memorial to the authorities, outlining what he was prepared to do to establish a settlement in Hull township, Lower Canada. He was able, as he had expected, to submit the endorsement of a number of reputable gentlemen of Montreal and Quebec City. The authorities were very slow in giving Wright an answer, but he was sufficiently hopeful to return to Woburn and make preparations that winter for a mass exodus to the pioneer lands of Hull township. Early in February, the heroic trek began. Wright set out with a party of "twenty-seven settlers, six double sleighs, two double teams of oxen to draw the implements of husbandry, mill irons, stores and other necessaries for settlement, to the value of about Two Thousand currency,"—in what must have been an epic chapter of pioneer settlement.

When the pioneers reached Montreal, Wright learned to his dismay that his title to the Hull township lands still awaited confirmation, so he was compelled to leave the whole party at Montreal while he made a hurried trip to the provincial capital. The news he received there was enheartening, however, and he returned to lead his settlers up the Ottawa, through the heavy snows, and on to the site of their new home. They reached the Chaudière Falls sometime in March, 1800. In the same month, the Council at Quebec passed an order issuing a warrant of survey in the township. In the following year Wright engaged a surveyor to make a township plan, and this was duly filed at Quebec City.

Wright combined sturdy Kentish stock with Yankee competence and ingenuity. He showed his good sense in attacking the wilderness with a fairly self-sufficient colony, with ample resources, and at a time of year when the least possible delay would occur until the first harvest could be taken off the soil.

"Spring came unusually early that year and vegetables and grain were planted in the small patches cleared and grew amazingly," wrote Lily Wright Cunningham, one of Wright's descendants, many years later. "The cattle thrived on the buds of the undergrowth." In his own later account before a parliamentary committee, "Squire" Wright went into greater detail: "We continued cutting down during the whole of March, April and May, building and putting in our vegetables and garden stuffs, and continued to do so, until we began to burn our fallows (which is the timber felled in rows) for Winter wheat." They produced a crop of 1000 bushels of potatoes that year, which unfortunately they lost during the next winter from rot, due to "putting them too deep in the ground". They sowed 70 acres of Fall Wheat. The following summer Wright built a large barn to hold the 3,000 bushels he harvested. On one measured acre he reaped forty bushels, an immediate assurance of the fertility of the soil he had chosen. That summer he surveyed the whole township of Hull, "placing 377 square posts in a township of 82,429 acres."

Almost immediately he had to branch out into other activities. He invested £1,300 in grist and saw mills. Until the grist mill was working he had to carry his grain 80 miles to be ground, and observed that it cost him twice as much to get his grain ground as it did to raise it in the first place. By 1803 he had 380 acres cleared, and he planted grass seed on the land which had given him two crops of wheat. In 1804 he began a blacksmith shop, with four forges, worked by water; a shoemaker's shop, a tailor's shop and a large bakehouse. He "commenced a tannery" the same year, "and I obtained from New York a cylinder for grinding of bark, also by water; also cleared a quantity of land, commenced making roads, and built several bridges."

This was impressive progress, but so far it was being supported by the capital resources which Wright had brought with him. If the colony was to prosper, some sort of export "cash crop" was imperative. A profitable export line had to be developed at once to pay for such further imports as were indispensable. The critical test of the settlement appears to have been reached in 1807-08, when Wright's original capital was about exhausted, and when the young settlement was ravaged by a costly fire. Some accounts say that as a result Wright went through a brief period of discouragement, and even despair, but that he was carried through it by the spirit and resolution of his sons.

Fortunately, Philemon Wright's desperate need for cash exports coincided with an international situation which offered, for a man of Wright's enterprise, a permanent and profitable solution.

By this time, Napoleon's blockade of European ports had succeeded in cutting off Britain from her traditional supplies of square timber in the Baltic countries. Without timber for her navies, Britain faced the loss of the war. It was a happy coincidence for Philemon Wright that the Ottawa River was potentially one of the finest sources of square timber in the world. There was one stubborn obstacle, however. No one had ever suggested any practical means by which the white pine forests of the Ottawa could be conveyed to the seaboard. Not a single raft had ever been exported from the Ottawa across the Atlantic. Some one had to pioneer the route. Philemon Wright determined to be that pioneer.

In the fall and winter of 1806-07 Philemon Wright began cutting white pine and assembling the 'sticks' into rafts and cribs on the Ottawa River below the Chaudière Falls. In the spring of 1807 he set off on a historic venture.

One completely unknown quantity was how to negotiate the chain of rapids between him and Quebec City—the Carillon, the Long Sault, and the Lachine. Lachine? Philemon Wright had some unorthodox thoughts about that. Why not by-pass Lachine by taking his timber via the north shore? "The habitants who had been settled there nearly two hundred years told me it was not possible to get timber to Quebec by the route on the north side of the Isle of Montreal, but I said I would not believe it until I had tried it." There spoke the true pioneer!

Philemon Wright tackled it and he made it, though on his first drive it took him 35 days to negotiate the Long Sault Rapids, before he even got to the Isle of Montreal at all. This particular obstacle yielded to some application of labor: when the Long Sault channel was improved, Wright ran rafts through it in 24 hours.

This was the beginning of a great industry, not only for Wright but for scores of others. The square timber trade for the British market became the most important single commercial enterprise in the Province; and eventually the square timber duties collected at the Chaudière became the biggest single source of revenue for the government of Upper Canada. That, however, is looking well into the future.

Wright's story by no means ends with the inauguration of the square timber trade of the Ottawa. His name bobs up everywhere in the records of those years. Only a few highlights can be mentioned here. He constructed the first Aylmer Road. Wright was host in 1819 to the Earl of Dalhousie, just appointed Governor General of the Canadas, and petitioned him for aid to establish an Agricultural Society. He also asked the Earl for £300 to help build a stone church. In 1819 he built the first steamboat on the Ottawa and started a regular service between the Chaudière Falls and Grenville. He was of service to the pioneer settlers of Richmond. In 1820 he built the "Columbia Hotel" at Wright's Landing, the best hostelry of those parts. When the Rideau Canal project was launched, Wright played a valuable role in its construction. He represented his county in the Legislative Assembly of Lower Canada from 1830 to 1834. When he died in 1839 the untouched wilderness he had found in 1799 had been transformed into a busy and prosperous Canadian community; and no one had done more to make it so than Philemon Wright himself.

8

While Philemon Wright was founding the settlement known for a time as Wright's Village (and which did not become the city of Hull for 75 years) there were a few much more modest beginnings of settlement on the south side of the Ottawa, in the area now embraced within the city limits of Ottawa.

Seven years after Wright had begun his establishment on the north side of the Falls, a Robert Randall, also an American (from Maryland), petitioned the government of Upper Canada for lots on the river at the Falls, where he proposed to develop the power and establish mills. In a letter dated October 8, 1807, he put forward the argument, which he thought would appeal to the Governor in Council at Toronto ('Muddy York' in those days) that an enterprise such as the one he contemplated "will be the means of settling the wild lands on the river, that is at this present a perfect wilderness, not one settler inhabiting the country." He was, obviously, referring to what is now the Ottawa side of the river. Randall's business ventures elsewhere were numerous but already over-extended; he soon lost financial control of most of them, and his mills at the Chaudière never materialized.

Settlement on the south shore began shortly after Randall's investigations of the power site, but continued to be slow and spotty. Several of the key properties in the heart of modern Ottawa were "drawn" by United Empire Loyalists, but never occupied by the owners. Ross asserts that a Mrs. Grace McQueen, a daughter of one of these Loyalists living in the County of Grenville obtained a Crown Patent for an area now bounded by Laurier Avenue, Gladstone Avenue, the Rideau River and Bronson Avenue—600 acres, then densely wooded and embracing some large swamps. This title was eventually acquired by Colonel John By in 1832 for £1,200. On May 17, 1802, a Jacob Carman obtained a patent for 600 acres right in the heart of modern Ottawa, paying "Ten Pounds, Halifax Currency" for it. This was later picked up by the Earl of Dalhousie for the Crown in 1823 at a cost of £750. There were no clearings or buildings attempted on either property. Somewhere about 1809 Jehiel Collins built a small store and dock at the Chaudière, on the south shore.

The first bona fide settler of Nepean Township is reputed to have been Ira Honeywell, son of Rice Honeywell (a Loyalist) of Prescott, who received about a thousand acres from his father on condition that he settle on it. "In February, 1811, Ira Honeywell and his wife, with their camp equipment and a few household effects on an ox-drawn sled, or 'jumper', bravely set out through the bush, travelled by way of the 'Putman Settlement' (eight miles above Merrickville), and came down the Rideau River to the Falls known as 'the Hog's Back'," relates A. H. D. Ross. "From here Ira cut out a trail to their home, three miles above the Chaudière Falls." Their son, John, is said to have been the first white child born in the township.

Bradish Billings (son of a Boston immigrant) is honored as the first settler of Gloucester Township. It appears that he entered the employ of Philemon Wright about 1807 and built his first shanty in Gloucester Township three years later. In November of 1812 he built a log house, and began combining small-scale farming with timber exports. He married Lamira Dow in 1813 and for six years they were the sole settlers in Gloucester.

John Burrows Honey was a native of Plymouth, England, who was trained as a civil engineer. He and his wife and his brother Henry emigrated to Canada in 1817. By October of that year they appear to have reached Bellows' Landing, and their cabin, which he located about where Wellington and Lyon Streets now intersect, must have been the first residence on the plateau which is now the heart of Ottawa. He received patent for his land on September 18, 1823, having completed his settlement duties. In 1826 he sold it to Nicholas Sparks, who thus acquired what afterwards became perhaps the most valuable single property in the history of Ottawa.

Nicholas Sparks was a native of County Wexford, Ireland, who seems to have arrived at Wright's Landing some time in 1816. He found work with "Squire" Wright and a few years later he had an opportunity to buy the lot earlier "proved up" by John Burrows Honey. The deed as recorded in The Registry Office shows that Sparks paid £95 for the property. Legend has it that when Sparks realized how much wild swampy land he had picked up in return for his hard earned money he broke down and wept. Since the land in question was bounded by the present Wellington, Laurier, Bronson Avenue, Rideau and Waller Streets, his opinion of the bargain must have brightened considerably as the years went by, and as its great potential value became apparent.

The stone house which he erected on what later became Sparks Street was the first in that part of old Ottawa. It remained there until very recently as a relic of the earliest settlements.

9

There is a fine vantage point in Ottawa on the riverside terrace below the Supreme Court Building, and the spectator who stands there and looks upstream toward the falls of the Chaudière can make out, to the left, the location of the oldest settlement on the south shore. It is a beach on a low peninsula, at present occupied by a series of round squat oil storage tanks. In the earliest days, just as the nineteenth century was beginning, it was a canoe landing. While the cliffs above and to the south east, where the government buildings now stand, were still a pathless tangle of beech and hemlock, it was the scene of a small but growing activity. As indicated earlier, a modest dock and log store were constructed there about 1809 by a certain Jehiel Collins. Soon afterwards, Collins sold out to his clerk, Caleb T. Bellows, a native of Vermont, and the dock area became known as Bellows' Landing. A decade after Collins's arrival, events occurred which had the effect of changing the name to *Richmond* Landing, a title it bore for several decades. Richmond Landing was the Ottawa terminus of 'the Richmond Road', and that name is still familiar to all residents of the national capital region.

The story of the founding of the village of Richmond, which preceded Bytown by seven or eight years, deserves at least a brief mention here.

The village of Richmond was one of a series of settlements deliberately planned and fostered by the Imperial Government as a combination defence and immigration measure intended to help secure the provinces of Canada against the threat of United States' invasion. The best account of these settlements in print appears to be that by Andrew Haydon in his *Pioneer Sketches in the District of Bathurst*.

The war of 1812-14 between Canada and the United States was waged, even in Canada, largely by British soldiers on land and by a British navy on the Great Lakes. (The Canadian militia in 1812 numbered only about 4,000 as against 25,000 British 'regulars'.) The total civilian population between Montreal and Detroit in 1812 was only about 75,000, and many of these were recent American arrivals whose loyalty to the British Crown was speculative. Under these circumstances it occurred to the British authorities that a movement of loyal emigrants to fill up some of the empty spaces of Upper Canada might stiffen up the local population, and at the same time provide an outlet for some of the surplus population of the British Isles then seeking a means of migrating abroad. An incidental advantage in the mind of the authorities was that such new settlements might provide recruits for the

Canadian militia and thus lighten the burden on the British regulars.

The Earl of Bathurst, who had become Secretary for War and the Colonies in 1812, initiated the move in a letter addressed to the Governor General in Canada (Sir George Prevost). In October, 1813, Bathurst advised Sir George that there were a considerable number of Scottish tenant farmers in Sutherland and Caithness anxious to emigrate, and that it had occurred to him "that the male part of this population might be rendered in some degree valuable both for the present defence and the future protection of Upper Canada."

Sir George Prevost passed along the Earl of Bathurst's suggestion to Sir Gordon Drummond, then administrator of Upper Canada. Drummond was enthusiastic, and replied:

"Independent of the advantage to result from the population being thus increased by such loyal inhabitants, the ranks of the militia will be filled with a brave and hardy race of men whose desertion to the enemy would not be apprehended." He then outlined for the benefit of the Earl of Bathurst the kind of equipment which should be supplied to such settlers, including tools and implements needed for the settlers in their pioneer task.

One strategic location for a group of such settlers immediately came to mind. The direct line of communication between the forts at Kingston, the key to the defence of Lake Ontario, and Montreal, the metropolis of the Canadas, ran along the St. Lawrence, which was at one narrow point immediately under the guns of Fort Ogdensburgh. (This consideration came up again later on when the capital of Canada was to be chosen.) It was imperative to secure a safer rear line of communications between Kingston and Montreal. This was available along the line of the Cataraqui River, the Rideau Lakes and the Rideau River. It was already known from the reconnaissance of 1783 that a continuous inland waterway between Kingston and the Ottawa River could be developed. It would be a useful first step to inaugurate a series of permanent settlements along this water route. Action was taken early in 1815, when a Proclamation was published in Edinburgh, and carried in certain Scottish newspapers, inviting prospective settlers to come forward and declare their desire to go out to Canada on a state-assisted emigration scheme. The first contingent occupied four ships: three of them sailed from the Clyde in July, 1815, and a fourth early in August. They had on board a total of about 620 emigrants. They were too late in the season to get on their land in 1815, and so they spent the winter in camp at various points along the St. Lawrence. In March, 1816, the first of these settlements was located "on a most beautiful site" on the Pike River, later called the Tay. This new settlement was given the name of Perth, and later made into a county town.

Meantime the Napoleonic War had ended and with it the armed conflict with the United States. A new problem then arose in the disbanding of many of the regiments, on both sides of the water. It would not do to turn the veterans loose to join the ranks of the unemployed, without compensation of some kind. British and Canadian governments alike were short of ready cash, after a long war, but there was ample land for all. Every soldier who wished was given a grant of 100 acres of land, and officers 200 acres. Provisions for officers and men, and their families, for one year, "implements of husbandry and tools" and "other comforts, according to the necessities of the individuals" were also pledged.

By the autumn of 1816 there were about 1400 immigrants in the new settlements using Perth as their supply depot. The following year the stream of immigration continued and an area to the north of Perth was gradually occupied. By the summer of 1817, the incoming settlers were struggling along the forest trails to homesteads as much as twenty miles north-east of Perth. They eventually reached an area where they were much nearer to the Ottawa River than to the St. Lawrence. At this stage the authorities decided it was imperative to open up another depot, and link it with the Ottawa. A site near where the Jock River flowed into the Rideau was chosen, and surveyed. The core of the new settlement was to consist of disbanded soldiers of the 99th Regiment of Foot, stationed at Quebec City.

Toward the end of August, 1818, therefore, these new settlers were brought up the Ottawa River from Lachine, where they had been temporarily encamped, and were disembarked at Bellows' Landing, at the foot of the Chaudière Falls on the south side. Since they had decided to call their new settlement Richmond, after the Duke of Richmond, who had been sworn in as Governor-in-chief of British North America only three months before, the logical name for their temporary camp on the Ottawa was Richmond Landing. From that point of disembarkation a rough trail was cut through the bush to the new site. This, of course, was the "Richmond Road", still a familiar name in Ottawa's geography.

The Duke of Richmond came on a visit to the military village named after him, about a year after its first settlement, and the trip turned out to be of such a tragic and unusual nature that it still looms large in the legends of the district. Many people of the Ottawa Valley know that the Duke of Richmond died from the rabid bite of a pet fox, and have visited the cairn on the Richmond Road which commemorates this sad episode. The story is often told in such a way that one pictures the whole incident as taking place in or around the little village of Richmond, — the snap of the diseased fox, the symptoms of hydrophobia, and the final convulsion. Contemporary accounts show that the injury had been sustained in a curious fashion at Sorel, Lower Canada, nearly two months earlier, and the incident had been entirely forgotten in the meantime. On August 26th, the Duke of Richmond gave a dinner in Sergeant-Major Hill's inn at Richmond Village, but complained of being ill and was treated by a surgeon. On the following morning the Duke's party set off by water for Wright's Village. At "Chapman's",—where the Richmond Road began—a double team of oxen sent by "Squire" Wright was to meet him. But before the Duke arrived at that rendezvous, he was fatally stricken, and died in a barn nearby. The corpse was put in a plain deal box, and the teamster sent by Wright to greet and carry the Governor General to Wright's Village had instead the mournful duty of taking the body to Richmond Landing, where it was subsequently placed aboard a batteau, and conveyed to Montreal.

All in all, the little bay below the Chaudière on the Ontario side saw much early history while it was the "port" of entry for all traffic between the Montreal-Ottawa route and the new settlements of March and Richmond. It saw the first encampment of the Richmond settlers and all their mail and supplies were later routed through it. The site was used in 1826 by Colonel By's construction gangs on arrival, while they were waiting for permanent quarters to be established on Barracks Hill and along the site of the new canal. Robert Legget, author of the fine book *Rideau Waterway*, even develops the theory that except for a bit of land profiteering by Captain John LeBreton the entrance locks for the Rideau Canal might well have been located near that point. If that had been the only consequence, it would not have mattered very much, except in its incidental effect on the pattern and symmetry of modern Ottawa. Dr. Lucien Brault and Robert Legget add the intriguing observation that if the entrance locks had actually been built from "Richmond Landing" there would almost certainly have been a short branch canal added for entry to the Ottawa River *above* the Chaudière Falls, and that this might have just been the extra stimulus needed to continue navigation up the Ottawa, this in turn leading to the development of the Georgian Bay waterway to the West—a scheme so vigorously and vainly proposed over the next three quarters of a century.

CHAPTER FOUR

Bytown is Born

Twenty-nine years after the journey of Philemon Wright and his Massachusetts neighbours to spy out the land of the Chaudière, a military engineer arrived on the spot who was destined to change the face and fortunes of the region even more than "the Squire" from Woburn had done. Colonel John By, of the Royal Engineers, veteran of the Peninsular Wars and with nine years earlier experience in Canada (1802-1811), had been given the task of constructing a waterway from the Ottawa River to the harbour of Kingston on Lake Ontario, a distance of 125 miles, chiefly to serve as a military by-pass to the vulnerable St. Lawrence River route to Montreal, commanded by the American guns at Fort Ogdensburgh.

Colonel By reached the proposed Ottawa River terminus of the waterway in September of 1826. The broad sweep of the lovely landscape, the smoking cauldron of the Chaudière, the bold cliffs over which the Rideau leaped and the promontory which today is crowned by the Parliament Buildings, were little changed from Philemon Wright's first glimpses, or, for that matter, Samuel de Champlain's. But a closer inspection of the region, especially on the north bank of the Ottawa, revealed some startling changes in a quarter of a century. The Industrial Revolution had begun to make its mark even on the remote stretches of the Ottawa River. A steamship service now plied between Grenville and Wright's Landing, which was at the foot of the Chaudière Falls. Wright's Village supplied a flourishing farm community, and between them they counted a population of about eight hundred. The Columbia Hotel, erected by Philemon Wright six years earlier, was a three-storey structure 83 feet long and 40 feet wide, with four stacks of chimneys and 18 fireplaces. It boasted "a very large parlour which was often used as a ball room."

Wright's Village itself boasted five mills, four stores, two hotels, three schools, two distilleries and a brewery. Limekilns, tanneries, blacksmiths' forges, and miscellaneous store houses and work shops were already built or were under way.

The export trade in squared timber for the British market, pioneered by Philemon Wright two decades earlier, had vastly expanded in the meantime, and hundreds of thousands of cubic feet of white pine, oak and other timbers were being rafted down the Ottawa annually. At the time of Colonel By's first visit, all this timber still had to be dragged laboriously around the falls (oak would sink if not supported on a raft of lighter woods) or sent through and over the thundering torrent of the cascades. Rafts and cribs had to be broken up above the Falls, and the bruises and scars on the "sticks" had to be removed by dressing before the rafts could be reassembled for the journey downstream to Quebec City.

As soon as he was conveyed by ferry across to the south shore of the Ottawa, Colonel By would find a much more modest settlement named Richmond Landing, consisting of an inn, a store, a log cabin which had been used as a distillery, and a warehouse or two. In the whole of Nepean Township in 1826, as assessment rolls show, there were only 682 acres under cultivation. There was in all Nepean Township one stone house, three houses made of squared timber, a number of log cabins, and two shops. The animal census recorded 47 horses and 83 cows. Taxes collected for the year amounted to only $85. The returns for Gloucester Township were of a similar modest nature.

As for the summit of the high cliffs on which the Parliament Buildings were to be built one day, Colonel By found only a forest of beech and hemlock, still untouched by man, and at the southern approaches to the hill there were dense cedar swamps and a beaver meadow. It would be difficult to credit the difficulty of traversing the Ottawa bush if the records were not so explicit. Two years earlier, Major G. A. Eliot, of the Earl of Dalhousie's Staff, had been instructed to survey a possible site for a fortified village or strong point in the general neighborhood of what we now call Lower Town, but he had found the swamps and tangles so impenetrable that his surveyors had given up the task. Very little clearing had taken place anywhere on the south shore of the river, although John Burrows Honey and Nicholas Sparks had opened up a few acres on the western side of the plateau, and an area around the Richmond Landing was partly cleared. A passable trail had been cut through to the west and south, leading eventually to Richmond Village 20 miles away.

An account written by John MacTaggart, Colonel By's Clerk of Works, describing his first trial survey run through the dense woods extending from Sly (or Sleigh) Bay, (later Entrance Bay) — below the present site of the Chateau Laurier — to the Hog's Back Falls on the Rideau is highly revealing. MacTaggart and a party of eight men spent three days just struggling through to the Rideau River, a distance of about four miles. To run a surveyor's level through the woods and swamps proved impossible until the ground froze. With frost came heavy snow. MacTaggart describes the slow progress in December 1826 through what is now the Glebe and Ottawa South area. "No matter; we started again, cut holes through the thickets of these dismal swamps, directed a person to go about half a mile before, and wind a horn,

keeping to one place, until those behind came up; so that by the compass
and the sound, there being no sun, we might better grope out our course . . .
Placed in thick and dark snow-covered woods, where, unless the axemen
cut holes, a prospect of five yards could not be obtained; doubtful what kind
of land lay on either side, or directly before; calculating at the same time
the nature of canal-making in such places, the depth to dig, or the banks to
raise; while the weather was extremely cold, and the screws of the theodolite
would scarcely move; these things all considered, were teasing enough to
overcome, and required a little patience."

2

The early days of Bytown have been the subject of much patient and tenacious
research by historians, annalists, and chroniclers. Readers who wish to
explore the matter more fully are referred to the works of Lucien Brault,
Harry J. Walker, Blodwen Davies, Hamnett P. Hill and others. A study of
much merit was written by A. H. D. Ross, a grandson of one of Colonel By's
engineers. *Ottawa Past and Present* is largely based on records passed down
to the grandson, and in it the story of the origins of Bytown can be vividly
traced.

On September 26th, 1826, the Earl of Dalhousie, Governor in Chief of
British North America, placed in Colonel By's hands "a sketch plan of several
lots of land" he had purchased for the Crown to serve as the site of the head
locks of the canal and such villages or other settlements as might be needed
to house the construction workers.

What was called "Upper Town" was laid out first, as early as mid-October,
1826. The Crown had acquired title to the plateau and cliffs extending from
what is now Bank Street west toward Richmond Landing, and as far south
as the present Wellington Street. This area is now occupied by the
Confederation and Justice Buildings, the new Supreme Court, some
'temporary' war buildings, and the power house on Cliff Street. All these
lots were spoken for very quickly. The first settlers to build in Upper Town,
according to Ross, were Dr. A. J. Christie (Bytown's first newspaper pub-
lisher), Captain Andrew Wilson, Michael Burke, Thomas MacKay, Thomas
Doxey, and Thomas Burrowes. If Bytown had its 'Founding Fathers', surely
these six must be considered as eligible.

"Lower Town" was at first bounded by Murray Street, the Rideau River,
Rideau Street and Sussex Street. It, too, was on Crown land. Contemporary
plans show that about a half mile of vacant property separated the two
settlements (as did the excavation for the canal entrance locks, until the
Sappers' Bridge spanned it). The land in between was in part Ordnance
property, in part owned by Nicholas Sparks, but Colonel By's plans called

eventually for a fortification of what we call Parliament Hill, and this vacant land below the hill would then be needed for a moat and other protective works. Colonel By accordingly used his powers at once to expropriate 104 acres of Nicholas Sparks' holdings, in what is now the heart of urban Ottawa. It was not until 1848 that this land reverted to the Sparks estate.

Before the "Lower Town" lots could be used for dwellings it was necessary to drain off the swamps which occupied most of the area. In February 1827, Col. By rented the first seven lots on Rideau Street to persons connected with the Civil Service. Jean St. Louis built the first log cabin in Lower Town, located on the east side of Cumberland Street. At about the same time Pierre Desloges from St. Eustache, P.Q., built a log house at the corner of George and Dalhousie Streets.

3

Though the first sod for the construction of the Rideau Canal was turned by the Earl of Dalhousie as early as September 29th, 1826, large-scale excavation and lock-building could not get under way until a number of key preliminaries had been attended to. Surveys, roads, camps, bridges, the letting of construction contracts, the recruiting of skilled artisans and the mobilization of workmen had to be arranged and dealt with first. Two companies of Royal Sappers and Miners were recruited in England especially for the Canal construction. The first contingent of these (81 to a company) arrived at Bytown on June 1st, 1827, and lived under canvas at the then Nepean Point, (later called LeBreton Flats) beside Richmond Landing, until barracks could be completed on the hill above the River. Advertisements inviting private contractors to submit tenders for the main construction projects were published in Montreal in the spring and summer of 1827. Montreal was able to provide some entrepreneurs and master builders already familiar with canal construction.

Meantime Colonel By had selected a site for his own residence, on what came to be known as "the Colonel's Hill", and in later years, when Major Bolton had succeeded Colonel By as commanding officer, as "the Major's Hill", and which is now Major's Hill Park north of the Chateau Laurier. The view from Colonel By's front porch and front yard, looking, as it did, over and up the Ottawa River and toward the Laurentian Mountains, excited the admiration of all visitors. Areas at the head of the bay up which the entrance locks were to be constructed were set aside as workyards and the building of stone workshops was begun.

There still exist some detailed descriptions of Bytown written in 1828 and 1829. In 1828, Joseph Bouchette, Surveyor General of Lower Canada, visited Colonel By's two townsites, and afterwards wrote: "The streets are laid out

with much regularity, and of a liberal width that will hereafter contribute to
the convenience, salubrity and elegance of the place. The number of houses
now built is about 150, most of which are constructed of wood; frequently
in a style of neatness and taste that reflects great credit upon the Inhabitants.
On the elevated banks of the Bay, the hospital, an extensive stone building,
and three Barracks stand conspicuous; nearly on a level with them, and on
the eastern side of the Bay, is the residence of Colonel By. From his verandah
the most splendid view is beheld that the magnificent scenery of the Canadas
affords."

Thomas Burrowes in 1829 counted 21 civilian buildings in Upper Town
and 126 in Lower Town. Some of the first lessees in Lower Town were James
Fitzgibbon, William Tornay, John Burrows, John Adamson, Thomas
Burrowes, Matthew Connell, Joseph McCloy, William Hall, William Clegg
and Isaac Berichon. During 1828 and 1829, Ross adds, some of the French-
speaking Canadians who settled in Bytown were John Amyot, Louis Audet,
Joseph Aumond, Pierre Baby, Luc Barrie, Charles Brassard, Erysonthe de
Brie, Joseph Chalifoux, Jean Baptiste, Couturier Andre Dandurand, Henry
Donic, Alexander Ethier, Joseph Galipaut, Jean Baptiste Homier, Louis
Xavier Homier, Paul François Homier, Jean Baptiste Lacroix, F. X. Labelle,
Joseph Lafontaine, Paul Lamothe, J. F. Montreuil, Joseph Nadeau, Pierre
Parantin, Michael Periad, Charles Rainville, Louis Rainville, Antoine
Robillard, Pierre Saucier, Antoine Seguin and Joachim Valiquette. It is clear
that Canadians of French origin mingled in Bytown with Canadians of other
origins from the very first day.

Bouchette's reference to the wide streets calls attention to Colonel By's
foresight in laying out Rideau Street with the then unusual width of a chain
and a half (99 feet). It was, of course, on Crown land. Wellington Street,
west of Barrack Hill, was partly on Nicholas Sparks' property, partly on
Crown land. Colonel By added a 33 foot strip from the Ordnance property
to the 66 foot allowance on the Sparks property to make Wellington Street
conform in width to Rideau, thus averting one headache for future capital
planners.

4

The earliest residents of any community come to acquire a special interest
for the historians later on. The human elements and ingredients of early
Bytown would merit a special study. They included personalities and characters of distinction in their own right, quite apart from the accident that they
were also first pioneers and charter citizens. Dr. A. J. Christie, mentioned
above, was an M.A. of Aberdeen and an M.D. of Edinburgh, a former editor
of the Montreal *Herald* and later of the Montreal *Gazette*, before he even set

eyes on Bytown. Captain Andrew Wilson, another pioneer builder in "Upper Town", was the author of a three volume naval history. Thomas Burrowes was an engineer from Worcester who served Colonel By faithfully during the construction of the Rideau Canal and later settled down near Kingston Mills. Thomas MacKay figures prominently in a later reference in this chapter. The prospects for financial gain, for employment, for a settled community, for opportunities in retail trade, in the professions, drew miscellaneous human stocks and strands from far and wide. The English engineers, sappers and miners of Colonel By's official staff were joined by Montreal contractors and their workmen, and a corps of skilled Scottish masons was induced to leave their own land and find work in Canada. The Ottawa Valley supplied native axemen and timber workers, many of them *Canadiens*. Several shiploads of Irish immigrants added color and zest to the construction works and the nearby camps.

It was a shifting and transient population, in part, bound to disperse when the canal was finished. But some of the artificers settled down permanently in the region, as did several of the contractors. The English sappers and miners were offered grants of land as an inducement to stay, when their services were no longer needed on the canal. Bytown, like other pioneer settlements, was founded by a mixed stock, rich in the virtues of courage, industry and ingenuity.

5

Annalists and historians have compiled a list of "firsts" in the history of Bytown. Some of these are well established, others may be more legend than history. The first white child was born at Bytown on September 25, 1826, to Mr. and Mrs. Thomas Burrowes, and was christened John By Burrowes. In 1827, Bytown's first house of worship was erected in Lower Town, a Methodist meeting house situated about where Rideau and Chapel Streets are now. The first school was started in the same year by James Maloney. The first civilian doctors (Christie, McQueen and Stewart) began practice in 1827. Several taverns and a local brewery opened in the same year. Merchants opened shops on a primitive Rideau Street.

Even a bare list like this throws some light on the emerging urban community of Bytown. In 1827, the first Catholic mass was celebrated "in a house at the north end of Bank St." In 1828 the first public meeting was held to elect public officers, and a sort of vigilant committee was chosen; in the same year St. Andrew's Presbyterian Church opened for divine service. In 1829 came the first public fair, the first market place and market building. In the same year the first timber slide was built around the Chaudière Falls. (One of Philemon Wright's sons had travelled to Sweden and Norway to see how they built such slides there.) In 1830, the first mill was drawing power from the Rideau Falls; and in the following year the first bridge was thrown over the Rideau River just above the Falls. Even more sophisticated developments were on the way. About 1835 the first bank agents settled at Bytown, the first newspaper appeared in 1836, the first social agency, the Bytown Dorcas Society, began work in 1837; the first theatrical performance is recorded in the same year. In 1838 the first reading rooms were opened; followed in 1841 by a circulating library; and in 1847 by a branch of the Mechanics Institute.

6

While the construction camp on the banks of the canal was coalescing with the two separate villages, "Upper Town" and "Lower Town", into a pioneer community (which without formal ceremony came to be called Colonel By's Town, or, more simply, Bytown,) there was new activity at the site of the Chaudière. Colonel By had seen at once the utility of a bridge or series of bridges across the Ottawa at this narrow point. His chief sources of food, fodder, hay, meat, dressed lumber, lime, and other building supplies would for a long time be the north shore of the Ottawa, and the general area served by Wright's Village. He asked the Earl of Dalhousie for authority to bridge the Ottawa just below the Falls. This was granted without difficulty, but the actual construction proved to constitute a series of major challenges; and two years were required to finish the seven separate spans.

The main span bridged a 212 foot channel through which the tumultuous waters of the Ottawa River poured. A wooden truss bridge supported by specially heavy chains brought up from the naval dockyards at Kingston was built to span this main channel, and it served the two communities until 1835. When it collapsed, the nearby residents were again compelled to depend on ferries. In 1843 a fine suspension bridge, designed by Samuel Keefer, restored convenient communication between Wright's Village in Canada East and Richmond Landing and Bytown in Canada West.

7

The Rideau Canal winds placidly through modern Ottawa, eloquent of an age long past, its banks carefully tended as parks, its borders forming modern motor parkways and driveways and boulevards, its still waters mirroring stately elms and deep-foliaged maples, spangled with flower beds, breathing peace and calm all along its pleasant course. What tourist of today can picture it as a military work thrown up in some haste to convey military stores and gunboats on a safe route between Upper and Lower Canada, away from the menacing American guns of Fort Ogdensburgh? And so thoroughly have the scars of construction been healed over that only the reader of history will guess the epic story of its building, the heroic mastery over almost impossible obstacles and handicaps. Without much more technology than the builders of Stonehenge commanded, Colonel By and his engineers built a 125 mile waterway through what was still a largely untamed stretch of Upper Canada rock and bush, infested with malarial mosquitoes and black flies. He and his workmen cut and blasted through massive rock ridges, gouged out deep channels in stiff clay, dammed the raging Rideau River at Hog's Back, carried the canal through 'Dow's Great Swamp' by massive earthworks, solved baffling engineering problems all along the 125 mile route, with hand power and ox power but nothing more. Nothing but dogged and heroic determination to see the project through.

The utility and indeed the feasibility, of such a waterway had been seen long before Colonel By arrived at the Chaudière in 1826. The need of it was urged by military engineers before the Revolutionary War was over in 1783. The Imperial Government hoped for a time that the financial burden of such a canal system could be borne in part at least by the new settlers, but pioneers are traditionally and inevitably hard up for ready cash. The establishment of the semi-military settlements along the Rideau River system from Perth to Richmond after 1818 lent new impetus to the promoters of the canal scheme. Such a waterway would incidentally provide the new settlers with a useful commercial route for transporting their supplies and export produce. By 1825, the British Government had decided that the project was necessary and should be proceeded with, even if the entire cost had to come out of the British taxpayer. The Royal Engineers were chosen to undertake the task, under command of Colonel John By.

8

A detailed account of the construction of the Rideau Canal falls outside the aim of this book. In any event, it has been so well done already that future historians can turn with a good conscience to other and more virgin areas. A. H. D. Ross, in the book already cited, gives a brief but graphic account of some parts of the story. Robert Legget's *Rideau Waterway* cannot be overpraised as a vivid, complete, popular account of the whole project. Legget's testimony to the great achievement of Colonel By and his staff and workmen comes with especial weight as being the opinion of a professional engineer. He rates the project as "the greatest work of British military engineers to be carried out in eastern North America," and "one of the great engineering works of the last century." He says that Colonel By "built locks and control dams on a scale previously unheard of, even in early American engineering circles." There were no bull-dozers, no giant earth-moving equipment, no air compressors, no modern explosives. There was not even horse power. The Rideau Canal locks and dams were built by stone masons, using small winches and hand cranes to place blocks of stone, which might weigh a ton or more. The excavations in clay were made by barefooted laborers with wheel barrows and picks and shovels. In rock the holes for gunpowder had to be tediously and laboriously gouged out, using rock chisels and sledge hammers.

The work thus began in the autumn of 1826 was finished, in spite of all setbacks and miscalculations, in the spring of 1832. The official opening took the form of a triumphal tour from Kingston to Ottawa, on a steam vessel, (originally called *The Pumper*, but re-named *The Rideau* for this special occasion), the party reaching the Ottawa wharf at the head of the flight locks (where the Union Station tracks are today) on May 29, 1832.

This remarkable waterway had been completed for £800,000, which sounds like a reasonable sum today, but it exceeded the original estimates by at least £300,000 and, even worse, a final item of about £82,000 appears to have been expended without prior authority. The investigations afterwards showed that there was not the slightest shadow on Colonel John By's probity: he had been authorized at the beginning to push ahead with the work without waiting for parliamentary appropriations, and he ended up a victim of the well-known phenomenon of our own day, of a public works project costing a good deal more than early estimates had foretold.

9

If there is any place in the modern capital haunted by the spirit of Colonel John By, I would guess that it is beside the west bank of the entrance locks, half way between the crest of Parliament Hill and the Ottawa River. One of the stone workshops erected close by the flight of locks still stands as it did when built in 1827,—the oldest existing building in Ottawa. It is now the Museum of the Historical Society, long known as the Women's Canadian Historical Society of Ottawa. The lease of the building was presented by the federal government to Mayor Charlotte Whitton of Ottawa, on the 125th anniversary of the beginning of construction of the Rideau Canal; and the Mayor in turn presented to the President of the Society the key to the premises. Among the thousands of relics owned by the Society, the By collection is of especial interest. "Perhaps the most personal of all the exhibits is upstairs," writes Robert Legget, "in the small room known as the By room, which overlooks the locks. Here is the Colonel's own chair, and here he regularly sat to write those reports on the building, which gave meaning, color and strength to the stirring history of the Rideau Waterway."

Colonel By and his engineers left their enduring marks on the landscape of Bytown, — the Waterway itself, the early construction roads, the Chaudière, Sappers' and Pooley's Bridges, the street patterns of Upper and Lower Town. There were other less intentional monuments and consequences. Everyone who has toured in the country bordering the Rideau Canal must have admired the many fine clean-cut limestone dwellings with their distinctive architecture and attractive doorways with fanlights above, which still testify to the skill and artistry of the stone masons Colonel By brought to the region to work on his canal locks and dams. Many of his artisans and laborers elected to stay on after the construction was over and their subsequent careers are intimately interwoven into the life of Bytown and the Ottawa Valley. It would be a fascinating project to trace the history of those families who first came to the region in this way and whose descendants constitute many of the 'old families' here. One interesting illustration must suffice.

Thomas MacKay was a native of Perth, Scotland. He migrated to Lower Canada in 1817 and four years later linked up with John Redpath to do contract work on the first Lachine Canal. By 1824 this work was finished, and both MacKay and Redpath had won a widespread and favorable reputation as builders and contractors. Redpath stayed on in Montreal and left his mark on the architecture of the city—Notre Dame Cathedral, McGill University, for example—while MacKay was invited by Colonel By to come to the Chaudière country in the fall of 1826 to give advice on the location of the flight of locks linking the Ottawa River with the upper reaches of the Canal. MacKay's masons contributed valuable service in the building of the Chaudière Bridges, and when the first contractor for the eight locks below the present Chateau Laurier was defeated by springs and difficult excavation, it was MacKay who took over and successfully completed that key section of canal construction. MacKay began to acquire property in the Bytown area as soon as the villages were surveyed. In the fall of 1826 he bid for a lot located about where the Justice Building now stands on Wellington Street. He was one of the officers elected to the first council set up to govern Bytown, being elected Bailiff. It was MacKay's corps of stone-masons who, during a lull in the construction of the canal locks, built "the Scotch Kirk," predecessor of the present St. Andrew's Presbyterian Church on Wellington Street. That was in 1828-9, and when the first "Kirk Session" was organized, MacKay was one of the first three elders. About the time Colonel By was packing up to return to England, MacKay built a grist mill and a saw mill at the eastern edge of the Rideau Falls. His operations expanded steadily in this area, which he called New Edinburgh. A ship called the *Thomas MacKay* was built by him at the foot of the falls on the Ottawa River. He erected a five-storey grist mill in the 1840's, followed by a carding mill.

With his profits from the construction work on the Canal and other enterprises, MacKay purchased 110 acres of wild land east of New Edinburgh (MacKay's Bush), and in 1838 he moved into a substantial stone house which became known as MacKay's "Castle". He himself called it Rideau Hall, and with many additions and alterations it is still there as part of the permanent residence of Canada's Governor General. MacKay also built the Bytown Court House and the Bytown Gaol. MacKay's manufactures found some temporary fame in wider circles: against world competition he won a gold medal for his blankets at the Great Exhibition of 1851. He was an active figure in the first railway link between Ottawa and the St. Lawrence River (the Bytown and Prescott Railway, 1854) though he lived just long enough to see the arrival of the first train to a siding not far from his New Edinburgh mills and factories. His commercial interests did not hinder him from serving as the representative of Russell County in the Legislature of Upper Canada, and when the two Canadas were joined in the Act of Union he was appointed to the Legislative Council of the Province of Canada, where he served until his death.

I find it a melancholy reflection, even today, that Colonel By's outstanding achievement was never adequately recognized by his own government. He went back to his homeland to face official investigations on the excessive cost of the Rideau waterway. He retired to his native village of Frant, near Tunbridge Wells, and fell into a state of ill health, almost certainly brought on in part by his exertions in the fever-ridden reaches of the Rideau waterway, dying at 53. He had hoped for military promotion; perhaps for a knighthood: neither was granted him. For a long time he was not much remembered by the residents of Upper Canada for whom he had toiled so valiantly. Is it symbolic that there still stands beside the canal an engraved stone, the base for a monument that was never built? In recent years some progress has been made in redeeming this neglect. There is Byward Market, Colonel By Drive, bordering the Rideau Canal from the Bronson Avenue Bridge to the Hog's Back falls, there is a memorial fountain below Laurier Avenue; and a rude monument of stonework from the old Sappers' Bridge stands in Major's Hill Park to mark the approximate site of his residence.

10

As we have seen, the construction of the Rideau Canal called into being almost over night the two settlements, Upper and Lower Town, supplemented for a while by construction camps and a scattering of squatters on lands for which no rental had to be paid. As many as 2,000 workers may have been employed in the Bytown area at the peak of construction, but once the contracts were complete most of these men and their families moved along to other portions of the work or to other employment elsewhere. The early prosperity of Bytown very largely was supported by periodic shipments of silver coins from the British Treasury, and the completion of the Canal works, the departure of the contractors, and the release of the hundreds of engineers, sappers, masons and carpenters left Bytown to its own local and regional resources. The peak of population must have fallen off considerably as a result. It seems to have declined to about 1,000 persons by 1832. This was about the same as the population of Wright's Village on the north side of the river. By 1837 the population of Bytown had modestly risen to 1,300, by 1841 it had risen again to 3,122 and by 1851 to 7,760.

The population figures suggest that after the completion of the Rideau Waterway, Bytown began to find its feet as a commercial and industrial centre of some importance. The potential wealth of the Ottawa Valley was, of course, prodigious. It appeared to some extent in the stretches of excellent farm land suitable for grain crops and dairying, in the boundless water powers available in the Ottawa and tributary streams, and most especially in the vast forest wealth of the Ottawa River watershed.

The Ottawa River is about 700 miles long and drains an area of over 55,000 square miles, about equal to the area of England and Wales combined. In its virgin state almost half of the entire Ottawa watershed was forested with white and red pine, and white pine was one of the most desirable woods to be found in North America. It was light, strong, soft, easily worked, obtainable in vast quantity, and suitable for large straight sticks, deals, or squared timbers. It was much sought after for ship-building timber, masts and deckplanking, for floors, interior fittings and even for engineer's patterns. Red pine was not so light and was less suitable for carpenter's wood, but it was stronger and highly acceptable for use in larger structures.

11

Commercial exploitation of the forests of the Ottawa Valley has gone through a number of interesting stages, the first of which began with Philemon Wright's famous pioneer drive of squared timber down to Quebec City in 1807 for the war-starved British market. The era of overseas export of square timber dominated the Ottawa industry until about 1850, when it began to be challenged by the new sawn-lumber export trade, with the U.S. as the chief market. The square timber trade thereafter shared the field with the new sawn lumber industry for half a century. As the one soared, the other fell off. The square timber trade reached a peak about 1865 but then declined, and by the end of the century it was just about finished. Meantime the manufacture and export of sawn lumber, mainly to the United States, began a rise to a position of dominating importance, until by 1870 Ottawa was the most important saw mill centre in Canada. Fifty years later, much of the best lumbering country having been 'logged over', there was a gradual change in the nature of the industry for the third time, as the manufacture of pulp and paper and other specialties emerged, but the Ottawa Valley will always be important for its woods products of one kind or another.

The effect of these several stages on the fortunes of Bytown (later Ottawa) was in every case substantial. The square timber export trade to Britain added much human zest and color to the Chaudière Falls and Ottawa Valley regions, but in the earlier years it brought only modest benefits to Bytown merchants. The white pine timbers were cut down and squared in the upper reaches of the river system, they were (after 1829) floated down the timber slides beside the Chaudière, reassembled into rafts and driven downstream toward Quebec City. Some of the money spent in extracting the square timber ultimately found its way into Bytown, of course, to pay for bush supplies needed upstream, or en route, or because the exporters lived in Bytown and spent some of their profits in the neighborhood. But the early square timber trade, with all its romantic and spirited atmosphere, could never support a large community at the junction of the Ottawa and the tributary streams, which was only a transit point.

In the period now under review, that is to say from 1832 to 1850, the elements of urban growth were, in the first place, this export trade in square timber, the retail market for farmers of the Ottawa Valley, and the forwarding and transport business using the new Rideau Canal and the Ottawa River both above and below the Chaudière Falls. A few modest local mills and factories got established during this period. For example, as early as 1830, Jean-Baptiste St. Louis had erected Bytown's first mill, on the Bywash near Cumberland and York Streets. Thomas MacKay had a grist mill on the Rideau in 1833, and some time later he purchased St. Louis' mill also. Grist and saw mills, and an oatmeal mill, are mentioned by Ottawa's chroniclers at least as early as 1843. But these were still small local enterprises, neither employing much labor nor bringing much outside revenue into the community. The big commercial break for Bytown arrived just about the time it was incorporated as a town. The subsequent decade was the most flourishing and most eventful in its earlier history.

12

The power possibilities of the Chaudière Falls had been eyed hungrily by ambitious promoters for many years, at least as far back as Robert Randall in 1807. There were no serious mechanical problems in the harnessing of the falls. The reason why nothing much was done between 1807 and 1850 was an economic one. What commodity could be manufactured at the falls which would find a profitable market in the outside world?

The first answer came about 1848 or 1849, when a successful lumberman of New England, Henry Franklin Bronson, appeared on the scene.

A story similar to that of Philemon Wright and his neighbours, was, in fact, about to be unfolded, with variations. Wright had come to the Ottawa seeking land for his family, from an older settled part of North America, where the virgin land resources had been thoroughly picked over. Bronson and his partner J. G. Harris had earlier developed an extensive lumbering business south of the line: they too were now facing a decline in their activities, as the forest resources of the Adirondacks were depleted. In the 1840's, Bronson, like Wright, came first on a reconnaissance. He liked what he saw, and made preparations to sell out his American interests, and move up to Canada. Other Americans at about the same time saw the possibilities for export mills at the Chaudière.

A. R. M. Lower, historian of the Canadian lumber industry, links the sudden "American invasion" of this period directly with the abrupt appearance of a profitable American market for sawn lumber at just this time.

One reason why in spite of its obvious water power advantages Bytown had not earlier become a sawmill town was that everyone interested in forest exploitation was already fully occupied in producing square timber for the Quebec market, and outside capital was not interested in investing in mills at Bytown until a promising outside market for sawn lumber appeared. Now, almost overnight, the 'hydraulic lots' at the Chaudière seemed highly attractive. By an order-in-council of September 30, 1852, they were placed by the municipality on the open market, with the condition that the buyers should utilize the water power for mills.

The next seven years were momentous. In 1851 Captain Levi Young from Maine built a small mill on the Bytown side of the river. O. H. Ingram and A. H. Baldwin soon followed. The latter is credited by Lower with the first shipment of lumber from the Chaudière to the American market. In the following year, Captain J. J. Harris, H. F. Bronson, and Messrs. Perley and Pattee, all Americans engaged in the lumber trade, began occupying the hydraulic lots and utilizing the tremendous power resources of the Falls. The speed with which the area was then occupied may be judged by the fact that by 1858 all available spots around the Chaudière were covered with mills and millyards.

Ottawa's export market in sawn lumber to the United States had been facilitated in the 1830's by the completion of a water route all the way to New York, via Montreal, the Richelieu Canal, Lake Champlain and the

Hudson. And about the time the Chaudière power was being harnessed and the old beauty spots on its banks were being obliterated by industrial plants, the first steam railway reached Ottawa from the St. Lawrence. It made its terminus, rather oddly, near the Rideau Falls rather than the Chaudière. The first locomotive and train via the Prescott to Bytown (later Ottawa) Railway reached Ottawa on Christmas Day, 1854. The enterprise was originally promoted by groups in Bytown and Prescott, and the Act of incorporation gave them the right to ply boats on the St. Lawrence, where they could link up with the Ogdensburg Railway. When local capital proved unequal to the task, capital from Boston came to the rescue. The promoters thought that if successful the railway line might be pushed still further north and west as far as Sault Ste. Marie, tapping the timber resources of a vast area and feeding the products to Boston and the Atlantic coast.

Thus the whole physical appearance of the Bytown-Ottawa region was being rapidly altered by the dramatic new turn given to the exploitation of the vast forest resources of the Ottawa River Valley after 1850.

The Chaudière sawmill sites were developed in the first instance by experienced men of substance, mostly Americans. Two other arrivals of the decade, however, came virtually without financial resources. Before long these two outdistanced any of their wealthy predecessors. One was a native of Vermont, Ezra Butler Eddy, who came to the Chaudière in 1854 and leased property from Ruggles Wright in December, 1856. The other, John Rudolphus Booth was born near Waterloo, Lower Canada, and opened his first mill at Ottawa, a single-saw plant, four years later.

Eddy first rented some space in a building from Ruggles Wright, and, with the assistance of his wife, began making safety matches. He soon branched out into making clothes pins, wooden wash bowls, and wooden pails. In 1866 he built a large sawmill, and four years later purchased from the Wright estate an island property on which he built a match factory. He eventually became known as the leading match manufacturer in the world. By 1873 he had become a millionaire. He served several times as mayor of Hull and represented the riding for four years at Quebec City.

John R. Booth is said to have arrived at Ottawa with $9. in his pockets. He rented a small mill from Alonzo Wright, and teamed up with Robert Dollar (destined later to become world famous as a U.S. shipowner) to manufacture shingles. Booth's enterprises prospered and flourished until at the time of his death he was the head of what was said to be the largest lumber business in the world. Already, by 1870 the Booth firm had an output of thirty million feet of pine. In the 1880's he built, with little outside help, the Canada Atlantic Railway, which eventually extended from Ottawa to Parry Sound.

Such men as these wrote exciting pages in the industrial story of the Ottawa Valley, and all of them traced back their beginnings to the momentous decade between 1850 and 1860.

The population of Bytown in 1851 was 7,760, and it doubled in the following decade. Civic pride swelled as the industrial expansion mounted, and in 1853 the Mayor of Bytown, which had been incorporated as a town only three years before, was authorized to petition the Executive Council of the Province of Canada for incorporation as a city. This privilege was granted, the effective date being January 1st, 1855. Colonel By's construction camp had come a long way in three decades. It was now the City of Ottawa. And the crowning development was still to come.

CHAPTER FIVE

Queen Victoria Chooses

Everyone knows that it was Queen Victoria who chose Ottawa to be the capital of Canada. Folk lore on the incident is uncomplicated, and in some versions beguiling. Far off across the Atlantic, the young Queen was invited to select for the honor one of a number of obscure but ambitious colonial towns. In this dilemma, did she, as cynics have sometimes pretended, merely bring her index finger down at random on the map, giving Ottawa the decision by pure chance? Or—a prettier tale—were her doubts resolved by a sketch of the cliffs above the Ottawa River, an admirable site for the new public buildings?—a sketch executed on the spot a few months earlier by Lady Head, wife of the Governor General, after a luncheon tendered by the corporation of the city of Ottawa to the Viceregal visitors?

Perhaps such a delightful legend should not be disturbed, but the historic record is more complicated. The 'seat of government' question, as it was commonly called, soured provincial politics for twenty years. It bred bitterness between rival cities, between Upper and Lower Canada, between Catholic and Protestant, English and French-speaking Canadians. Prestige, status, cultural and social advantages, local purchasing power, increased local employment, future growth, these and other factors were at stake in the choice. Ministries were reshuffled as a result of the issue, individual cabinet ministers resigned, governments were overthrown, legislatures debated the issue for many weeks, the capital of Canada was moved back and forth several times in fifteen years, and the Queen was only appealed to at last when everything else seemed to have failed. Even after she had chosen, the issue was violently revived, and her choice almost repudiated.

One more point. All this to-do was not about the capital of the federal union of Canada, the Dominion of Canada. Most of it occurred years before a federal union was even a subject of serious debate. The capital Queen Victoria chose—the one which a later legislature almost repudiated—was the capital of the United *Province* of Canada. When the Fathers of Confederation met at Charlottetown and at Quebec in 1864, the issue revived. Which city should be the capital of the new federal Dominion? Perhaps fortunately for the future of Ottawa, over two million dollars of borrowed money had meanwhile been invested in provincial capital buildings overlooking the Ottawa River. What was not yet the functioning capital of the *Province* of

Canada—since the buildings were not yet ready—was in 1864 chosen *a second time* to be a capital city, this time the capital of the federal union of Canada, a *Dominion* soon to extend "from sea to sea".

Even that does not quite terminate the story. There is substantial evidence that as late as the winter of 1866-67 there was some opposition among the Fathers of Confederation to the choice of Ottawa as the Dominion capital. We might suppose that after July 1st, 1867, at any rate, it could be taken for granted that Ottawa would remain the capital, and that even Viscount Monck —a leading critic of the choice—would resign himself to the inevitable. But the son of a deputy minister of 1867, in some reminiscences prepared for the Women's Canadian Historical Association of Ottawa, wrote a paragraph which suggests otherwise:

"For the first few years after Confederation there was much doubt as to the wisdom of having selected Ottawa as the capital," Colonel C. P. Meredith recalled, " and the after dinner talk at Rideau Hall in Lord Monck's regime was frequently on this topic, and it was felt that it would be impossible for the Government to remain here and that the Parliament buildings would be sold to a religious order." (!)

2

The complete story from 1840 to 1867, adequately buttressed by historic documents, would fill many pages, and as it is an issue now long dead and buried, that would be out of proportion here. But the highlights deserve inclusion.

During the years while Bytown was growing up from a canal construction camp into a lively commercial village, and from that into an industrial and manufacturing centre of some importance, as outlined above, political skirmishing in other parts of the province of Canada was playing fast and loose with its ultimate national destiny, alternately raising and dashing hopes.

Rivalry for the seat of government began with the Act of Union in 1840. Up to that time there were two separate provinces, two capitals. Quebec City had been unchallenged as the seat of government for Lower Canada: its historic claims dated back to 1608. The newly created province of Upper Canada had begun with a capital at Newark (Niagara-on-the-Lake). Governor Simcoe had turned a brief wistful glance westward to London on the Thames, but on imperial instructions had moved the capital to 'Muddy' York—Toronto as it was called after 1834.

The union of the two Canadas in 1840 under one government, with one legislature and one council, created the problem. Only one capital was now required. Where should it be located? Quebec City was too far east: Toronto, it was thought, was too far west. Upper Canada had entered the Union with the understanding that the new capital would be located somewhere within its territory. The Act of Union conferred on the Governor General the right to decide.

Lord Sydenham chose the scenic and historic community of Kingston, where Lake Ontario runs into the St. Lawrence. Kingston had a population of about 5,000 in 1841. It possessed no public buildings suitable for housing a provincial government, but that could soon be remedied.

Lord Sydenham's choice of Kingston soon proved to be highly unpopular with the majority of the Legislature. French-speaking members were in favor of moving the capital back to Canada East (the new name for Lower Canada). They proposed Montreal. In the autumn of 1842, there was a long debate on the subject in the Legislature, in which the limitations of Kingston as a capital were rudely exposed. The Colonial Secretary at Westminster was opposed to a change, however, and the citizens of Kingston fought a stout rearguard action. Nevertheless, in October 1843, the provincial legislature introduced a formal motion to transfer the capital to Montreal, and after a lengthy and heated discussion the resolution passed. In November, 1844, the first session at Montreal opened in a re-modelled market building in a square now called Place Youville.

3

A dispassionate observer from the outside might well have regarded Montreal as in the main the most suitable place in the province of Canada for the seat of government. At any rate, once there, it appeared likely to stay. But in 1849, a bad year for the citizens of Montreal, the riot aroused by the Rebellion Losses Bill, the burning of the Parliament Buildings, and the physical attack on Lord Elgin in the streets of Montreal forever destroyed, as it proved, Montreal's hopes for a permanent seat of government. The Annexation Manifesto of 1849 did not help matters either.

The decision to move out of Montreal opened up the old sores, and for another decade the "seat of government" question, as it was called, was almost constantly under public debate, with all the rivals for the honor in full cry.

The first arrangement by the Canadian government, after the Montreal fire, took the form of an ambulatory or oscillating capital, shifting back and forth between the two historic capital cities, Toronto and Quebec City. The seat was first moved to Toronto in 1849, then to Quebec City until 1855, then back to Toronto.

An ambulatory capital turned out to be expensive and inconvenient. Every time a change was imminent the old jealousies between Upper and Lower Canada flared up again. A capital had symbolic significance, and neither

Jack nor Jacques would give up easily. The hope and dream that the Act of Union would result in a spiritual as well as a constitutional congress of diverse peoples was failing to materialize. Some officials and legislators professed to see merit in the necessity of residing by turns in the heart of the old French-speaking Catholic Canada, and then in the newer Protestant English-speaking metropolis. Sir Edmund Walker Head, Governor General, in a dispatch of 1855, reported that during four years of sessional residence at Quebec City the Upper Canadian members had learned more about that part of Canada and its people and had shed some of their prejudices "by living in good fellowship and brotherhood with their French brethren." He thought that the reverse benefit would accrue when the Quebec members went to reside in Toronto.

But events in the following year changed the Governor General's view. In April, 1856, after prolonged debate, the Legislature 'finally' decided that Quebec should be the permanent capital, and that the erection of parliament buildings should begin there at once. But there was nothing 'final' about the decision, as it proved. A pair of 'want of confidence' amendments connected with the 'seat of government' question dragged on through the first half of May, 1856. On one of the divisions a majority of the Upper Canada members voted against the government. Under the convention of 'double majority' in force at the time, this was interpreted as equivalent to a government defeat. Advantage was taken of the adverse vote to recast the ministry, though a general election was averted. Nothing had been done to rescind the motion choosing Quebec as the permanent seat of government, but further progress was blocked when the Legislative Council, which had not been consulted in advance, struck out of the Supply Bill the sum of £50,000 placed there by the government to finance a start on the erection of permanent government buildings at Quebec City.

So the session of 1857 began with the whole issue still in the air. The majority of the Upper Canada members were still determined not to agree to Quebec City as the capital. Sir Edmund Head suggested a petition to the Queen asking Her Majesty to settle the matter. John A. Macdonald, government leader for Canada West in the Assembly, accepted the suggestion. The Council also found the suggestion palatable. There was further debate, at the end of which two addresses were forwarded to the Queen, each of them praying "that Your Majesty will be graciously pleased to exercise your Royal Prerogative, and select some place for the permanent seat of Government in Canada."

There was a general election expected in the late fall, and the young John A. Macdonald was already a sufficiently shrewd politician to write a private letter to the Permanent Under-Secretary at Westminster, advising that it would "not be expedient" that the Queen's decision should be given for eight or ten months. He did not want this hoary and highly contentious issue injected into the Canadian election campaign of 1857.

4

Sir Edmund Head forwarded the petitions with a covering dispatch, in which he carefully refrained from expressing any official views about which city should be chosen, though he did voice his own personal conviction "that the matter ought to be definitely settled."

Also, since he felt that he would be expected to supply the British Government and the Queen with all the data possible to help the Queen make a wise decision, he supplemented the review of the issue in his public dispatch with a carefully written private memorandum. This confidential paper may well have been decisive in shaping the Queen's choice, and for any student of the subject it is compulsory reading. The language is so terse that extracts from it will serve better than any summary.

Sir Edmund Head's memorandum opened with a reminder that the Legislature in 1856 had voted against the periodic transfer of the seat of government. Thus the adoption of a fixed seat of government was now a necessity. To keep the matter open was to supply "a constant stimulant to the hatred of race and the conflict of religious feeling". Irrespective then of the periodic expense, the suspension of public business and the personal inconvenience caused by the change from one place to another, the interests of Canada as a whole, and the security of the Union, demanded a solution of the difficulty.

"Ottawa is the only place which will be accepted by the majority of Upper and Lower Canada as a fair compromise," Sir Edmund continued. "With the exception of Ottawa, every one of the cities proposed is an object of jealousy to each of the others. Ottawa is, in fact, neither in Upper nor Lower Canada. Literally it is in the former; but a bridge alone divides it from the latter. Consequently its selection would fulfil the letter of any pledge given or supposed to be given, to Upper Canada at the time of the Union. The population at present is partly French, English and Irish. The settlement of the valley of the Ottawa is rapidly increasing, and will be at once stimulated by making it the capital.

"This circumstance is an incidental advantage of great value. Canada is long and narrow; in fact, all frontier. The rapid extension of settlement up the Ottawa, and on each side of it, would give breadth and substance to the country.

"Ultimately, indeed in a short time, the question will arise 'which is to predominate, Upper or Lower Canada?' Upper Canada is conscious of its increasing strength, and of the fact that it pays the larger share of the taxes. The cry for increased representation to the most populous and the richest portion will soon be heard, or rather it is already raised. The only solution of the difficulty will be the chance that the district of Montreal, and the English population about it and in the townships, may be got to side with Upper Canada, and thus turn the scale in favor of that section, which, for reasons beyond our control, must in the end prevail. All real conflict would then be useless, and Quebec must succumb. It is most important therefore that the middle district should be made to feel its importance, and should connect its interests with Upper Canada. This object will be greatly promoted by the choice of Ottawa, linked to Montreal by its trade, and literally in Upper Canada but close on the border of the other section of the Province."

Sir Edmund Head went on to consider the claims of Montreal, Quebec, Kingston and Toronto; and the objections to the choice of any one of them.

"The main objection to Ottawa is its wild position, and relative inferiority to the other cities named. But this wild position is a fault which every day continues to diminish. The present population may be called 8,000 or 10,000, not of the best description. It will be six years before the Government can be actually transferred thither, and the settlement of the fertile country on the Ottawa would be accelerated by the very fact of the certainty of such transfer, even before it took place . . . .

"Ottawa is accessible by water from Montreal and from Lake Ontario. In the former communication there are still some difficulties, but they are not important. It is accessible too by a branch railroad from Prescott, where the line joins the Grand Trunk. The distance from Montreal may be called 100 or 120 miles, but its connection with Montreal is such as to cause its selection to be readily acquiesced in by that great city. I have heard persons of influence at Montreal say they would as soon have the seat of Government at Ottawa as at Montreal itself. The latter city considers itself as the natural outlet of the Ottawa country, and believes that the opening of the valley of that river would establish its own communications with the western lakes, independently of Lake Ontario. In this they may be wrong, but the impression undoubtedly exists, and it is important for our present purpose.

"In a military point of view (I speak of course with submission to higher authorities), Ottawa is advantageously situated. Its distance from the frontier is such as to protect it from any marauding party, or even from a regular attack, unless Montreal and Kingston, which flank the approach to it, were previously occupied by the enemy. Stores and troops could be sent to Ottawa either from Quebec, or Kingston, without exposure on the St. Lawrence to the American frontier.

"A secondary consideration, but one of some importance as affecting the popularity of the choice, is the fact that the Rideau Canal, now handed over to the Provincial Government, would probably increase its traffic and become more productive by the transfer of the seat of Government to Ottawa. At present this great work is a dead loss so far as money is concerned.

"On the whole, therefore, I believe that the least objectionable place is the city of Ottawa . . . . The question, it must be remembered, is essentially one of compromise. Unless some insuperable bar exist to its selection, it is expedient to take that place which will be most readily acquiesced in by the majority . . . . If Ottawa is chosen, Montreal will acquiesce in the choice, and the majority of Upper Canada will not in any way resist, for to them it

Copy

To the Queen's Most Excellent
    Majesty

Most Gracious Sovereign

        We your Majesty's dutiful
and loyal subjects, the Legislative
Council of Canada in Provincial
Parliament assembled, beg leave
to approach your Majesty with
renewed assurances of devotion
and attachment to your Royal
Person and Government.

        We desire, may it please
Your Majesty, to express our
opinion that the interests of
Canada require that the Seat
of the Provincial Government
should be fixed at some certain
place.

Facsimile of the final draft of the petition to the Queen from the Province of Canada, asking her to make a choice of a Capital. Written by E. P. Taché, dated Monday, March 16, 1857. From the Public Archives of Canada

We therefore respectfully pray that your Majesty will be graciously pleased to exercise Your Royal Prerogative and select some one place for the permanent seat of Government in Canada.

Legislative Council
Monday 16th March 1857.

(signed) E. P. Taché
Speaker L. C.

is a partial triumph. The whole matter is a choice of evils, and the least evil will, I think, be found in placing the seat of Government at Ottawa. Whichever section predominates, and however far westward the commerce of Canada may extend, Ottawa will be a convenient position.

"If the Red River settlement and the Saskatchewan country are finally to be annexed to Canada, the Ottawa route to Lake Huron and Lake Superior will be available, and may possibly turn out the shortest and most advantageous of all."

5

This interesting private document throws light on a number of incidental points. Sir Edmund Head labored under the same delusion as Lord Durham had nearly two decades earlier, that the French-speaking Canadians were destined to be assimilated, and that eventually "Quebec must succumb".

This was an unrealistic reading of the situation, and Sir Edmund Head had less excuse for a failure to appreciate the tenacity of the French-language culture than had Lord Durham two decades earlier. What would have happened if the two parent stocks had been forced to get along indefinitely within the one legislature is hypothetical. In time one element might have become dominant, or there might have been open revolt. Events, as it proved, drove the leaders of Canada West and Canada East to the solution of a federal union, an attempt to combine unity and diversity, in which cultural autonomy was preserved for both 'nations', and yet within a single state.

Sir Edmund Head's unflattering reference to the citizens of Ottawa as being "not of the best description" was contained in a confidential memorandum, and no one's withers are wrung by it today. Presumably he had in mind the unsavoury reputation which a small and in part transient element had given to Bytown early in its history, and which had persisted until just before the date of his private communication. There was some basis for his comment. As early as 1829, for instance, a correspondent described the lumbermen of the Ottawa River from Hull upwards as being "a mixture of Irish, Scots, English, in short you will find some amongst them from every part of Europe, the very dregs of those respective countries, and the most depraved and dissipated set of villains on earth. For my own part the Ottawa would be the last place in America I would choose for a future residence." (Cuthbert Cumming to James Hargrave, Chats, April 20th, 1829). Between that date and 1852 there were frequent clashes and riots in Bytown between bigots of both Catholic and Protestant faiths. J. H. Gray, one of the Fathers of Confederation, admitted that people like himself, from New Brunswick, knew Ottawa only as 'Shanty Town', "where lumberers resorted and where faction fights were wont sometimes to take place." The story of the "Shiners" as told in the works of Ross, Brault, Blodwen Davies and others leaves no doubt about the existence of a lawless element. Disgraceful episodes were not rare in the early days. What is quite clear is that the great majority of the residents of Bytown were similar to the pioneers who built up other parts of Canada, and that the population of Ottawa included some sterling stock. I suspect that in Sir Edmund Head's comment there was a little of that unconscious snobbery many aristocratic visitors from the cultural centres of Britain and Europe displayed when they faced the rugged and relatively unlettered stock of North American pioneers.

6

Though his own private views were so overwhelmingly in favor of Ottawa, Sir Edmund Head caused a circular to be sent out to each of the rival cities inviting the corporation of each to send to the Secretary of State for the Colonies "a full and fair statement" of their respective claims. So it cannot be said that the British Government was inadequately briefed, in the event the Queen sought advice from her ministers. Head's memorandum and the original correspondence on the subject were specially printed for the use of the Colonial office. The Royal Archives at Windsor Castle contain a memorandum dated October 16, 1857, by Colonel Charles Grey, the Queen's private secretary, which gave additional support to Ottawa: "An attentive perusal of the papers relative to the seat of government in Canada leads to the conviction that the choice of Ottawa will be the right and politic one," Colonel Grey wrote. Quebec, he agreed, was the strongest and most acceptable point for communication with the Mother Country, but Ottawa was reported "as by no means deficient in natural strength." Colonel Grey thought it ought to have a Citadel planned on the best military design, commanding the town. He also urged the building of two fortified posts in advance on the St. Lawrence, say at Prescott and Cornwall, "which an American force crossing the St. Lawrence to attack the new Capital could not with safety leave in their rear."

The preoccupation of Sir Edmund Head and Colonel Grey with the menace of American invasion is difficult for readers in another century to understand unless they remember that U.S. feeling against Britain and British North America had been greatly excited in 1855 by a recruiting campaign to enlist residents of the United States for the Crimean War. This campaign had been imprudently pressed by Joseph Howe and others, to the great annoyance of the American authorities. Sir Edmund Head found "the aspect of affairs in the U.S. very ugly." The seat of government (Toronto) lay open to U.S. attack in the event of war. "There is nothing as yet to hinder my being taken prisoner any day," he wrote to Sir George Cornwall Lewis in March, 1856, "for as things now stand the Yankees would have command of the Lakes." He added, in a semi-serious vein: "If I am carried off to Boston or New York, I will apprize you of the change in my address."

All in all, Queen Victoria and her Imperial advisers were well briefed on the situation in British North America and supplied with solid arguments in favor of choosing Ottawa as the capital. Which is not to say, of course, that Lady Head's sketch of 'Barrack Hill', or the personal enthusiasms of the Governor General and his wife, conveyed directly to the Queen during their visit to England in the late summer of 1857 may not have been influential in their own special way.

The British government honored John A. Macdonald's request that the decision be held up until about the end of the year. In his official communication of December 31st, 1857 to Sir Edmund Head, Henry Labouchere, the Colonial Secretary, stressed two points, that both the Queen and the British government had played a part in the events leading up to the decision, and that the question had been considered "by Her Majesty and by Her Government with that attention which its great importance demanded." Labouchere added that "the statements and arguments contained in the various memorials laid before them in consequence of your invitation to the Mayors of the several cities chiefly interested, have been fully weighed." And the communication closed with the fateful words: "I am commanded by the Queen to inform you that in the judgment of Her Majesty the City of Ottawa combines more advantages than any other place in Canada for the permanent seat of the future Government of the Province, and is selected by Her Majesty accordingly."

> "I am, yours &c.,
>
> "H. LABOUCHERE."

7

Rumours of a favorable decision had excited citizens of Ottawa during the autumn, but it was not until mid-January of 1858 that the good news became official. The City Council at once offered to "furnish the necessary buildings to accommodate the Legislature and the offices of the Government" until permanent buildings could be erected.

Any jubilation turned out to be slightly premature. For a time the powerful forces opposing the choice of Ottawa refused to give up, in spite of the royal arbitration. Before January 1858 was out, George Brown was expressing the view, in a letter to Luther Holton, a *Rouge* of Lower Canada, that the Queen's decision could still be upset. Six months later, Brown's opportunity to test his belief arrived. Donald G. Creighton suggests that Brown saw in a revival of the whole seat-of-government question in 1858 an ingenious way of detaching from the Macdonald-Cartier administration a substantial block of Canada East supporters, thereby threatening its overthrow in the Legislature. This proved to be a shrewd guess. On July 28th, 1858, the controversy was tossed back into party politics. U. E. Piché moved in the Legislature that "in the opinion of this House the City of Ottawa ought *not* to be the permanent seat of government of this province" and when the vote was taken the government found itself defeated 64 to 50. It elected to place its resignation in the hands of the Governor General, even though it had been sustained immediately afterwards in another want-of-confidence motion. George Brown was then asked to undertake to form an administration, and he did so, but the Brown-Dorion regime lasted only two days, when that ministry was in turn defeated. Brown at once asked for a dissolution and a new election, but Sir Edmund Head decided instead to see if Macdonald and Cartier could re-constitute their ministry and carry on the affairs of the country. After all, there had been an election only seven months earlier. The famous 'double shuffle' followed; the Cartier-Macdonald administration, as it was now called, was formed, met the Legislature, and was sustained. It was able to complete the session without further mishap.

(One important aftermath of this stormy session was the government's determination to study the possibility of forming a federal union, so as to bring to an end the combination of weak ministries, bitter rivalries between Canada East and West, the 'double majority' convention, and the persistent state of deadlock and *impasse* which had bedevilled the Province for several years.)

As soon as the session of 1859 opened, the seat-of-government question came up once more. Sir Edmund Head had proposed, and the Cartier-Macdonald government had agreed, to insert in the Speech From the Throne an assertion that the reference to the Queen, the voting of funds for the erection of parliament buildings, and the Queen's decision in favor of Ottawa were alike binding on the government of the province. "I cannot doubt that you will recognize a selection made by Her Majesty at your own request." To placate Quebec City to some extent, it was proposed "to carry out the understanding which existed at the time when the reference was made, by which the Government will be transferred to Quebec for a fixed period, until the necessary arrangements shall have been completed."

L. V. Sicotte, the most powerful politician in Lower Canada next to Cartier himself had resigned from the government when he found out what was afoot. He was not awed by this attempt to clothe the issue with the dignity attached to the Address from the Throne. He promptly moved a want-of-confidence amendment which—if passed—would once more have eliminated Ottawa from the contest, and would have re-opened the whole controversy.

In his motion he recalled that the legislature in the previous year had passed a resolution declaring that Ottawa should *not* be the seat of government.

For a time indeed, Ottawa's chances seemed to be in grave jeopardy. George Brown's Toronto *Globe* raged against the whole Cartier-Macdonald policy on the seat of government question. It saw in the reference to an interim move to Quebec City an attempt to bribe some Lower Canada legislators into supporting the Speech From the Throne, and thus the choice of Ottawa. "Ministers could tell their English-speaking followers that they honored the Queen's decision and would quite soon go to Ottawa; they could tell their French followers that the final move would be several years away, and that if a confederation were achieved in the meantime, its new capital might well turn out to be Quebec. Besides being a mere dodge to get the maximum number of votes, the *Globe* protested, this 'insane project' of a double move would cost close to two million dollars. It was done to please Lower Canada; Upper Canada was simply to be ignored, since the ministry could not hope to get control of that section. And once again, the West's only portion would be to pay the increased taxes produced by ministerial waste and trickery."*

Sicotte's amendment, seconded by Hector Langevin, provoked a bitter debate which lasted nearly a fortnight. Had his motion carried, Ottawa would have lost the capital. A realization of this aroused Richard William Scott, sitting in the Legislature for Ottawa, and his fellow members from Carleton and the adjoining counties, to organize a determined lobby to make sure that Sicotte's amendment would be beaten. The judgment of history appears to give Scott, a former mayor of Ottawa (and later Sir Richard), a large part of the credit for mobilizing the vote against Sicotte's resolution, and so saving the seat of government for his city.

One last feeble effort was made, a year later, to debate a reconsideration of the seat-of-government issue. In May, 1860, a motion to that effect was moved and seconded, and put by the Speaker. But it was defeated by the decisive majority of 88 to 24, every member of the Legislature from Canada West voting against it. The carping and criticism did not wholly die down, but the plans for the erection of government buildings at Ottawa and the arrangements for the transfer thereafter went systematically forward.

Brown of the Globe, by J. M. S. Careless.   (Macmillan of Canada.)

Retrospect

The technology of the Algonquin was primitive,
but his birch bark canoe was a marvelous means
of travel and conveyance in his circumstances
and way of life." From an oil painting by
Frances Ann Hopkins, in the Public Archives of
Canada.

The residence of Lt. Colonel John By during the
construction of the Rideau Canal. Built in 1827
of rubble stone on Colonel's Hill, it was later
occupied by Major Daniel Bolton when the
area became known as Major's Hill. From a
water colour, probable author J. Jebb, R.E., in
the Public Archives of Canada.

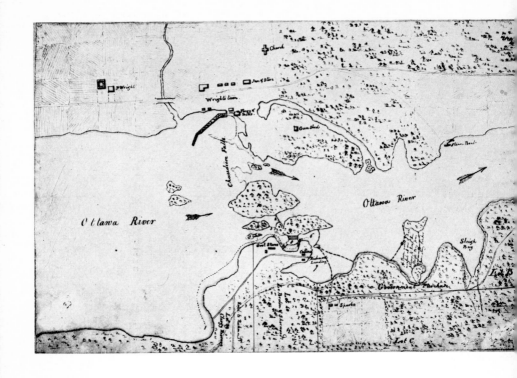

This map, by Major G. A. Eliot, dated 1825, is one of the earliest maps of Ottawa and region. The original is in the Public Archives of Canada. It shows Wrights Town on the Lower Canada side of the river, and Richmond Landing on the Upper Canada side.

view of the Mill and Tavern of Philemon
ight at the Chaudière Falls, on the Ottawa
er, Lower Canada," H. Y. DuVernet,
23, from a painting in the Public Archives of
nada. The City of Hull was known as
ights Town until 1875. Named after its
nder, Philemon Wright, of Woburn,
assachusetts. In 1800 Wright, accompanied
five families, 14 horses, 8 oxen, 7 sleighs,
ether with provisions and implements
essary for settlement, arrived at the
audière Falls. The erection of buildings
nmenced at once and by 1823 there were 5
lls, 4 stores, 2 hotels, 3 schools, 2 distilleries,
rewery, and a population of approximately
). Wright initiated the square timber trade and
s the first man to float a raft of square
ber down the Ottawa River.

Although Philemon Wright's settlement had
reached a population of approximately 700 by
this date, there were far fewer people settled
upon the site of the present Ottawa. Some of the
personalities of the day were: Robert Randall,
original patentee of the Chaudière water lots;
Ira Honeywell, pioneer settler in what is now
Nepean Township; Bradish Billings, pioneer
settler in what is now Gloucester Township;
John Burrows Honey, Lewis Williams, Captain
John LeBreton, Caleb T. Bellows, Daniel
O'Connor, Captain Andrew Wilson. The present
Capital of Canada was originally known as
Richmond Landing, then Bytown (1827), and
finally Ottawa (1855).

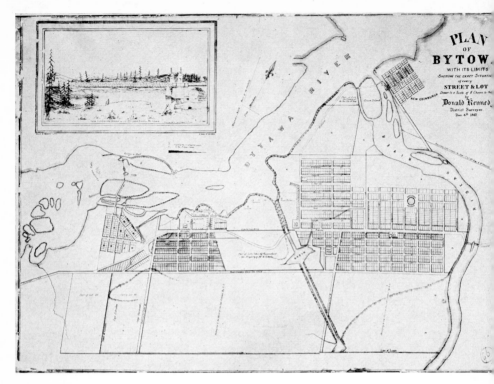

*Plan of Bytown, 1842, by Donald Kennedy. The
original coloured map measures $23\frac{3}{4}$ inches
by $33\frac{1}{4}$ inches, and is drawn to a scale of 6 chains
to an inch. It clearly shows the division of
Bytown into Upper Town, Lower Town, New
Edinburgh and Mount Sherwood. The inset
sketch shows the new Union Suspension
Bridge which was opened to traffic in 1843.
The bridge was designed by Samuel Keefer,
C.E., constructed under the direction of
Alexander Christie, and was the first
suspension bridge in Canada.*

MacKay Estate, Park, Villa, and Village Lots,
1864. The original is a coloured lithograph by
W. C. Chewett, Toronto and measures $17\frac{1}{2}$
inches by $34\frac{3}{4}$ inches. Thomas MacKay was the
successful stone mason contractor on the eight
Ottawa locks of the Rideau Canal. "With his
profits from the construction work on the canal,
and other enterprises, MacKay purchased 110
acres of wild land east of New Edinburgh, and in
1838 he moved into a well-built stone house
which became known as MacKay's Castle. He
himself called it Rideau Hall. The MacKay
Estate was rented to the Government from 1865
until 1868 when it was bought as the Vice-Regal
residence.

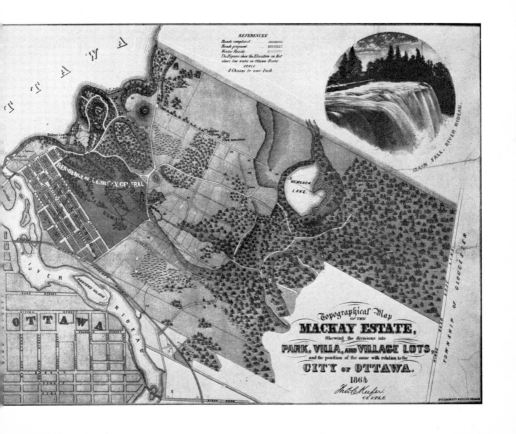

Oil painting of the Parliament Buildings from the Quebec side of the Ottawa River, by Frances Ann Hopkins, 1871. The original is in the Sigmund Samuel Gallery of Canadiana, in Toronto. Mrs. Hopkins (1838-1918) was the daughter of Rear Admiral Frederick William Beechey and grand-daughter of Sir William Beechey, the famous portrait painter. She was married to Edward Martin Hopkins, private secretary to Sir George Simpson of the Hudson's Bay Company, and accompanied her husband on many of his travels in Canada. Authentic paintings of canoe travel in the great days of the northern fur trade are few and far between. Mrs. Hopkins' paintings of voyageur life are rated as being the most reliable historically, as well as the most artistic of those that have survived. This painting accurately portrays the Parliament Buildings in 1871. The Library of Parliament has not been built. The present East Block is still only two sides of a rectangle, the other two sides being added to form a square early in the twentieth century.

"Rideau Falls near Ottawa, May '56".
Original water colour by W. A. Austin, an
Engineer in Lower Canada 1855-56, is in the
Public Archives of Canada. Samuel de
Champlain first saw these spectacular Falls on
the 4th of June, 1613. His description reads:
"There is an island in the center, all covered with
trees, like the rest of the land on both sides and
the water slips down with such impetuosity that
it makes an arch of four hundred paces; the
Indians passing underneath it without getting
wet, except for the spray produced by the fall."
Subsequent explorers gave the name le rideau
or "the curtain" which became Rideau Falls.
Thomas MacKay's five-storey grist-mill,
carding-mill, and saw-mills are shown in the
picture, together with stacks of sawn lumber
on the shore and a square timber raft in mid-
stream.

r Edmund Head, Bart. (1805-1868). From the ublic Archives. Sir Edmund Head was overnor-in-Chief of Canada from 1854-1861, ad played a key role in the events leading to the lection of Ottawa as the Capital of the ovince of Canada in British North America. is carefully written private memorandum on e subject is believed to have been the chief fluence in the Queen's choice. He was the son the Reverend Sir John Head, Bart., rector of ayleigh, Essex, England and succeeded to the aronetcy in 1838. Educated at Winchester and riel College, Oxford and a Fellow of Merton ollege, Oxford, from 1830 to 1837. From 48 to 1854 he was Lieutenant-Governor of ew Brunswick prior to his appointment as overnor-in-Chief of Canada.

Lt. Colonel John By, R.E. (1783-1836). From the Public Archives. Veteran of the Peninsular Wars and with nine years experience in Canada (1802-1811), he was given the task of constructing a waterway from the Ottawa River to the harbour of Kingston, Ontario, a distance of 125 miles, to serve as a military by-pass to the vulnerable St. Lawrence River route to Montreal. Col. By laid out Lower Town and Upper Town, and must be considered the first planner in what was to become the Capital of Canada. His foresight in laying out Wellington Street, 99 feet wide, has been appreciated by successive generations of planners.

"Houses of Parliament, Ottawa", from a Chromo Lithograph in the Public Archives of Canada. The lithographer was Burland Lasricain of Montreal and artist's license has been employed as the fountain and stairs are not the same as existing photographs reveal. It has been observed that the lines of the original Parliament Building were less severe than the present soaring Peace Tower. Jacques Gréber felt that the original building was more consistent with the genius of Gothic architecture.

"The Falls of the Lièvre River at Buckingham",
Edwin Whitefield approximately 1855. The
original water colour is in the Sigmund Samuel
Gallery of Canadiana in Toronto. This picture
accurately records the beauty of autumn.
It is a typical scene of the period and may still
be observed today at small saw-mills up the
Gatineau River. The mills shown here are
probably Bowman's Mill and Bigelow's Mill.
These two amalgamated in 1860 and passed
through a succession of owners until acquired
by the James MacLaren Company in 1901, a
firm which still operates on the Lièvre. Edwin
Whitefield was both artist and engraver. It is
estimated that he did over forty prints of the
more important or historically interesting citi
and towns of the United States and Canada.
Most of his work was done in pencil, and it is
probable that his water colours were done for
his own amusement. His two large views, 35
inches by 19 inches, "Ottawa City, Canada
West, Upper Town", and "Ottawa City,
Canada West, Lower Town", published in 185
are well known for their extreme accuracy.

CHAPTER SIX

The Crowning of the Cliffs

I t took the provincial legislature eighteen years to make up its mind about the site of a permanent capital, as we have seen. But once the choice of Ottawa had been settled by the defeat of the Sicotte-Langevin amendment in February, 1859, the authorities moved rapidly. Too rapidly in some respects, as events proved.

On May 7th, 1859, an advertisement was widely published by the Department of Public Works inviting architects to submit plans and designs for four public buildings to be erected in Ottawa: a parliamentary building, two departmental buildings, and a residence for the Governor General. The sum of £225,000 (about a million dollars) had been voted in the 1859 estimates for the Ottawa projects, including landscaping and extras; and for the buildings themselves the architects were instructed to aim at a cost not exceeding the following figures:

The Parliament Building	$300,000
Two departmental buildings	240,000
Residence of the Governor General	100,000

A substantial cash premium was offered for the most acceptable designs. The final date set for considering plans submitted by architects was August 1st, 1859.

Despite the short notice, no fewer than thirty-three separate designs, prepared by eighteen different architects, were filed with the Department of Public Works before the August 1st deadline. Sixteen designs were for the Parliament Building, submitted by fourteen competitors. Ten of these were in the Classic or Italian style, six in the Norman or Gothic. For the two departmental buildings, four were Classic, three Gothic. For Government House, there were ten designs, of various styles.

By the 25th of August, the Chief Architect of the provincial government and the deputy commissioner of public works had examined and weighed the several designs. The first and second choices for the Parliament Building were in what was described as 'Civil Gothic' style. The first and second choices for the departmental buildings were also in 'Civil Gothic'. The first choice for Government House was Grecian, and the second Norman.

The site for which the architects had been instructed to plan the buildings was the promontory above the Ottawa River known then as Barrack Hill. It was Ordnance Land, and was said to occupy 29 acres.

Reproduction of a portion of a page from the Ottawa Citizen, vol. 1, number 1, October 4, 1859 and the first advertisement to contractors for the construction of the Parliament Buildings. From the Public Archives of Canada.

Comments on the designs submitted for the buildings are in existence and are still interesting. F. R. Rubidge, assistant chief engineer, remarked that an impression seemed to have prevailed that an "edifice of the sternest architectual style" was best adapted to the site. He personally thought it would be a mistake to erect a gloomy pile of buildings for Legislative Buildings on so commanding a position.

Samuel Keefer, deputy commissioner of Public Works, noted that there was one set of plans of Lombard Venetian Style, one Norman, one Elizabethan Tudor. One of them had a "heavy castellated style" which Keefer thought rendered it "prison like" and "defiant in its aspect" and "therefore unsuited to become the seat from whence should emanate the laws of a free country."

Of the two designs which survived the preliminaries, the second choice "had a conventual and collegiate appearance" which seemed to Keefer to associate it with the business of devotion and learning "rather than with purposes of Legislation."

When the identity of the architects submitting the first choice for the Parliament Building was revealed by the opening of a sealed envelope, they were disclosed to be Thomas Fuller and Chilion Jones of Toronto. Fuller was a native of Bath, England, who had come to Canada only two years earlier. He had won widespread reputation as designer of the cathedral at Antigua. He has been described as the best architect in the Gothic style living on the North American continent at the time. He later designed the State Capital at Albany, and in 1881 was appointed Chief Architect for Canada. The Langevin Block was later designed by him. He remained in office at Ottawa until his retirement in 1897.

The Fuller-Jones firm also won second place for their design of the Departmental Buildings. The first award for the East and West Blocks, as they are now called, was given to the firm of Stent and Laver. Frederick Warburton Stent was a native of Lincolnshire, who had arrived in Canada in 1855. Both Stent and Augustus Laver in later years became successful and prominent architects in the United States.

It is not difficult to surmise why Gothic was chosen for the Parliament Buildings, quite apart from the admitted beauty and harmony of Fuller's drawings. Not only was a romantic and picturesque type of architecture generally thought most suitable for the incomparable setting on the high promontory above the Ottawa River, looking across to the blue Laurentian Hills, but in Gothic there was a sentimental link with Westminster. The Houses of Parliament of the United Kingdom had been completed in 1852, only seven years before. Alan Gowans, in his book *Looking at Architecture in Canada*, contends that Fuller and Stent felt that "it was practically mandatory on them to express the country's close ties with Britain by taking as their model Westminster New Palace, home of the 'Mother of Parliaments'." But the Canadian buildings were not slavish copies of those or any other earlier buildings, Gowans points out. The creations of Fuller and Stent displayed an eclectic advance or development from the already somewhat obsolete Gothic of Westminster, and if they had a model at all it was to be found in the newly erected University College at Toronto and the University Museum at Oxford.

John Page, chief Engineer for the Canadian Department of Public Works, writing at a time when the Ottawa buildings were well advanced, justified the design in these words:

"All the Buildings are constructed in what may be termed the Pointed Gothic Style of architecture, and from the bold, broken line they present— their numerous towers, high-pitched, variegated slate roofs, pierced by dormers and surmounted by ornamental wrought iron cresting and terminals, together with the quaintness of the carved figures, combine to produce an imposing and picturesque effect."

3

Over the years many visitors and residents have praised the buildings and the site. A favorite comment for quotation is that of Anthony Trollope, the English novelist, who visited Ottawa in 1861. Since the buildings were barely well begun at the time, I cannot help feeling that he was basing his compliments partly on the magnificent site, and partly on the architects' designs,— on what was pending, not on what he actually saw.

The Parliament Building, Trollope wrote, "stands nobly on a magnificent river, with high, overhanging rock, and a natural grandeur of position . . . . The glory of Ottawa will be—and, indeed, already is—the set of public buildings which is now being erected on the rock which guards, as it were, the town from the river. I take it upon myself to say that as regards purity of art and manliness of conception the work is entitled to the highest praise . . . . I have no hestitation in risking my reputation for judgment in giving my warmest commendation to them as regards beauty of outline and truthful nobility of detail . . . . I know no modern Gothic purer of its kind, or less sullied with fictitious ornamentation, and I know no site for such a set of buildings so happy as regards both beauty and grandeur." Years later the American editor Charles Dudley Warner was quite as warm in his praise: "The group of Government Buildings is surpassingly fine. The Parliament House and the Departmental Buildings, on three sides of a square, are exceedingly effective in color, and the perfection of Gothic details, especially in the noble towers. There are few groups of buildings anywhere so pleasing to the eye, or that appeal more strongly to one's sense of dignity and beauty."

Such sentiments must have been gratifying to architects Fuller and Stent in time to come, but there were years of grave stress and bitter recriminations while the buildings were in course of erection. Tenders were called for the buildings to be in by November 1st, 1859, a date later extended to November 15th. The contracts were awarded on November 22nd, and the first sod was officially turned on December 20th, 1859.

The actual laying of the corner stone was deferred until the visit of Edward, Prince of Wales, (later Edward VII) on September 1st, 1860. This was the most ambitious and impressive ceremonial occasion to date in the youthful city of Ottawa. Some amusement was expressed by such visitors as the correspondent of *The Times* of London at the actual inscription on the corner stone. The uncertainty still felt by many Canadians over the choice of Ottawa finds reflection in the carved wording which describes it as the "corner stone of the building *intended* to receive the Legislature of Canada." The editor of *The Times* pontificated on the matter in his issue of September 20, 1860, as follows: "With the account of this ceremony, our correspondent has combined a description of the city of Ottawa, which we confess has filled us with very serious misgivings as to the wisdom of the step which Her Majesty has been advised to take in selecting it as the capital of Canada." The editor "rejoiced" that the question had "not gone so far that it is too late for reconsideration."

4

Contracts had been let for the government buildings in 1859 without adequate preliminaries or preparations. No test borings were made down to the foundation rock, and no provision was made for an adequate system of heating. The fireproofing of the buildings was an afterthought. The contractors were soon in trouble. It was found necessary to excavate to a much greater depth than had been expected, because of faults, fissures and cavities in the underlying rock. The quarrying and transporting of the local stone needed for the basic structures of the buildings turned out to be more difficult and expensive than had been expected. Any rock brought from the Hull side of the river had to be ferried across and handled twice en route. In the end, most of the stone for the walls was quarried about 12 miles from the site, in Nepean township.

As the municipality of Ottawa was not yet able to provide a water supply, provision had to be made for drawing it from the Ottawa River. A six horse power steam engine and pump were installed at the base of Parliament Hill for this purpose.

By May 3rd, 1861 there was already in sight an expenditure of $1,436,408, according to Samuel Keefer. This was $400,000 over the original vote. At that time Keefer was confident that no more unexpected contingencies would arise, but this turned out to be wildly optimistic. Keefer attempted to soothe his minister by recalling that it had cost fourteen million dollars to build the Houses of Parliament at Westminster, covering $4\frac{1}{2}$ acres. If the Canadian buildings, covering $3\frac{3}{4}$ acres, could be completed for one and two-thirds millions of dollars, it could not be held to be an excessive figure, he contended.

By September 1861 the sum appropriated by the Legislature two years earlier had been completely exhausted, bills were piling up, and an order went out to suspend all work on the buildings. This caused great consternation and distress in Ottawa among the contractors, engineers, craftsmen and all others engaged on the project. The halt threw out of employment between 1,600 and 1,700 workmen, supporting between five and six thousand people. A particularly disturbing aspect was the departure of many skilled mechanics, who had been recruited from Great Britain, Germany and the United States, and who now left the capital for other cities, or returned to their distant homes.

Departmental and parliamentary investigations followed. So did a Royal Commission of inquiry. In April 1862 it was estimated that it would cost $2,600,000 to complete the buildings, of which $315,000 might be deferred. The Royal Commission, reporting in January 1863, recommended that the original contractors should be given new contracts for renewal of construction on the buildings. The annual votes by the legislature indicate the rate of progress, $688,344 in 1862, $100,000 in 1863, $400,000 in 1864, $300,000 in 1865, and $500,000 in 1866. By this time the buildings had already cost three times the original estimate, and there was still much to be done,—the tower was still under construction, and only the foundations of the Library had been laid. But by the spring of 1865 the essential accommodation for the legislative chambers and the departmental offices was approaching readiness, and orders went out to prepare for a move from Quebec City to Ottawa in the fall. In October 1865 the first contingent of civil servants began to arrive, and plans were made to call the first session of the Provincial Parliament at Ottawa in the spring of 1866.

5

The familiar jibes of Hon. George Brown about the extravagance of the project and how far in advance of the times the buildings would be, were made during the latter period of construction,—when the cost was mounting alarmingly, and when ways of reducing or deferring the heavy demands on the provincial treasury were being debated. For example, the original plans called for three impressive but costly fountains,—could they be eliminated? Was the great tower really necessary? Could they get along for a time without the Library? Read in the light of these considerations, Hon. George Brown's famous letter of August 15, 1864, to Hon. John A. Macdonald, seems less unreasonable than when taken out of historical context:

"The buildings are magnificent; the style, the extent, the site, the workmanship, are all surpassingly fine," Brown wrote. "But they are just *five hundred years in advance of the time*. It will cost half the revenue of the province to light them, to heat them, and to keep them clean. Such monstrous folly was never perpetrated in this world before. But as we are in for it I do think the idea of stopping short of completion is out of the question. I go in for tower, rotunda, fountains and every conceivable embellishment. If we are to be laughed at for our folly at least let us not be ridiculed for a half-finished pile."

It is an interesting detail that the plans provided for a total of 255 offices in the three buildings. It was expected and intended that these would accommodate all the provincial civil servants required at headquarters, in the provincial capital. Seating in the Legislative Chamber itself had been planned to hold the 65 members from Canada East and the like number from Canada West, or 130 all told. No one knew that before it was finished it would have to accommodate the Dominion House of Commons. Fortunately the Legislative Chamber had been made large enough for considerable expansion. As it turned out, it housed the Provincial Legislature for one session only. By the time it was occupied for a second session, the Province of Canada had been joined in federal union with Nova Scotia and New Brunswick; and provision had to be made for 181 members of the first federal House of Commons. This, incidentally, required an enlargement of the Chamber, which was completed during the summer and early autumn of 1867. And even so, the old House of Commons was crowded from the first day of occupation until the fire of 1916 destroyed it.

6

The choice of Ottawa as the capital had provoked much derisive and ill-natured comment, as we have seen. It was "the Westminster in the Wilderness". The erstwhile Oxford don Goldwin Smith later saw in Ottawa "a sub-arctic lumber-village converted by royal mandate into a political cock-pit." American editors, noting that Ottawa had been chosen because it was less vulnerable to U.S. attack, agreed that Ottawa was safe, because invading soldiers would get lost looking for it. Americans even had a formula for finding it: "Start from the North Pole; strike a bead for Lake Ontario;

Reached Ottawa at 6 — mayor
of the city waiting with his
carriage "cum & so on" — very
civil — went at once to
the Public Buildings where
met Mr Page the Architect
in charge & went all over
the buildings. They are really
magnificent. Fit for the
British, French & Russian
Empires — were they all
Confederated! A hundred
years hence, the people
will fancy the men of these
days were giants in conception
at least if not in ability. The
architecture is something
like the Toronto University
but infinitely finer — the
work is beautiful & of

*Facsimile of two pages from a letter by George Brown to his wife,
August 15, 1864 commenting on the new Parliament
Buildings at Ottawa. From the Public Archives of Canada*

the most substantial character. There is one main
pile for the Legislative
departments — & two enormous
side piles for the Departmental
buildings. Any one of the
three would be quite large
enough for the whole. The
three piles form three sides
of a grand square covering
23 acres! The centre is
to be laid out within
in ornamental grounds
fountains & so forth. The
whole stands on a high
promontory, seen all
round for a great distance
& amid scenery no where

and the first spot where the glacier ceases and vegetation begins—that's Ottawa!" The correspondent of the *London Times* in 1860 was sure that nothing could ever develop on this remote and unpromising site. As for the buildings, already begun, they might serve as lunatic asylums, "whenever the town is sufficiently prosperous to require them for that purpose." Ottawa could afford to smile at such comments: it was in the thick of an industrial boom, it was 400 miles closer to the equator than Goldwin Smith's Oxford, and exciting days lay ahead.

Not that Ottawa had much to show yet in the way of urban grace or maturity. In response to the lumbering and manufacturing upsurge of the 1850's and 1860's the city had spread like a bed of mushrooms, outdistancing all efforts to provide even the most essential municipal services. Noisy saw-mills, foundries, untidy lumber yards and ugly commercial houses sprang up almost overnight on no particular plan, until the industrial sprawl masked much of the city's original scenic loveliness. As late as 1854 a distinguished visitor summed up his impressions in these words: "There has been as yet no time to pave the streets, and in bad weather they are in a desperate condition. Only near the houses there are run what is called 'plank roads'. As for gardens, fruit trees, or flowers, no one has had time so much as to think of them, and the old rough boulders and masses of rock are lying about still, among the groups of houses, and firs and other forest trees are springing up again out of the stumps. Here and there amongst elegant colleges and churches are to be seen fragments of the primeval forest, lofty pines and firs and thick underwood that may occasionally give shelter to a bear. By and by they will be changed into gardens, but as yet the unbroken mass of the primeval forest fences the town on all sides and if you get a view of it from a high point you see for miles and miles nothing but a sea of wood in which the town lies like the nest of a heathcock."

A perusal of the records collected by historians like Harry Walker and Lucien Brault enriches the detail. In that year, 1854, Ottawa boasted ten miles of plank sidewalks. Sparks Street still lacked walks on one side in 1857, and Rideau Street remained in like case as late as 1859. The Byward Market was given a paving of macadam in 1860. They coated Rideau Street with gravel as far east as King Edward Avenue in 1859-60. By 1862 heavy borrowing was necessary to finance the draining and macadamizing of extensions to the street system. The first Ottawa department of engineers was not created until 1866, and the paving of streets in the modern manner did not begin until 1895.

Gas lamps had been introduced in the 1850's, superseding whale oil lamps. To supplement communal wells and pumps, carriers brought water up from the Ottawa river, and the first aqueduct was not ready until 1875. Firefighting was tackled by volunteer companies. There was no salaried police force until

1865. The first tramways, powered by horses, did not begin operations until 1866. There were some drains and sewers along Wellington and Rideau Streets by 1857. The first Ottawa park seems to have been Major's Hill, which was not turned into a civic garden until 1874. The city hall was modestly housed over a market building. There were old established weekly newspapers, but the first daily newspaper was not published until 1865. Ottawa had a Mechanics Institute as early as 1847, and *L'Institut Canadien Francais* had opened in 1852. The Ottawa School Board managed with rented rooms until 1857, the first school house built specifically for that purpose being occupied in that year. Ottawa churches dated back to 1827. The College of Bytown, the forerunner of Ottawa University, began instruction as early as 1849. There was no house-to-house delivery of mail until 1875.

But civic progress was only a matter of time. Ottawa was getting wealthy from the lumber trade; it was rapidly becoming the most important sawmill centre in British North America. In 1857 the amount of sawn lumber produced in the Ottawa-Hull area was 34 million feet, board measure. Ten years later the output had increased to 80 million feet, and by the end of the century it was 180 million. John R. Booth alone had an output of 30 million feet of pine in 1870. His firm maintained as part of its winter operations three hundred teams. In 1871 the seven mills of Ottawa City employed about 1,200 men and produced lumber valued at over $1\frac{1}{2}$ million — the highest in any census division in Ontario.

7

The rising tide of commercial prosperity in the late '50's was accelerated by the construction of the government buildings. This project expanded the working force of the city by upwards of 1,500 workmen, and the expenditure during 1859-65 of over $2,500,000 boosted local purchasing power. In 1865-66 nearly three hundred civil servants took up their permanent residence at Ottawa, relieved that the ambulatory system of shuttling back and forth between Toronto and Quebec City was over. The sessional arrival of 130 members of the Legislature of the Province of Canada in June, 1866 gave Ottawa a further foretaste of what would come when the Dominion was created.

From 1840 to 1867 it must have been particularly difficult for the city fathers of Bytown and Ottawa to make firm plans for the future. Between 1840 and 1857 there was only a fluctuating hope that the final choice of capital would fall on their city. The Queen's choice of 1857, when it came, was almost too good to be true. And indeed, the seat of government was almost lost to Ottawa again in the Legislature in 1858 and 1859. The letting of tenders for the parliament buildings and the beginning of construction must have brought a new sense of relief. But before the buildings were finished additional anxieties arose. It began to look as though the Province of Canada itself might undergo a radical change in the structure of government. One of the possible changes would reduce the importance of Ottawa, the other would greatly enhance it. By 1864 there was widespread belief that a federal union with the maritime provinces could be consummated. But if that failed, it might be necessary to set up a federal union of the two Canadas—Canada East and Canada West. Again, if Confederation did become a possibility, there was a distinct likelihood that Ottawa would be chosen as Dominion capital, but by no means an assurance. As a matter of fact, the proposals for Confederation revived the claims of Quebec City, since it would be about half way between Cape Breton and western Ontario, the inhabited ribbon of the proposed Dominion.

The actual arrival of the Canadian provincial civil service at Ottawa in the autumn of 1865, and the opening in June, 1866, of the first—and, as it proved, the only—session of the Provincial Legislature to meet at Ottawa must have been re-assuring. But uncertainties continued. By this time the Quebec Conference had definitely selected Ottawa to be the capital of the new Confederation—but the prospects of federal union with the Maritimes grew dark for a while in the latter half of 1865 and the early part of 1866. New Brunswick became lukewarm and Nova Scotia actually hostile. Prince Edward Island had decided to remain outside, and so had Newfoundland.

The Province of Canada was the most enthusiastic area of British North America on the subject of Confederation, but even there a dissident rump became vocal. In June, 1866, A. A. Dorion introduced a motion as amendment to the Address on the Speech From the Throne, contending that federal union was too momentous a step to take without a direct appeal to the voters. If it had succeeded, it might have delayed negotiations by many months. Fortunately for the progress of the Confederation movement, Dorion's resolution received only 19 votes in a Legislature of 130.

By measures which need not be detailed here, but which form part of the essential story of Confederation, the opposition in New Brunswick was overcome, and the opposition in Nova Scotia was in effect ignored. By the autumn of 1866 the delegates from the Province of Canada, Nova Scotia and New Brunswick were ready to meet in London to draw up the terms of Confederation.

The official arrival of the Governor General in May, 1866, must have been comforting to the people of Ottawa. They would not, however, have felt so sure about their future if they had been privileged to inspect his private correspondence with Westminster.

Perhaps Monck had been somewhat spoiled by the amenities of Spencer Wood at Quebec City, where he had been residing, and annoyed at the inconveniences of travel between Ottawa and the seaport at Quebec which linked him with 'home'. At any rate, only four days after his official arrival at Ottawa, he wrote a confidential letter to the Rt. Hon. Edward Cardwell at Westminster, in which the following appeared:

"It seems like an act of insanity," he wrote, "to have fixed the capital of this great country away from the civilization, intelligence and commercial enterprise of this Province, in a place that can never be a place of importance and where the political section of the community will live in a position of isolation and removed from the action of any public opinion. My confident belief is that, notwithstanding the vast expense which has been incurred here in public buildings, Ottawa will not be the capital four years hence." One of Viscount Monck's particular grievances was the execrable state of the road between Rideau Hall and his office in the East Block. I have already alluded to a tradition that to circumvent the dusty ride to his office he used a navy gig or cutter manned by blue jackets to take him from the Ottawa River at the foot of the Rideau Hall grounds to Entrance Bay below the Parliament Buildings.

Though the official records of the several conferences preceding Confederation do not disclose any hint of it, some remarks made by the Hon. John A. Macdonald on his return from London to Ottawa in May, 1867, give color to the belief that some political opposition to the choice of Ottawa persisted right up to the enactment of the British North America Act. Macdonald is quoted in a contemporary account as telling the citizens of Ottawa on May 10, 1867, that "he had some doubts before going to England as to whether the seat of government for the Dominion would remain in Ottawa, but he was now happy to say there was no question Ottawa was confirmed as the capital of the new Dominion. Those present [to welcome him on his arrival] and their children would live to see it the metropolis of British North America."

8

So, as it turned out, the citizens of Ottawa were able to celebrate the first Dominion Day in a mood of jubilant expectation. Ten years of stubborn opposition had failed to shake its claim as permanent capital, whether of Province or Dominion. It was written into the British North America Act that 'until the Queen directs otherwise' the seat of government should be Ottawa. The working quarters of the government buildings were completed and largely occupied. The Governor General was in residence at Rideau Hall, having returned just in time to take part in the official Confederation Day ceremonies. The first Dominion Cabinet was being sworn in that very morning, in the Privy Council Chamber of the East Block. Many of the Fathers of Confederation were there in their midst, and would become permanent residents. There would be a general election soon, and the first Parliament of the Dominion of Canada would be opened in the Senate Chamber on the Hill. The thousands of excited citizens who gathered to hear the Dominion Day proclamation by the Mayor of Ottawa, or who assembled on Parliament Hill to admire the military parades and Viscount Monck's review of the troops, could indulge to the full their admiration of the noble structures crowning the heights above the Ottawa River, and let their imaginations anticipate freely the great days for Canada and Ottawa that unquestionably lay ahead.

CHAPTER SEVEN

A Capital Takes Root

The story of the founding of the capital of Canada possesses the fascination of all organic birth and growth. Just as every towering white pine tree in the Ottawa Valley existed once in embryo as a tiny seed, the whole of the modern capital region with all its developments and ramifications in physical space and national symbolism was contained in 1867 in a short section of the British North America Act and a partly-finished cluster of Gothic buildings on the old Barrack Hill. But the imperial statute which had located the federal capital at Ottawa had already begun to set in train a long and inevitable series of changes, bound to be increasingly dramatic and momentous as the nation grew. The bustling and prosperous lumber town on the Ottawa could not escape the revolution imminent and potential in its change of status. There were major transformations lying ahead—architectural, social, political, cultural. Ottawa was now the symbolic and administrative heart of a federal union rapidly reaching transcontinental dimensions. Its future fortunes must have been beyond the imagination of all but the most far-sighted of its citizens in 1867.

Some of the early physical changes have been already sketched. By 1867, the government buildings on the Hill were substantially finished, except for the circular Library and the upper section of the lofty tower. Rideau Hall was being enlarged. Several hundred civil servants had taken up residence. The 72 Senators provided for in the British North America Act were being summoned. The first Dominion general election was held in August, and it sent to Ottawa 181 members of the House of Commons for the opening of the first parliamentary session on November 7th,—a fascinating cross-section of the pioneering families of British North America, as the Parliamentary Companion for 1867 establishes by chapter and verse.

The division of powers outlined in the British North America Act made it necessary to sort out the civil service. The headquarters staff of the Province of Canada, located since October of 1865 in Ottawa, was now divided up between the Dominion and the provinces. Those civil servants who had been dealing with matters reserved to the provinces under Section 92 went back to the provincial capitals. But additions to the federal civil service had to be made to provide federal service for the whole Dominion. In 1867 the territory to be served stretched from the Head of the Lakes to Cape Breton. By 1873 the Dominion civil service was responsible for administration of national affairs from ocean to ocean. The first census of federal civil servants numbered 264 persons, with Post Office (56), Public Works (30), Secretary of State (25) and Agriculture (25) heading the list. Additions were immediately necessary. The growth of the federal civil service appears in the steady expansion of departmental office space and the record of the construction of new government buildings. They reflected the growth of government activities, the rise in the population and area of Canada, and the gradual shift in the reigning philosophy of the state: from the negative, regulatory government of 1867 to the positive 'social welfare' state of the present day.

2

Thus the establishment of the federal capital in Ottawa caused tangible and measurable changes: new buildings, additional population. But more elusive and more subtle changes in the *quality* of the life in the Ottawa community were also pending.

Overnight, Ottawa became a viceregal seat. Into this bustling sawmill centre and Valley market town, with its lumber barons, its successful merchants, and its nucleus of struggling professional men, the arrival of the highest social court of the land must have been electrifying. Not that all the sturdy pioneers were overawed by viceregal visitors or even by members of the royal family. Republican sentiments were not confined to the American states. The sycophant, the critic, and the snob were all to be found. Social climbers were not likely to ignore the opportunities provided by Rideau Hall. More than once in the early history of Government House there seemed to be more of a democratic spirit there than in the drawing rooms of Ottawa. The presence of Rideau Hall set up social tensions, and created cliques and classes. But on the whole, the arrival of the viceregal establishment seems to have been a leavening influence. Whatever their personal idiosyncrasies, the incumbents of Government House were, in the main, a great credit to the institutions they represented. They were men and women of education and refinement. Several of the viceroys deserved the title of statesmen. They were graduates of Eton and Oxford, Harrow and Cambridge, Trinity College and St. Andrews. Several of the Viceregal appointees, and two at least of their Chatelaines, were authors or artists of some distinction. Most of the Governors had held high ministerial office in England, or were destined to do so, or both. Three of Canada's early Governors General were later singled out for the high honor of serving as Viceroy of India. The steady cumulative effect of this procession of cultured, lettered and seasoned envoys cannot be brushed aside as unimportant. They took their duties in Canada seriously, and they lent a hand in the formation and fostering of a number of valuable scientific, artistic and literary associations.

The Province of Canada had originally intended to build a new residence for the Governor General, as was mentioned in the last chapter. Architects' drawings for a vice-regal mansion were submitted in the summer of 1859, at the same time as the designs for the government buildings. A controversy then arose over the site. The present Nepean Point was considered: it would, indeed, have made a magnificent location. But opposition developed. And by the time a site could be agreed upon, the expense of erecting the parliament buildings had run so far above the original estimates that the whole Government House project was allowed to lapse. By the summer of 1865, some kind of action became imperative. Viscount Monck would be expected to take up residence in Ottawa in the early future. Lacking a new building, the authorities looked around for at least a stop-gap, and the historic 'castle' of Thomas McKay in New Edinburgh was found to be available for rental. On August 7th, 1865, "MacKay's Castle", and spacious grounds of 87 acres, were leased for twelve years by the Provincial Government, with the option of buying. (Three years later both house and estate were purchased.) During the year 1867-8, Rideau Hall—as MacKay had called it—was substantially enlarged. A report by F. P. Rubidge, architect and assistant engineer of the Department of Public Works, explains that "the old unpretending stone house, the former abode of the late Honourable Thomas MacKay, having a superficial area of about 3,700 feet, afforded merely eleven rooms, most of which were of very limited dimensions." To this edifice, Rubidge reported, "a new main building and domestic wing of picked and dressed limestone, covering 10,200 superficial feet, or nearly three times larger than the old building, have added some 49 more rooms, most of them of large area." The rooms were carpeted and fitted up "in a handsome modern style, with highly finished furniture, made of the various Canadian and other woods." In 1868, cottages were built on the grounds, wells were sunk, fencing was completed, and other suitable improvements made to the property.

Even with the additions and improvements mentioned above, Rideau Hall failed to impress the earliest incumbents. W. Stewart MacNutt says that when the Earl of Dufferin arrived (in 1872) "he had almost, in disgust, driven back to the station. 'Nothing but a small villa such as would suit the needs of a country banker' "—such was his first reaction to it. Dufferin added a fine ballroom, and in preparation for the coming of Princess Louise, daughter of Queen Victoria, further improvements were made in 1878. MacNutt reports that the Marquis of Lorne found it a "far finer residence" than he had expected. In any event, whatever its aesthetic merits or its level of material comfort, its occupants began very early to dominate the social life of the Canadian capital.

Confederation had brought together into the new capital the outstanding political figures of British North America. Ottawa was, for shorter or longer periods, the home of some of the leading Fathers of Confederation, Macdonald, Cartier, McGee, Tupper, Tilley, Chapais, and Galt. Joseph Howe spent much of the last five years of his life in Ottawa. The location of the Supreme Court of Canada at Ottawa guaranteed the residence there of eminent and experienced jurists, and also periodic visits by leading counsel of Canada. Canada's parliamentary library was staffed by such distinguished scholars and constitutional authorities as Alpheus Todd, Sir John G. Bourinot, Benjamin Sulte and A. D. DeCelles. As a saw-mill town Ottawa would have waited a long while to add such celebrities to its population.

From the very beginning the government service began to make its mark on Ottawa cultural life. Many of the civil servants were routine clerks and book-keepers, but they also included some of the ablest administrators and executives in the country. For the historian there is an interesting link between the Ottawa service and Canadian letters.

The peculiarly hopeless economic position of *belles lettres* in a young and materialistic pioneer society was recognized to some extent by the appointment of poets, historians and essayists to the civil service. It was better than letting them starve to death, or migrate, and the idea prevailed that the relatively light hours of work would leave them some freedom for literary creation. Whether in the main the routine also stifled their literary inspiration is another matter. In any event, Charles Sangster arrived in Ottawa in 1868, W. D. LeSueur a bit later, Archibald Lampman and Duncan Campbell Scott in the early 1880's, and William Wilfred Campbell in 1891. Charles G. D. Roberts sought an appointment in 1884, but was persuaded by his father to give up the idea. William Kingsford, after a long career in the Dominion civil service, settled down at Ottawa to write his ten-volume *History of Canada*. Several pioneer scientists added stimulus and prestige to the cultural life of the capital. In 1881 the Geological Survey was transferred from Montreal to Ottawa, Alfred Selwyn superintending the move. George M. Dawson, son of Sir John W. Dawson, became assistant director of the Survey shortly afterwards. The aggressive and redoubtable John Macoun was appointed botanist to the Geological Survey in 1882. When the Experimental Farms Branch of the Department of Agriculture was founded in 1886, that eminent scientist William Saunders was appointed director: he and his son Charles revolutionized Canadian cereal breeding. Sandford Fleming made Ottawa his home for many years. The assassination of Thomas D'Arcy McGee deprived Ottawa of an illustrious addition to these names: just before his death in 1868 he had agreed to accept the light post of Commissioner of Patents, with the intention of devoting all his spare time and energies thereafter to literary work.

The "Fourth Estate" in Ottawa was supplemented in 1866-67 by the arrival of the first contingent of the parliamentary press gallery. Small at first, mainly sessional in attendance, it grew sufficiently to require an enlargement of the Press Gallery accommodation in the House of Commons in 1879. Before the end of the century, its membership had included such talented writers as George Johnson, later Dominion statistician, Carroll Ryan, author and poet, Martin J. Griffin, later parliamentary librarian, W. T. R. Preston, controversial author, John Wesley Dafoe, great Liberal editor, Robert Smeaton White, editor of the *Montreal Gazette*, P. D. Ross, editor and owner of the *Ottawa Journal*, Fred Cook, later Mayor of Ottawa, A. H. U. Colquhoun, biographer and educationist, Sir John Willison, author and editor, Hon. Charles Marcil, later Speaker of the House of Commons, and Louis P. Kribs, a spirited polemicist of his day.

Confederation brought into being at Ottawa a new breed of people, with new interests, new loyalties, new relationships. These were the first *Canadians* —using that word in an original and special sense. The coincidence that the new *Dominion* was given the name of the old *Province* obscures the point I am trying to make. Before 1867 there were Upper Canadians, and Lower Canadians or *Canadiens*. There were also Nova Scotians, and New Brunswickers and Prince Edward Islanders. There were Manitobans and Northwesters and Pacific Coast settlers. But beginning on the 1st of July, 1867 a new national sentiment began to emerge, and Ottawa was the most favorable breeding ground for it. These were the citizens of the new federal union, the Canadians of national horizons. Ottawa began to offer a home to men and women of the most diverse geographical, political, racial, religious and cultural backgrounds, who mingled in one community; who began to create one heterogeneous society, and who dreamed of a greater Canada. In the Halls of Parliament and in the Civil Service, in the Russell Hotel and in private boarding houses, on the same streets and in the same clubs, the elements and nucleus of a Canadian people began to form.

4

All these were in the nature of social, cultural and intellectual seedlings planted into the soil of the Ottawa community and likely to contribute to the enrichment of future generations. There was at the same time one inherent flaw or source of future friction inherent in the terms of Union, which so far as I can discover aroused little or no apprehension at the time. It does not appear to have come up for extensive discussion at the 1864 Conferences, and only one of the Fathers of Confederation published any important comment about it. In the Confederation Debates at Quebec City in 1865 only Christopher Dunkin drew attention to the anomalies and objections inherent in it.

The point is that the constitutional position of Ottawa as the capital was materially altered by the decisions of 1864-67; and the change in that particular respect was a retrograde step. As capital of the *Province* of Canada, no serious jurisdictional problems could possibly arise between the Crown and the Town in Ottawa, for the municipality of Ottawa would have continued to be under the direct control of the Provincial Government on Parliament Hill. Nor would any problem arise if government activities spread into adjoining municipalities, or even across the Ottawa River into Canada East, since between 1840 and 1867 the Ottawa River merely separated two geographical divisions of one Province.

But Confederation changed all that. Now Ontario and Quebec were autonomous states within their defined powers, and these powers included the exclusive control of municipal and local matters. Now Ottawa, by the B.N.A. Act, was a federal capital located *within a provincial municipality*, and the latter took its orders, not from Parliament Hill, but from Queen's Park, 275 miles away, and from a jurisdiction separate and autonomous and independent in broad respects from the central federal government. And the Ottawa River had once again become a boundary between two autonomous governments.

The difficulties inherent in this new situation did not show up for some time, but they were there from the beginning.

The most acute and prescient observations on this matter came from the pen of John Hamilton Gray, the Saint John lawyer and New Brunswick Father of Confederation, who wrote an interesting analysis and recommendation with respect to it. The general poverty of the surviving records of the events and conferences of 1864 gives added value to Colonel Gray's published recollections of that period.

John Hamilton Gray dedicated his *Confederation of Canada* to his fellow members of the House of Commons. (He was a member of the first federal parliament 1867-72). The book was published in Toronto in 1872. It was intended to be a history of Canada from 1864, the year of the Quebec Conference, to 1871, the year when British Columbia entered Confederation, and it was planned in two volumes, but the second was never published.

Gray described the Conference at Quebec, and the 'Grand Tour' of the Fathers which followed, to Montreal, Ottawa, and the other cities of Ontario. He praised the choice of the capital, and credited Sir Edmund Head with far-seeing judgment. "Few cities," he wrote, "possess greater local advantages. Watered in front by the Grand River, on the right by the Rideau, and intersected by the canal, it possesses, for sanitary arrangements and sewerage, the very greatest facilities. Originally well planned and laid out by Colonel By, who foresaw its future destiny as a large town, its broad parallel streets, and reserves for public purposes, afford accommodation and security."

Colonel Gray was deeply moved by the natural grandeur of the site. "Built on a lofty table-land, eighty or a hundred feet above the river, with bold escarpments in front, the eye is arrested on every side by scenes of unequalled beauty," he declared. "The Gatineau Hills, the first amid the primeval up-heavings of the great Laurentian range...bound the horizon to the north, and the spreading plains to the south afford scope for unlimited expansion.

"But its importance lies not simply in its attractive appearance. It is the centre of a rich agricultural district, and its great water powers on the Chau-dière and Rideau have given it the largest manufacturing establishments in lumber at present on the North American continent. This latter circumstance is due, in a great measure, to the energy and enterprize of American citizens, who, seeing its immense natural advantages, and knowing the unlimited ex-tent of its forests beyond, and the water tributaries of those partially un-explored regions, made it their home."

Gray recalled the coming of the lumber barons and industrial promoters like Bronson, Pattee and Perley, Harris and Eddy. "The river was put in harness; and now the spot, which at that time was simply known as a scene of beauty, is crowded with mills and machine shops, and, including both sides of the Falls, affords unceasing employment to twenty thousand people, daily creating untold wealth, and, with its schools and churches, spreading the comforts of life around."

Colonel Gray was impressed by Ottawa's central location. "Its position with reference to the entire Dominion, as extending from the Atlantic to the Pacific—an achievement brought about far more rapidly than at the time of the Convention [the Quebec Conference] was conceived—is admirable. On the line along which the Canadian Pacific Railway must run, it will command equal facilities for access to Quebec and the Maritime Provinces on the one side, and the Western Territories and British Columbia on the other."

But after all these words of praise for the capital, Gray, the New Brunswick lawyer, lodged one important demurrer. It was apparent, he said, that the Fathers of Confederation had made one mistake at the Quebec Conference. "*No provision was made for creating a federal district for the capital, and with-drawing it from the exclusive control of the local legislature of one of the Prov-inces.*

"That which was destined to be the capital of the Confederation might fairly rest its claim for support upon the people of the Dominion," he continued. "Its order, well-being, sanitary arrangements, police regulations, adornments and improvements are essential to the comfort and security not only of the representatives who attend Parliament, but of all those who are compelled to resort to the capital of the country in the discharge of the various duties attendant upon the administration of public affairs. Its reputation should be national, not provincial. It belongs no more to Ontario than it does to New Brunswick, Nova Scotia, Quebec, or to any of the Provinces constituting the Confederation."

The New Brunswick Father of Confederation showed a keen insight into the whole problem:

"The expenses incident to its civic control must necessarily be far greater than would devolve upon it if merely an ordinary municipality. It is no answer to say that the increased value in property is sufficient consideration for the increased burden put upon the inhabitants. That does not meet the question. They may not choose to accept the responsibility; and the Dominion Parliament, under confederation, has no power to legislate upon the matter. The legislation for the capital in all civil matters is entirely under the control of one province, differing in its laws from the others. The employees and officials of the Dominion Government, residing at Ottawa, numbering almost two thousand men, in every respect competent as voters, and, under other circumstances, capable of enjoying and exercising their franchise, are wisely interdicted, by the policy of the Government of the Dominion, from interfering in the local Provincial politics, or taking part in the elections for the Provincial Legislature. Yet they are subject to the taxation imposed upon them by that legislation; and bluff old Harry the Eighth never unfrocked a bishop with more satisfaction than the Ontario Legislature, for local purposes, taxes a body of men whom they do not pay, and who are debarred from exercising any influence upon the selection of their body."

Colonel Gray then reviewed at some length the history of the District of Columbia, and drew the conclusion: "Americans have their capital, Canadians have no capital for their country."

He thought the matter could still be rectified: "The City of Ottawa, with a certain area around it, should be created a Federal District; the laws for its future government (not interfering with private rights, or the city's present municipal privileges without adequate consideration) should be passed by the Dominion Parliament, and carried out by officers responsible to the Dominion Government, and through it to the people of the whole Dominion; or by a territorial arrangement, as in the District of Columbia, the legislatures of Ontario and Quebec ceding such portion of territory on both sides of the river as would make the District thoroughly unprovincial, and stipulating such terms in the cession as would preserve existing rights and interests."

5

When a capital city is created from the ground up, in hitherto unoccupied territory, as at Canberra and Brasilia, the national or federal government must perforce proceed to establish a new community from scratch. There are no taxpayers yet to levy upon for municipal services, and the central government must construct and operate and pay for its own. In such circumstances, a 'federal district' comes into being almost automatically.

But that was not the case with Ottawa. It was already a city of 18,000 persons by 1867. The rudiments, at least, of essential municipal services were already in existence. There was a well established tradition of self-government in municipal matters, long predating Confederation. The government of the province of Canada in 1859 never proposed to set up a separate or rival municipality, when it began erecting the Parliament Buildings. Nor did the government of the Dominion of Canada in 1867. It is true that pending the strengthening of Ottawa's municipal services the Canadian government undertook to provide some utilities of its own. In 1859, the city of Ottawa still had no water supply except that provided by private carriers freighting water from the river. The Provincial commissioner of public works put in a small plant down below the Library to pump water for the buildings. A separate sewerage system was built by the provincial government when the buildings were under construction. Some elementary fire protection was also provided, and the policing of the hill was under provincial and then federal control.

In several respects the effect of the planting of the Canadian capital within the municipal limits of Ottawa was not unlike that of the location of a large private corporation. Both operations require massive new construction, create new jobs, and, before long, additional municipal burdens. But in two vital elements there is a sharp contrast. Government properties are given permanent exemption from municipal taxation by the terms of the British North America Act. And governments possess contingent powers no private company ever enjoyed. One is the power of expropriation.

Gray's proposal of a federal district for Ottawa found few converts, especially in the early years. The problems he foresaw did not immediately grow irksome. The activities of the federal government did not impinge very much on the municipality of Ottawa for the first fifteen years. The city corporation was not very conscious of either actual or potential costs or inconveniences arising out of the presence of a seat of government, while the advantages were all too patent. The early government buildings were physically confined to Parliament Hill, which from the beginning had been Ordnance Land, and which had never been taxed for municipal purposes. And at first, as has been said, the government buildings even provided their own utilities.

The incipient conflict of interests between Town and Crown was therefore not tested for some time. The day would come when the federal government would find it necessary to expand beyond the limits of the old Ordnance property on Barrack Hill into the heart of the business section of Ottawa, when the municipal services needed in the enlarged government buildings would begin to lay heavy new burdens on the City Fathers. Then the problems foreseen by J. H. Gray at Confederation would emerge in growing magnitude.

6

The first few years of Confederation were intoxicating and prosperous in the main, a great impetus being derived from the exciting achievement of Confederation and the accession of great new areas of North America as the outlines of the new Dominion were filled in. Railway building could foster booms: it could also wreck budgets and create political crises. The Intercolonial Railway was begun at once and vigorously prosecuted: by 1876 Central Canada was linked with six Atlantic ports. The Canadian Pacific Railway proved to be a more formidable undertaking: before it was finished in 1885 several political and financial crises shook the young country. After six or seven years of buoyant times and balanced budgets, the federal government began to be plagued by a prolonged international dislocation which economists call 'the Great Depression'. This began about 1875 and lasted for twenty years. The Riel Rebellions of 1870 and 1885 threatened to drive a permanent rift between the two historic parent stocks of Canada. Sir Richard Cartwright said that the volley that killed Thomas Scott in 1870 cost a hundred million dollars, and nearly broke up the young Confederation. The execution of Riel in 1885 was a sort of *riposte* for Scott's death, and for a time it threatened to finish off what the first Riel Rebellion had begun.

There were indeed some highly discouraging times before the 20th Century was reached. A motion urging secession was passed by the British Columbia Legislature in 1877. Nova Scotia elected a secession government in 1884. Cartwright, looking back at the end of a life which had spanned the early years of the federation once wrote: "The plain, if disagreeable truth is that from 1866 to 1896, Canada as a whole, with one or two brief interludes, retrograded in every way, physically, morally and materially." Even Wilfrid Laurier went through a period of profound discouragement. Writing to Edward Blake in 1891 he expressed a fear that the premature dissolution of the country was at hand. Looking back from the vantage point of 1960 such comments seem unduly pessimistic. But the first thirty years of Confederation undoubtedly brought their own deep-seated problems, and the impact of events was in turn written on the sluggish progress of Ottawa on its way to becoming a stately or impressive city.

For the first eighteen years of Confederation the numbers of the federal civil service at Ottawa rose at a modest pace. About 400 persons were added between 1867 and 1885, or at a rate of a score or so a year. For the first 15 years it was possible to accommodate all these officials on Parliament Hill.

A brief review of early building is in order here. When the first Parliament of Canada met at Ottawa, very little construction work had yet been done on the Library Building, and by an order-in-council of 29 February 1868 it was ruled that construction should not be proceeded with. (The Buildings had already cost three times the original estimate). Meantime the large 'Picture Gallery' in the Parliament Buildings was used as a library room. Then in November 1870, a contract was called to complete the walls of the Parliamentary Library, and in 1873 work began on the roof. By 1877 the Library was ready for occupation. This in turn relieved some of the pressure on office space within the Centre Block.

Meantime the original Western Block, as they called it, was being enlarged. The contract for the extension was let in 1874 and the work was completed in the year 1875-6. The enlargement added 59 offices and ten rooms in the basement.

About the same time a temporary building west of the West Block was made into a permanent workshop for architects and engineers. The subsequent fate of this workshop was unusual. In 1880 it was converted into a Supreme Court Building. For a time it also served as an Art Gallery. The Supreme Court and the Exchequer Court were accommodated in it for half a century.

By such devices as these the problem of accommodation was kept within the confines of Parliament Hill until 1880. In that year the Geological Survey was moved from Montreal and housed in a former hotel building on Sussex Street. But the tempo of staff additions in the civil service was already beginning to rise. By 1883 it was apparent that a major addition to the group of government buildings was mandatory. This time the government had no choice about location. For the new building it had to find a site outside of the Ordnance Land on Parliament Hill. Yet it was desirable to build it as conveniently as possible to the centre of government business. The solution adopted was to take over commercial property on the south side of Wellington Street, and build there. The so-called Southern Block, which became known as the Langevin Block, was the result. For the first time the needs of the federal government had led to the pre-emption of a block of valuable commercial property and had thus removed it from the assessment and tax rolls of the city of Ottawa.

The completion of the spacious Langevin Block in 1885 eased the problem of office accommodation for 20 years. In designing it, Thomas Fuller (who was by now Chief Dominion Architect) departed from the 'Civil Gothic' of the other buildings on the Hill to employ a modification of the Italian Renaissance style. New Brunswick sandstone was used in the walls. Sir James Edgar, speaker of the House in the late 90's, wrote that the change from the Gothic was made to provide more space and light in the offices. No more major projects for departmental buildings were necessary until after the turn of the century, but it was during this period that the Central Experimental Farm was being established as an important agricultural laboratory.

8

As seen from City Hall, the gradual expansion of federal government offices and the increased government demands upon municipal services raised the issue of adequate compensation. The federal government properties could not be taxed, but neither could the municipality be expected to provide municipal services free of cost. Discussions between the corporation of Ottawa and the federal government began at an early date.

Two years after Confederation, the City of Ottawa negotiated with the federal Department of Public Works an agreement under which the City was permitted to draw on surplus water passing over the Chaudière Falls to supply the city with water and drive the necessary machinery. In 1877 the Government Buildings were connected with the City Waterworks. An agreement dated March 6, 1877 was reached between Crown and City covering the fee to be paid to the City for water services to the government buildings and to Rideau Hall. The price was $9,000 a year. This rose as the number of government buildings increased, and between 1877 and 1899 (the date when a bill was introduced to provide for new financial arrangements) the sum fluctuated between about $9,000 and $15,400 a year.

In 1883 the City Corporation made representations to the federal government that it should receive compensation for the loss of tax revenue from the expansion of government property across Wellington street into the heart of the commercial area, and to reimburse it for the additional burden laid on it in maintaining civil services because of Ottawa being the seat of government. The federal government rejected the idea of a grant for this purpose, but agreed instead to assume certain liabilities. In 1883 the government agreed to pay for the maintenance of Dufferin and Sappers Bridges, and the timber slides and bridges over them at the Chaudière Falls. It agreed to drop toll charges on the suspension bridge at the same site. Two years later the government agreed to take over the maintenance of Major's Hill Park.

Also in 1885, the City asked the federal government to take over the cost of the police force in Ottawa. This was refused, as was a request to maintain the MacLaren Bridge over the Rideau River at New Edinburgh. But the federal authorities accepted the responsibility of maintaining the Laurier Avenue Bridge and the sidewalks in front of Cartier Square.

9

We have already seen how the 'Industrial Revolution' came to the 'meeting of the waters' about the middle of the 19th century. The harnessing of the Chaudière followed the building of wheels and mills on the Rideau. The city of Ottawa became a regal capital on the old Barrack Hill, but elsewhere it took on the drab and smoky appearance of a prospering lumber town and industrial community.

The first railway had been inspired by the hope of exporting sawmill products in quantity to Ogdensburg and eventually to the Atlantic seaboard at Boston, as we saw. It reached Ottawa in 1854, and for a long time was the only link by rail with the outside world. After a pause in the 1850's the railway age got into high gear again, and by the end of the century Ottawa had become an important railway centre. The promotion of new railway companies was encouraged and supported by most municipalities, which saw in the railway the road to commercial prosperity. The steam locomotive brought in its train major changes in the landscape and pattern of every city in North America, and Ottawa and Hull did not escape.

Railways encouraged the establishment of new factories; factories spelled new payrolls and an increase in steady jobs; jobs meant more business for the shops and other retail services. But the factories and railways also brought smoke and grime, vast extensions of ugly buildings and sprawling yards. The railways sought the cheapest and most convenient entrances and exits from the urban centre: they were favored clients, and they blighted wide strips and large areas of the cities they served. The railway companies were fiercely independent of one another—keen rivals for civic favors. City fathers were little inclined to dictate terms to railway promoters holding out the golden prospect of enhanced industry, greater population, more wealth, higher employment. The grim trend was inevitable. The Ottawa-Hull area had a great potential future because of the lumbering wealth of the Ottawa Valley and the tributaries to the Ottawa, because of the rich farm lands, because of the vast amounts of hydro-electric power right at the doorsteps of the national capital—one of the greatest concentrations of hydro power sites anywhere.

The effect of the Industrial Revolution on some of the grandest natural scenery in eastern Canada—on the Chaudière Falls, the banks of the Ottawa river opposite the Parliament Buildings, Nepean Bay, the Rideau Falls—can be readily seen by comparing early drawings and engravings with photographs of the same regions a century later.

The proliferation of railway lines created the greatest headache for future city planners. Even a bare recital of the new companies and projects conveys a sense of the profusion of new projects. The first railway, the Bytown and Prescott Railway Company (later Ottawa and Prescott) ran its tracks across the city to a terminus at New Edinburgh, near Thomas MacKay's manufacturing plants. In 1871 a branch line was built, again across the city, to the Chaudière Terminal at Broad Street. In 1879 the North Shore line linked Quebec City with Hull and Ottawa. Three years later this was acquired by the Canadian Pacific Railway Company. The Canada-Atlantic at about the same time erected a terminal on the west side of the Rideau Canal at the end of Elgin Street. The Canada Central crossed the city to use the same terminal as the Canadian Pacific Railway. In 1896 the Ottawa, Arnprior and Parry Sound Railway Company linked Ottawa with Georgian Bay. In 1898 the Montreal and Atlantic Railway Company provided a new shorter route between Ottawa and Montreal. In the same year the Ottawa and New York Railway Company completed its line to a new terminus at Nicholas Street and Mann Avenue. Early in 1901 the Royal Alexandra Railway Bridge linking Ottawa and Hull was opened for traffic. An amalgamation of two earlier companies, the Pontiac Pacific Junction Railway Company and the Gatineau Valley Railway, used this bridge to link Ottawa by rail with Maniwaki and Waltham, P. Que.

Such was the railway situation up to the point where the Ottawa Improvement Commission was beginning its program. But the railway building era was still at its peak of activity and in the following decade several additional complications of the railway and terminal spiderweb were introduced.

The Ottawa-Hull urban areas would in any event have faced serious problems of communication as traffic increased in density. They were built upon a network of intersecting waterways, — the Ottawa River itself, the Rideau River, the Rideau Canal, the Gatineau River, and Brewery Creek, which converts much of the older portion of Hull into an island. This network of water courses of itself made necessary many expensive bridges and bridge approaches. When upon this water network there was superimposed an almost chaotic collection of railway lines, spurs, yards, termini and warehouses, the effect on the flow of traffic throughout the region, can be imagined. Railways crossed streets at hundreds of points, and scores of dead end streets marked the points where no crossings were provided.

10

Is it only a coincidence that national pride in the capital region seems to have been at low ebb in the last quarter of the 19th century, in the years preceding the first concerted effort to preserve and enhance the natural beauty of the area? Even the Hon. Wilfrid Laurier, later to be associated with the dream of making Ottawa "The Washington of the North" said in 1884: "I would not wish to say anything disparaging of the capital, but it is hard to say anything good of it. Ottawa is not a handsome city and does not appear to be destined to become one either." And W. L. Mackenzie King, who was ordained to play a considerable part in changing matters for the better, wrote in his first impressions, in July 1900: "The first glimpse of the city was from the lately fire swept district and it was gloomy enough. The business part of the town is small and like that of a provincial town, not interesting but tiresome...I will miss greatly the University Society and the pleasant surroundings of Cambridge. Ottawa is not a pretty place save about the parliament buildings."

CHAPTER EIGHT

"Washington of the North"

By the end of the 19th century, Ottawa was a flourishing industrial centre. It was still the hub of the lumbering industry of eastern Canada. It had the largest paper mills in Canada and the leading match factory in the world. It had pioneered in the use of hydro-electric power, and there was known to be nearly a million horse power of potential energy within a fifty mile radius. Its population had doubled in the past fifteen years.

But there were two Ottawas. Ottawa as an Ontario industrial city could hold its head high. Ottawa as the national capital—the symbolic heart of Canada—was another matter. There was increasing dissatisfaction by national leaders at its failure to grow into the proud and beautiful capital of a great Dominion. Comparisons with other world capitals were depressing.

The 1890's witnessed a great quickening of interest throughout North America in city architecture and planning. It was precipitated by the impressive designs of Daniel H. Burnham, John W. Root, and Frederick Law Olmsted for the World's Columbian Exposition held at Chicago in 1893. The exposition was housed in a planned group of 150 buildings, in Romanesque, Greek and Renaissance architecture, and because the main edifices were constructed of a composition resembling marble, it became known as the *White City*. Echoes of this imposing example of what was possible in large-scale landscaping and city planning appear to have reached the Canadian capital.

If Ottawa was ever to become a stately and beautiful capital, costly outlays could not be escaped. National, not local, resources must be tapped. But until after 1895—the end of the 'Great Depression'—the federal government was chronically hard up. Easier times would encourage national projects. It was Wilfrid Laurier who was destined to inherit both the clamor for national action and the budgetary surpluses to make action feasible and acceptable.

In June of 1893, while leader of the opposition Liberal party in the House of Commons, Wilfrid Laurier had arrived at Ottawa to attend a national Liberal convention. He was presented with an address by the Ottawa Reform Association, and in his reply he said:

"Let me tell you now that I will continue to keep a green spot in my heart for the many kindnesses I have received from the people of Ottawa, not only from my political friends, but from my political opponents as well...and when the day comes, as it will come by and by, it shall be my pleasure and that of my colleagues, I am sure, to make the city of Ottawa the centre of the intellectual development of this country, and the Washington of the North."

Three years later Laurier was elected Prime Minister of Canada, and he remembered what he had promised. On August 5th, 1896 he was presented with an address of welcome in a great political demonstration on Cartier Square in Ottawa, and he repeated and amplified the observations which he had made at the time of the Liberal convention.

When he came back from the Diamond Jubilee celebration at London in 1897, the Prime Minister was once more hailed by the people of Ottawa. A great streamer had been stretched across Wellington Street, bearing the words: WELCOME HOME. Sir Wilfrid used this as the text for his reply. Ottawa *was* his home and would continue to be so, and he would not forget the undertaking he had given in public at least twice before.

2

Meanwhile the future of the capital was being debated in Ottawa's City Council. Shortly after Laurier's accession to office, Fred Cook and Robert Stewart, city councillors, proposed the appointment of a civic committee to make a study of the principal capitals in the British Empire, to see what sort of grants were made by the national governments to the municipal authorities, and what plans were being made to beautify and embellish the several capital cities. Fred Cook, in his reminiscences, recalls that the current attitude on the improvement of Ottawa was one of apathy, and that both in City Council and in the federal government there was reluctance about spending money for public amenities. Cook thought it might strengthen Sir Wilfrid's hand in proposals to embark on an improvement scheme if he knew what was being done in other parts of the Empire. By October of 1897 considerable information had been accumulated, and the City forwarded a petition to the Laurier government.

This document went into the budgetary problems of an urban municipality which was at the same time the seat of a national government. It listed the sums expended and obligations incurred by Ottawa for public works and municipal improvements, including payments for the protection of federal property. The annual revenue of the corporation from taxes was represented as being entirely inadequate for its needs as the seat of government. By 1897, the properties owned by the Crown within the city limits of Ottawa (and as such tax exempt) were valued at $14 million. The memorial stressed that the city had received no compensation from the federal government for the city's large outlay on public works, in contrast with the practice in other parts of the world. A strong point was the fact that the United Kingdom government paid municipal rates to the city corporation of London on all its properties, including the Houses of Parliament. The petition closed with the suggestion that a fixed annual grant might be set up for the city of Ottawa, in return for which the city would undertake to furnish an adequate water supply, provide efficient fire protection to all government property, and such other services as might be agreed upon.

There was no immediate response from the Laurier government, but the subject was placed on its agenda. Hon. W. S. Fielding, former Premier of Nova Scotia and now federal Minister of Finance, began to look into the quite complex financial and jurisdictional relationships between a federal capital like Ottawa and the provincial municipality in which it was located. Early in November, 1898, Fielding prepared a memorandum for his chief, expressing the hope that while Laurier was in Washington, he would make some inquiries about the system of government of the District of Columbia. He expressed sympathy with those "friends" who wished to improve the capital of Ottawa, and added that he "would not be disposed to object to moderate contributions from the Dominion Treasury" under a proper system of government.

An extract from Lady Aberdeen's diary written ten days later implies that by a "proper system" Fielding had in mind something like a federal district for the Canadian capital. The whole Aberdeen reference is illuminating on the climate of Ottawa opinion prevailing just before the introduction of the first legislation on the subject—the 1899 Act which created the Ottawa Improvement Commission.

The occasion for the diary entry was Lord Aberdeen's farewell address at the Russell House, in which he spoke of the capital and its natural advantages.

"I must own," Lady Aberdeen wrote on the following day, "to beginning to feel a sneaking fondness for the place itself, in spite of its shabby old Government House put away amongst its clumps of bushes and in spite of dirty old tumble down Sussex Street, to drive over which always needed an effort, although it was an effort almost daily repeated.

"Perhaps this fondness is not altogether unconnected with a scheme for a general improvement of Ottawa which lies very near our own hearts and which if carried out would make her one day a very queen of capitals. The idea is to get a plan made and adopted whereby a beautiful stately drive or esplanade would be constructed from Major's Park right down Sussex Street, along which only buildings of an approved type would be allowed, that only on one side, leaving the river side free and open and terminating on the Government House ground with a new and worthy Government House overlooking that lovely view of the river which may be had from the Governor General's Bay— then throwing a bridge over to the Gatineau which would enable a drive to be made all round the other side of the river and coming back to Hull.

"Of course the same drive would have to be considered west of the

Parliament Buildings to the Chaudière Falls. It would make a glorious place of it and there is nothing now to prevent it. Then Nepean Point should be made a public park with open air skating and facilities for toboganning across the river and a building which would be the rendezvous for all the sports for which Ottawa is famous both in winter and summer.

"This would make up fully for that site having been made impossible for Government House, first by the Printing Bureau and then by the dreadful C. P. Railway Bridge which is mauling it to pieces, which Sir Wilfrid laments over as much as everybody. It was allowed whilst he was in England.

"Sir Wilfrid is quite taken with the idea and came over the place with me to inspect it one day—so did Mr. Tarte and he was most enthusiastic about it but seemed to think it possible to undertake it at a much earlier date than we had ventured to hint at. We only said, 'Look fifty years ahead and get a plan made whereby such a scheme may ultimately be developed and which will prevent eye-sores of buildings being put up meanwhile and thus preventing it, and, to begin with, the new geological museum as the first beautiful building.'

"Mr. Tarte thinks it would be a good thing to get a plan and an opinion from the architect who put up those beautiful Victoria Parliament Buildings and as he is now in London on Klondike business, I am to try to see him. Mr. Edwards the great lumber merchant is another ally, and a very necessary ally too—but he thinks the lumber works will not remain where they are for so long.

"Mr. Fielding says, 'Get Ottawa put under a Commission like Washington and I am with you.' Probably he is right for the Ottawa authorities have not been very wonderful up to now.

"Altogether it does not seem impossible for some such plan to be carried out and it is certain that the last two or three years have seen a great advance in the sort of *esprit de corps* which exists amongst Ottawa citizens. The city seemed to possess no soul before and to be composed of people who had no special interest in hanging together, but all this is changing and the formation of the Ottawa Tourist Association to develop the means of getting to the various charming places around about Ottawa and which are but little known will help in the same direction and will promote pride in the place.

"As Montreal is now hopelessly lost as a capital everything possible should be done to push Ottawa and Sir Wilfrid is anxious to redeem his promise of making it the 'Washington of the North'. He also thinks that a new Government House is quite a question within the range of practical politics in the next year or two if the revenue keeps up."

3

The following year Mr. Fielding introduced legislation to create the Ottawa Improvement Commission, to consist of four commissioners, three chosen by the federal government and one by the city of Ottawa.

Section 15 of the statute stipulated that the annual grant of $60,000 to the city of Ottawa would be in full payment, satisfaction and discharge, of all claims and demands in respect to water services for the government buildings, grounds, parks and the Dominion Experimental Farm.

The debate that followed indicates that there were still many members of the House lukewarm toward the expenditure of any money for the beautification of the national capital. There was a frugal if not niggardly approach to the matter. Members from right across Canada complained that their constituents would be opposed to taking money raised by general taxation, from farmers and others, and handing it over for special concessions to one city. If Parliament Hill undertook to develop special parks and driveways in Ottawa, that would be equivalent to easing the tax load on the Ottawa city ratepayer, they said. Every other city in Canada would come to Mr. Fielding and ask for a similar handout. The grant of $60,000 was criticised as being extravagant, despite Mr. Fielding's explanation that the increase was really only $45,000, since the old annual grant of $15,000 for water services was to disappear. One member wanted to cut the $60,000 vote in half. Much was made — by members from other parts of Canada — of the "immense advantages" Ottawa city already derived from the presence of the national capital. Any other city in Canada would be delighted to receive the national capital, and that "without any bonus". Indeed, other cities might be prepared to put up a substantial annual sum for the privilege of housing the national capital. And so on.

Mr. Fielding, aided by one of the Ottawa city members, succeeded in meeting all of these objections, and the bill was passed in due course. But it is a reflection on the defensive and almost apologetic attitude of the Laurier administration at the time, that Mr. Fielding promised that he would try to find a secretary for the Ottawa Improvement Commission from among the civil service, who would perform his duties in his spare time, after hours, "as a labour of love", at no cost to the federal treasury! And it is interesting that one member should warn that by this bill the national government was entering into a perpetual partnership with the city of Ottawa, that another member should contend that "we have already enough government property around here," and that a third should object to a Commission acquiring city property, on the ground that it would create "an imperium in imperio", blocks of public land over which the local municipality had not the slightest jurisdiction.

In no sense could the bill be described as authorizing a municipal grant to the city of Ottawa as compensation for the tax-exempt properties within the municipal boundaries, or as compensation for the exemption of federal civil servants from municipal income tax. Indeed, as has been said, by the legislation the city lost the annual grant which had been paid since 1877 for water services to federal government property. Nor was any claim put forward in the debate that such a compensation in lieu of taxes should be paid. But it did come out for the record that there were costs and debits as well as gains to the municipality because of the presence of the federal government. The city had been compelled to go in for much larger expenditure for water mains and drains. A recent fire in the "Western" Block had led the city to double its expenditure for fire protection. The Ottawa member, N. A. Belcourt, made the point that Major's Hill Park had been handed over to the federal government after the city had spent $35,000 on it. If the corporation had taken a purely commercial attitude, it could have subdivided that property, sold it for a large sum, and obtained substantial amounts of tax revenue from it ever after, he said. Mr. Belcourt also raised, perhaps for the first time in a Commons debate, the complicated problem of the effect on city revenues of federal government expropriation of municipal property. In order to build the Langevin Block on Wellington St., the government had taken over private properties. The city had, Mr. Belcourt argued, thereby lost the tax revenues it had previously been deriving from those private properties.

The member for Beauharnois (Mr. Bergeron) immediately interposed with what has since become a familiar rejoinder. Not so, he said,—the merchants and others who sold the Langevin site property to the Crown had proceeded to build again somewhere else, and were again paying Corporation taxes, with no net loss to the Corporation.

In passing it may be noted that Mr. Fielding's undertaking that the Secretary of the Ottawa Improvement Commission would be a civil servant discharging the duties without special compensation continued until 1919. From that date until 1921, when a full-time Secretary was appointed, an official of the Auditor-General's office (William Kearns) received part-time remuneration.

4

Mr. Fielding had introduced his proposals to spend some federal money on the beautification of the capital at a favorable juncture. Though no one could be sure of it in 1899, Canada was in the early stages of a great era of expansion. The background for the advance was described by the authors of the Rowell-Sirois Report (1940) in the following language:

"For twenty-five years the new nation had languished and even the most sanguine were troubled by forebodings about the success of Confederation. Then a fortuitous juncture of world circumstances brought with a rush the fulfilment of hopes long deferred. Life began to stir in the frame erected years earlier for a trans-continental economy. Directed by the national policies of all-Canadian railways, western settlement and protective tariffs, it grew with a rapidity surpassing all expectations. A vast and sudden transformation was wrought by the magic of wheat. The wheat boom brought a flood of settlers into the West and created two new and flourishing provinces. It precipitated a new era of railway development and spurred on the industrialization of Central Canada. Immense capital expenditures were necessary to equip the West and the growing metropolitan areas of the East."

The national capital soon responded to these stirring events. From 1896 to 1913 the expenditure of the federal government on national services multiplied seven times. The civil service rose proportionately. In that seventeen year period the following new government buildings were erected in Ottawa:

A Laboratory at the Experimental Farm, the Dominion Observatory, the Printing Bureau, the Archives Building, the Victoria Memorial Museum, the Royal Canadian Mint, a Fuel Testing Plant, an Instrument Testing Building, additional Laboratories at the Experimental Farm, the Connaught Building, and a Geodetic Building in connection with the Observatory. This was in sharp contrast with the first thirty years of Confederation, during which the Langevin Block and the Geological Museum were the only additions of importance. All of the new structures except those on the Experimental Farm were built within the business or residential areas of the city of Ottawa, thus removing further valuable properties from the city tax-rolls.

5

Meantime Ottawa as an industrial and commercial city was also responding to the new era of national boom, and Crown and Town began, willy nilly, to get in each other's way. It was inevitable that the era from 1896 to 1913 would see a growing awareness of new capital problems. On the one hand the new national pride and consciousness and the new buoyancy in federal revenues led to a determination to create in the capital region, if not the "Washington of the North", at least a setting worthy of the great new Canada. And on the other hand the councillors of the city of Ottawa became increasingly aware that the realization of such ambitious national plans would call for expenditures far beyond the means of the Ottawa taxpayers. Who was to foot the bill for these national schemes? Apart from direct costs, the new national plans for the capital might clash with Ottawa's own corporate hopes of becoming a great industrial and commercial city. How could these conflicting ambitions be reconciled? In the main, Town and Crown had so far gone their own separate ways, without much interference one with the other. But with both city and capital expanding in a dynamic fashion, the future would demand some new and constructive solutions.

6

There was no lack of desirable "improvement" to be tackled when the Ottawa Improvement Commission began its work in 1899, with an annual grant of $60,000. In the early years of its operations, it began to clear up the banks of the Rideau Canal, still cluttered with warehouses, sheds, lumber yards and piles of construction material right up to Parliament Hill; and turn the west verges into a pleasant driveway, beginning at Laurier Avenue and pushed along by stages past the Exhibition Grounds, past Bank Street to Bronson Avenue, with the intention ultimately of linking it up with the Experimental Farm. King Edward Avenue was converted into a boulevard, and the first stage of Rockcliffe Park was developed. An additional 100 acres of land was acquired for the expansion of Rockcliffe Park, and a boulevard planned between the two sections.

The Commission was a voluntary body operated with a negligible overhead. After three years of activity, lacking a landscape architect or professional planner on its own staff, it engaged the services of Frederick G. Todd of Montreal, a native of New Hampshire, to outline a general scheme for Ottawa's parks, boulevards and driveways. This was completed in August, 1903.

A controversy grew up later on about the use made of the Todd Report by the Ottawa Improvement Commission. The airing of the whole problem of planning a national capital which came out of this controversy paved the way for the appointment of the Holt Commission in 1913. For this reason a synopsis of the Todd Report is useful here. In any event it enables us to look at Ottawa and the surrounding area of the time through the eyes of a trained landscape architect. In the introduction to his report Frederick Todd emphasized that since he was dealing with a national capital he had paid but little attention to the purely arbitrary boundaries of the region. He expressed boundless confidence in the future of the capital, and pleaded for a far-sighted policy, looking ahead as much as a hundred years. Older cities had paid heavily for lack of foresight, he reminded the Commission.

"Not only is Ottawa sure to become the centre of a large and populous district, but the fact that it is the Capital of an immense country whose future greatness is beginning to unfold, renders it necessary that it shall also be the centre of all those things which are an index of man's highest intellectual attainments, and that it be a city which will reflect the character of the nation, and the dignity, stability, and good taste of its citizens."

Todd was concerned that the fashionable phrase "Washington of the North" might be taken too literally. What had made the beauty of one might mar the beauty of the other. The Government Buildings at Washington were built in a Colonial architecture suitable for the terrain.

"Your Government buildings are pure Gothic, the style which is perhaps better suited than any other to a picturesque site." He deplored the lack of an earlier plan for Canada's capital. "With a natural location which cannot be compared with that of Ottawa, the original plan of Washington took advantage of every natural feature which the location possessed, and made the most of it, and from this plan has evolved a beautiful city. When we consider what a very ordinary city Washington might have been if allowed simply to grow up as so many other cities have, and when we think of the beauties which Ottawa might have possessed had its growth been directed by the same wise forethought, we must realize the benefits of a well conceived plan not only from an aesthetic, but also a purely business viewpoint." This last remark showed that he did not brush aside the industrial values. Later on he emphasized the importance of Ottawa's manufacturing future. "We should not wish to take land for parks which will be needed for manufacturing purposes, nor should we wish to build a boulevard through land, be it ever so attractive now, which is certain to be built up with factories at some later date. To preserve the great natural beauty of the city as a heritage for the Dominion of the future, and at the same time to allow of the development to the greatest possible extent of the magnificent industrial opportunities of Ottawa, presents a problem of such magnitude that to attempt to discuss it in this report would be practically impossible. It seems to me, however, that this question must be faced sooner or later."

Frederick Todd's *detailed* proposals are, perhaps, of limited interest today. But two or three of his major recommendations should be stressed. He urged the preservation of large natural parks or forest lands, adjacent to the capital. "The Dominion of Canada is famous the world over for the extent and beauty of her forests, and for this reason it would seem appropriate that there should be reserved in close proximity to the Capital, good examples of the forests which once covered a great portion of the country." A reserve of about 2,000 acres "between Wright's Bridge and Chelsea" was one suggestion; the lands and woods around Meach Lake was another. To balance Rockcliffe Park, which he greatly admired, he suggested a similar park on the Ottawa River to the west, near the present approaches to the Champlain Bridge. He deplored the fact that Hull had no parks and proposed a fine site west of the mouth of the Gatineau River. He urged the building of an impressive boulevard linking Rideau Hall and the Parliament Buildings, to skirt the banks of the Ottawa River wherever possible. He grew lyrical over this proposal. "The views which may be obtained are magnificent. The Parliament Buildings, rising above the cedar clad Nepean Point, dominate the view cityward, while the views up and down the Ottawa River and over the City of Hull to the Laurentian Mountains are so grand and so diversified that it is impossible we should ever tire of them. They change with every turn of the road, with every whim of the elements; they change with the time and the seasons, and though changed in details, in light and shade, and in coloring, they remain still the same impressive views. Paris may spend a fortune on her grand avenues, Washington and Chicago may spend millions in constructing boulevards, but none of them can equal in grandness or impressive scenery, a boulevard constructed along this bank of the Ottawa River."

7

Sir Wilfrid Laurier, as Prime Minister, continued to take a benevolent interest in the beautification of Ottawa, and he received suggestions for further improvement from many quarters, including the highest. Among the Laurier papers there is an interesting letter from Earl Grey, when Governor General, written in April, 1908. Earl Grey had conceived of a novel plan for Nepean Point, and had taken the Hon. Raoul Dandurand and his wife, and Robert (not yet Sir Robert) Borden and Mrs. Borden to the site to outline his idea. He invited Sir Wilfrid to come and have lunch with him and then permit him to take the Prime Minister to Nepean Point for a similar inspection. Earl Grey thought that a Gothic structure in harmony with the Parliament Buildings should be built there, to serve as an official hotel for legislators and distinguished guests. Earl Grey wrote that he was sorry for the M.P.'s who had to leave their homes as much as 3,000 miles away "for whom that miserable Russell House looking on Sparks with its eternal tramcars is apparently the only accommodation."

What Sir Wilfrid thought of this idea has not come down to us. Shortly afterwards, the Grand Trunk Railway found a solution of its own in the stately Chateau Laurier, to accommodate which, incidentally, a site at the southern extremity of Major's Hill Park was made available.

8

The early work of the Ottawa Improvement Commission drew many compliments. Anyone who has contrasted pictures of the Rideau Canal banks before and after its development of the first Driveway will find no mystery in this. Anson A. Gard's *The Hub and the Spokes*, published in 1904, contains ample evidence of five years of achievement in a number of attractive photographs. "What with the pretty walks, tree embowered Ottawa is becoming a veritable beauty spot," wrote Gard, "and I would have my people know it. This will be especially worthy a visit, when the Driveway, of frequent mention, is completed. Only today have I fully appreciated its beauty. I leisurely walked along through its miles of flower borders, here a miniature park, there a lakelet spanned by a rustic bridge with ever and anon forms of park and lakelet, and all so pleasing that I forget distance in the ever changing scenes around me. The rustic work of bridges, bannistered steps, and various forms into which small cedar stems were worked, was so marvellous in design that I hunted out the man who had executed it all. I found him at work on the Driveway in front of the Papal Delegate's mansion to the west of Bank

Street, where he was putting up some steps of a design more artistic than I
had ever before seen in rustic work. I had expected to find a man living on
his reputation, and overseeing others, as they did the labor, but instead I
found Thomas Craig, a day carpenter, working out with his hands the intri-
cate and beautiful designs of his brain. He said he was shortly to begin a
rustic summer house, thirty feet square, a little further along beyond the
Papal Delegate's grounds. It is all to be of small round pieces of cedar, in its
natural form, and from his description it will be very pretty."

When the rustic gardener turned to larger designs, such as the planning of
Lady Grey Drive, there was less enthusiasm from the discriminating. And of
course the Ottawa Improvement Commission had no authority or resources
to tackle the basic flaws in the traffic pattern of the city. Professional architects
and town planners began to deplore the lack of anything like a radical long-
term program which alone could guarantee an impressive and beautiful capital
some day. Soon after the Royal Architectural Institute was created in 1907
it registered its protest on this point with the Laurier government. The Institute
was particularly critical of the fact that after holding a national competition
for designs of some new government buildings, the Department of Public
Works had ignored the successful plans and was proceeding to build from
an entirely different set of plans designed by its own architect. Resolutions
were passed by various provincial associations of architects and forwarded
to Ottawa, but the situation failed to change. Finally, soon after the defeat of
the Laurier Government in September, 1911 a deputation of members of the
Royal Architectural Institute of Canada waited upon the Rt. Hon. Robert
Borden.

"The wish of this deputation," they told him, "is to impress upon you and
your Government the fact that for a considerable time past there has been
a growing desire throughout the country, that in the civil improvements of
Ottawa, the greatest forethought and care should be taken."

"Ottawa, the Capital City, gifted with a magnificent natural site and an
abundant water power has an undoubted future. Now on the threshold of
its metropolitan life it would be wise not to leave to haphazard, changes that
have become a pressing necessity. The difficulty of finding a decisive site for
the new buildings, the question of a proper entrance into the city of the railways which are constantly increasing in number, the proper development of
the park system, and what is equally obvious and even more difficult of
solution, the need for future amendments to the street system of the city
itself, all point to the necessity of careful consideration of the matter."

The delegation wanted Mr. Borden to agree to the appointment of an honorary technical commission to plan the future of Ottawa and district, citing
the action taken at Washington for a similar purpose many years earlier.

The delegates handed to the Prime Minister, among other documents, a resolution by the Ontario Association of Architects passed at their annual meeting at Ottawa two months earlier. This used some blunt language about the inadequacies of the work being done by the Ottawa Improvement Commission to date. The resolution said the Ontario architects desired to express their appreciation of the measures being taken to add to the dignity and beauty of Ottawa but suggested that the time had arrived for a broader outlook, for coordination of the several works in progress and for planning for future works.

"The Association, after a careful inspection of the work that has already been executed, feels that much which has been done, will have to be undone, as it neither meets the needs of the situation in design or execution. The association would respectfully point out that in many cases the fundamental principles of the disposition of masses and of consideration for natural features, have given place to a striving after effect by over-elaboration of detail and the use of a quantity of meretricious ornament quite devoid of artistic quality."

9

What the architects were getting at comes out in detail in a later criticism of the Ottawa Improvement Commission's work, this time from within the Commission itself.

In 1910 a practicing architect of the city of Ottawa, Major Colborne Powell Meredith, was appointed to the Commission. He was soon at variance with some of his fellow commissioners on the quality and status of the work being done for the capital by the commission and the government. In the January following the architects' representations to the Prime Minister, there was a debate in the House of Commons on the work of the Ottawa Improvement Commission, and Sir Wilfrid Laurier, defending what had been done, said that the Commission had had the services of a professional landscape artist as far back as 1903, and that it had been acting on his recommendations.

C. P. Meredith at once took issue with this statement. After speaking to Hon. Martin Burrell, Minister of Agriculture, he sent him a confidential letter in which he said that "It is quite evident Sir Wilfrid has been misinformed." Actually, Mr. Meredith continued, "after the report was presented it was too big apparently for the Commission to grasp, and it was consequently pigeon-holed."

"Constantly through this preliminary report Mr. Todd makes suggestions and mild criticisms, but looking at what the Commission has done after the lapse of these nine years I fail to see a single instance where they have acted on his suggestions." Major Meredith charged that the work of the Commission had been "so crude and inartistic" that it had drawn the severest criticism of experts, and he added that he wished the Prime Minister could be made more familiar with the situation before it came up again. "I may say that as a Commissioner," he concluded, "I consider that the Commission has, from the first, carried on its work in a most unbusinesslike way, and persists to continue doing so, notwithstanding all the criticisms that have been made, and are content to have the general park scheme, the engineering work and the designing of structures requiring artistic training done by a so-called superintendent, who is nothing more than a bricklayer."

Meantime the Rt. Hon. Robert Borden had forwarded to the Ottawa Improvement Commission the criticisms of the Royal Architectural Institute, and at a meeting held in February, 1912, they had answered some of the strictures. The Commission had, they contended, carried out the general plan outlined by F. G. Todd "as fully as the financial resources at the disposal of the Commission would permit." This answer was incorporated in a Commission resolution, but C. P. Meredith as a Commissioner refused to vote for it. He wrote shortly afterwards to the Prime Minister, saying that he disagreed with his own Commission and explaining why. He sent with his letter a summary of the Todd Report, and scathing comments upon the limited extent to which Todd's recommendations had been carried out. He noted that nothing had been done about large natural parks for reserves, nothing done about Meach Lake, nothing done about Chaudière Park, nothing done about a Park on the right bank of the Rideau, nothing done about a park in Hull. He criticised severely the actual construction of Lady Grey Driveway. "As an example of the way in which the work should not be done one could not find anything more complete." He was severe, too, in his criticism of the treatment of Patterson's Creek Park and some of the smaller parks and squares taken by the Improvement Commission from the city.

The Ottawa Improvement Commission was handicapped by insufficient funds, restricted powers, and possibly, by lack of imagination. As it was not created as a town-planning body, and in any event lacked authority in that field, its remedies were bound to be superficial rather than basic. And the magnitude of the problem was rapidly growing. The importance of its work was meantime recognized by an increase in annual vote from $60,000 a year to $100,000 a year in 1910, and in 1917 to $150,000 a year. It always had its critics, in detail, as can be seen by reading the Commons debates year after year on the amendments to the Act under which it operated. But many tributes were paid from time to time for its accomplishments in changing the outward face of the capital.

10

The Borden government met the growing criticism of the architects and town planners by the appointment of a 'Federal Plan Commission' in 1913. The chairman was Herbert S. Holt of Montreal (later Sir Herbert). The other members were Alexandre Lacoste, K.C., Frank Darling, R. Home Smith, and the mayors of the cities of Ottawa and Hull, ex officio.

The terms of reference of the Commission were wide and searching. The order-in-council, dated September 12, 1913, instructed the commission to "take all necessary steps to draw up and perfect a comprehensive scheme or plan looking to the future growth and development of the city of Ottawa and the City of Hull, and their environs, and particularly providing for the location, laying out and beautification of parks and connecting boulevards, the location and architectural character of public buildings and adequate and convenient arrangements for traffic and transportation within the area in question."

This was a tall order for the Commission, and it was not until 1915 that the Report was tabled. Like the Rowell-Sirois Report a quarter of a century later, it was ill-starred in its timing. The outbreak of the First World War intervened. Anyone who reads the Holt Report today may be convinced that if it had been presented in more normal times it would have led to early action on the part of the federal government, in which case it is reasonable to suppose that Sir Robert Borden would have shared with Sir Wilfrid Laurier a prominent niche in the national capital story. Even from the few references given above it is clear that Sir Robert was deeply interested in the subject and that his government at least set up a strong commission instructed to grapple with the fundamentals of the growing problem.

11

The Holt Report makes impressive reading, even today. Its observations are outstandingly acute, and its forecasts have stood up, in the main, very well. Many of its recommendations have since been adopted, and it foreshadowed some of the problems which are still plaguing the authorities. Of course its members were not omniscient: for example, they predicted that the population of Canada by 1955 would be thirty million, just about double what was attained. They proposed some measures that were more costly than the federal taxpayer would have supported, even in peace time; and they recommended a political reform (a federal district with over-riding powers) which the population of the local municipalities would have resisted stoutly. Some of their proposals were fortunately not adopted, in the light of what has happened since. But on the whole this strikes me as one of the outstanding state documents of Canadian history, and no subsequent capital planner has been able to ignore it.

Its main recommendations were condensed into short space in the letter addressed to the Hon. W. T. White, Minister of Finance, which accompanied the final report:

(I) We are of the firm opinion that the future improvements in the area about the Capital at Ottawa and Hull should not be attempted without first establishing a Federal district and securing for the Federal authority some control of local government.

(II) We are of the firm opinion that the pivot, on which hinges the success or failure in carrying out any comprehensive plan, lies in the proper solution of the problem of steam railway transportation.

(III) In order that proper administrative and office accommodation may be provided for the work of the Government, the extension and development of the Government Buildings should be carried out on a comprehensive plan.

(IV) There should be proper control of residential and manufacturing districts by enforcing building restrictions.

(V) The highly commendable work of the Ottawa Improvement Commission should be extended and enlarged by the development of a broad and forceful policy as to further park lands, and there should be established a National Park or Forest Reserve in the Laurentian Hills, under the control of Dominion Government.

The fate of these strong recommendations can be even more laconically summarized: (I) Politically unacceptable or premature. (II) A brilliant diagnosis, but requiring decades to cure. (III) Increasing attention was paid to this. (IV) A matter for municipal action, and in part gradually implemented. (V) Steady progress made on this program.

In a brief history it may be out of proportion to dwell very long on the Holt Report. But what they had to say about the "pivot" on which hinged the success or failure of the basic plan, is still of live interest today.

The Commission examined the cause of the unplanned railway "jungle" which, superimposed on existing geographical obstacles in the natural and artificial waterways of the capital region, raised such a serious problem in city planning. It was not, of course, a problem confined to Ottawa. No attempt was made to blame either the railways or the municipal authorities. "The cities were small and anxious to thrive. The railways were in a precarious business, and often it was essential to their construction that they should obtain bonuses or grants from the Federal Government, from the Province, or from the cities or towns. It was not to be expected that men would look ahead fifty or seventy-five years to see whether or not a certain location would hurt the city at a time far in the future. The cities needed the railways and took the least line of resistance to obtain them. So we find areas, occupied by railways, in what has become the most valuable business districts of a city...The lines naturally built terminals at points most advantageous from the point of view of railway operation. There was no control or direction by the city looking to the future...With the railway lines firmly established and no means provided for re-locating and unifying them, it was logical for the city to grow around and between them. The railway lines, in a large measure, fixed and established definitely the development of the city...

"The railway lines were able to penetrate a city from almost every direction. Along these lines, industries, warehouses and local distributing centres have been established. Instead of a logical division of railway and industrial areas and of residential areas, industries have been scattered indiscriminately and have detrimentally affected in their immediate neighbourhood a much larger area than they themselves occupy. Tenement areas have grown up between the arms of the railways, close to the centre or heart of the city, where property values are high and it is necessary to crowd the population in order to secure adequate returns."

The Commission explained that the earlier railway lines were usually permitted to enter the city at the least cost to themselves, which usually meant at the grade of the surrounding country or of the city itself. This made level crossings common and grade separations rare.

"Absence of experience, foresight and control led to the lack of provisions for the opening of streets. It led to the use of then unimportant streets by the railway companies, to the placing of yards within the city, close to the central development, and to the closing of streets where they interfered with yard and track lay-outs."

Then, as time went on, this lack of street communication blocked the efforts of the city to grow into areas outside and beyond the railway lines.

"The railways, when they had closed up streets, were reluctant to allow of re-opening them across their property. When leave was granted, it was usually at the expense of the municipality. Where streets existed at grade crossings, the railways were usually reluctant to provide subways or bridges. Passage across grade crossings was dangerous and often inconvenient, and consequently the city grew in directions where there was a minimum of obstructions of this kind."

The Commission was able to illustrate all of these undesirable developments in the cities of Ottawa and Hull:

"The several main railway entrances into Ottawa, and the minor lines, giving means of access to special localities, have cut the city up into many parts. They have the effect of placing, by their presence, and by the presence of the yards and industrial developments which they induce, strong barriers between the divisions.

"This multiplicity of entrances and minor connecting lines has had the effect of indiscriminatingly spreading industrial works throughout the city."

The problem of remedying the above conditions without seriously interfering with the legitimate and desirable growth of railway transportation has preoccupied the planning authorities ever since that date, although it was not until after the presentation of the Gréber Report that bold action to relieve the railway situation was begun.

CHAPTER NINE

In and Between Two Wars

Nothing much was done for ten years about the recommendations in the Holt Report. No effort was made to introduce a "Federal District" type of government for the national capital. No new city plan was adopted. The proposal to deal drastically with the railway problem remained in complete abeyance. However, the annual grant to the Ottawa Improvement Commission was raised in 1917 from $100,000 to $150,000 a year. With these sums the Commission continued its improvement program: it built Island Park Drive, and developed Hampton Park; and it made plans for the extension of the Driveway system into the Province of Quebec by the proposed construction of a new bridge (Champlain) across the Ottawa River.

The failure of Sir Robert Borden and his government to act, after demonstrating a keen interest in the beautification of Ottawa by the creation of the Federal Plan Commission, is largely explained by contemporary events.

The Holt Report is dated 1915, but it was not in print until the following year. The Parliament Building burned down on February 3rd, 1916; and it required ten years and twelve million dollars to rebuild and enlarge and furnish it.

Meantime Canada had been plunged into the first global war. Before an Armistice was signed on November 11, 1918, it had exacted a fearful toll of young Canadian lives, had made prodigious demands on Canadian energies, and had driven a serious rift between Protestant Anglo-Saxon Canada and the French-speaking Catholic Canadians of Quebec.

Between 1914 to 1924 an unremitting and unprecedented series of deficits in the National Budget increased the net National Debt from $335 million to $2,417 million.

On top of the colossal war costs the federal government had to find funds or guarantee loans for another $700 millions to salvage from bankruptcy the Canadian Northern, the Grand Trunk and the Grand Trunk Pacific Railway systems.

Canada's finance ministers were at their wits' end how to terminate this series of massive annual deficits without resort to deliberate inflation or to new tax imposts of a crushing nature. Demands for inescapable expenditures were so great that anything which could be shelved or deferred had to wait for happier times.

Once the budget was balanced again—as it was for seven successive years beginning in 1924—the resumption of expenditures on the 'improvement' of the Ottawa region could be confidently expected.

In 1927 Canada would be celebrating the Diamond Jubilee of Confederation. The easing in the national finances and the desire to celebrate the national anniversary in some appropriate fashion explain such events as the completion and dedication of the Peace Tower in 1927, the nation-wide broadcasting of the anniversary celebrations and the first carillon concert on July 1st of the same year; and the replacement of the Ottawa Improvement Commission by the Federal District Commission, also in 1927.

Duncan Campbell Scott wrote in 1916 that the fire which burned down the Parliament Building "was terrible and tragic; it was the most terrifying and beautiful sight I have ever seen." It began in the Reading Room while the House was in session listening to a debate on the marketing of fish. Though alarms were sounded at once seven persons lost their lives; and others, including the Librarian, Hon. Martin Burrell, were severely burned. Some portraits and records were saved; and the Parliamentary Library suffered only from water damage.

At first an examination of the outer walls of the Building indicated that it could be restored rather than reconstructed. Further inspection led to a decision to rebuild, so as to increase the height by one storey and to add about 50% to the original floor space; and later on to construct a lofty Tower as a memorial and monument to symbolize the Victory of 1918 and the future Peace which the "War to End War" was then expected to secure and perpetuate.

The House of Commons met on the 4th of February, 1916, in the Public Auditorium of the Victoria Memorial Museum, without losing a day, and by the following Monday, quarters had been fitted up for members of both Houses, and the essential parliamentary staffs.

The first meeting of the House of Commons in the rebuilt Centre Block took place on February 2nd, 1920.

2

While nothing had been done to implement the main recommendations of the Holt Commission, another comprehensive and sweeping plan for the improvement of the national capital was published in 1922. It was the work of Noulan Cauchon, planning assistant to the City of Ottawa. He proposed a modified "Federal District" which would give a federal government commission authority over the physical features and public utilities of the capital region, but would preserve provincial and municipal autonomy in other respects, and leave the residents of the area with undisturbed rights of franchise. Since the Cauchon Report was never acted upon it is probably unnecessary to say more about it here than that it recommended a number of dramatic alterations and developments, similar in several respects to the general pattern of the Holt recommendations. Undoubtedly it helped prepare the way, by influencing public opinion, for the later work of the Federal District Commission, and the National Capital Commission.

3

In 1927 the Ottawa Improvement Commission was reconstituted as the Federal District Commission, with broadened powers and the extension of its interests into the province of Quebec. The eight members of the older Commission were increased to ten, of which one was to be a resident of Hull. The Honorable Thomas Ahearn, P.C., who had made a major contribution to national sentiment in his organization of the national broadcast of the Diamond Jubilee Celebration, was appointed first chairman. The annual grant was raised in the Act from $150,000 to $250,000.

The new Commission had hardly come to grips with its enlarged tasks before a situation arose in the heart of Ottawa which forced the federal government to intervene, and led to the amendments of the Federal District Commission Act of 1928. These reduced the annual grant to $200,000 but provided an immediate capital sum of $3,000,000, for a national project which could not be tackled on a piecemeal basis.

The reasons for the change were set out in detail in the House of Commons by the Prime Minister, W. L. Mackenzie King, in one of the historic expositions of the national capital problem. The text of his address can be read in the verbatim Hansard report for April 24, 1928.

The Prime Minister explained why an immediate appropriation of three million dollars was proposed for the Federal District Commission. More than half of the sum was needed to buy property in the municipal heart of Ottawa, so that a plan might be realized to create the open space now known as Confederation Square or Place. The crisis involved the old Russell House, an historic hostelry. This was currently being demolished, and the owners had applied to the city of Ottawa for a permit to erect a new modern hotel on the site.

The city council had advised the Federal District Commission that unless a good reason could be found why such a permit should not be given to the hotel owners (Mr. Mackenzie King reported), the Board of Control would be obliged to authorize the new construction. Aware that once a large new hotel had been located on the site of the old Russell House any dream of creating an impressive approach to the Parliament Buildings from the south east would be delayed for many years, if not permanently frustrated, the government had decided to grant authority for the expropriation of the Russell

House property. The sum allocated to the Commission would cover the cost
of the Russell House property and other properties still needed to open up
the area where Confederation Place now stands. The remainder would finance
the continuation of the Driveway system as already projected.

The Prime Minister told the house what was in the mind of the Federal
District Commission: It proposed "to make a large circular space around
which the traffic of the city will have to move in one direction in the area
through which Sparks Street runs at the present time and which is bounded
on the south by the present Russell House and on the north by the square
that has already been expropriated. The idea would be to have something
corresponding to what in the city of London, England, one sees at Piccadilly
Circus or Oxford Circus whereby in the centre of the city the traffic would be
obliged to move one way around the sides of a circle and into which particular
area the different streets would run. That centre would be virtually the heart
of the capital."

Mr. Mackenzie King added that he thought the national war memorial
should be placed in the centre of that circle.

An additional reason for the determination to do something about a vista
of the Parliament Buildings from the *south-east* lay in the lack of any open
space to the immediate *south* of the Parliament Buildings; and the improb-
ability, having in mind the value and substantial nature of the buildings
already located between Metcalfe and O'Connor Streets, from Wellington St.
south, that a broad avenue in that direction would be opened up in the early
future. The Prime Minister referred to it in these terms: "Take the main
approach to the front entrance of these buildings, already referred to, Metcalfe Street. It ought to be a magnificent boulevard and a grand approach to
these houses of parliament, but as viewed from the main entrance it is pretty
much in the nature of a country lane; it is not very much larger. There is
practically no approach to Parliament Hill from Metcalfe Street at the present
time. The same is true of O'Connor Street at the western end of the grounds;
and the same was true of Elgin Street until the changes made last year had
come into being." Mr. Mackenzie King made reference to the magnificent
approaches to the Legislative Buildings in some of the provincial capitals.
"If we had an avenue running up to Parliament Hill comparable to University
Avenue in Toronto, this city would take on an entirely different complexion.
My view is that parliament would not only be justified in taking but really
ought to take steps immediately to make an approach to the main entrance
of the Houses of Parliament similar to that which has been made with respect
to the legislative buildings in Toronto. I am not, however going to advocate
that at the moment."

Three years earlier, Mackenzie King had thrown out a hint that he favored the creation of a federal district, designed after the Washington pattern in some respects. He returned to the idea in greater detail in this debate: "There is one further step," he said, "which I think will be necessary, namely, that the capital of Canada be placed under the control of a federal district commission. When that step is to be taken is not for me to say at the moment. It might involve changes in the representation in parliament and might more appropriately be considered at the time when a redistribution measure is before the house. But I do think that sooner or later, and perhaps, having regard to the future, the sooner the better, this capital of the Dominion should be placed under the control of a federal district commission. The present action may prove a step in that direction."

The proposal to vote a substantial sum to tear down a business block in the heart of Ottawa and thus open up a vista of the Parliament Buildings met with considerable opposition in the House of Commons, and three divisions were forced before the bill passed. Familiar arguments were heard. The Hon. R. B. Bennett, leader of the Opposition, wondered if the country could afford it, wondered if the expenditure of a similar sum on other purposes would not be of greater benefit to the people of Canada. He advocated caution in view of the colossal national debt, and the heavy annual deficit of the national railways. John Evans (Rosetown) argued that parliament should confine its activities to Parliament Hill: it had no business crossing Wellington Street and interfering in the affairs of the city of Ottawa. T. L. Church (Toronto) contended that every year the Dominion was contributing to the municipality of Ottawa the equivalent of five or six mills of local taxation, lifting part of the burden off the Ottawa taxpayer and spreading it over the whole country. T. E. Kaiser (Ontario) said he would oppose spending any more money on the beautification of Ottawa until a supply of pure water was provided for its residents. Peter McGibbon (Muskoka) opposed the vote because "the people in the rural municipalities of the province of Ontario get practically nothing from this government." J. C. Brady (Skeena) wanted the Prime Minister to exert his influence on the city of Ottawa to see that the streets near the parliament buildings be made safer in the winter months and that a better water supply be provided.

G. G. Coote (Macleod) regretted that the money had not been appropriated to open up an approach directly in front of the buildings. A. M. Carmichael (Kindersley) suggested holding up the matter until a federal district was created. W. A. Boys (Simcoe North) considered it an extravagance to spend over a million dollars razing a commercial block in the heart of Ottawa to turn it into a park; he too thought the money would be better spent in widening Metcalfe Street to the south. R. J. Manion (Fort William) challenged the idea that in any commercial sense the acquisition of the property in the heart of

Ottawa could be called a national investment. H. H. Stevens (Vancouver Centre) criticised the condition of the streets and the quality of the drinking water. J. H. Harris (Toronto Scarborough) thought Ottawa business men would object to a park area being opened up between one part of the city and another: it would delay business men in getting back and forth. He was in favor of having another first-class hotel erected on the site of the old Russell House. E. J. Garland (Bow River) said that while no one was more susceptible to beauty than he was, he felt it his duty to his constituents to urge that the sum of three million dollars be spent instead to relieve poverty and misery and unemployment throughout Canada.

Agnes Macphail (Southeast Grey) thought that Ottawa was quite well supplied with parks and driveways as it was; she did not think very highly of a 'slanting view' of the parliament buildings; she thought more attention should be paid to child welfare, and less to the beautification of an already beautiful capital; and she moved an amendment reducing the sum from three million dollars to one million seven hundred and fifty thousand dollars. Miss Macphail's amendment was defeated.

4

The Federal District Commission made substantial if not spectacular progress from its appointment in 1927 to the outbreak of the Second World War. It was still essentially a parks development commission. It completed the purchase and clearing of the Russell House site and adjacent properties, the creation of Confederation Square or Place, the location in it of the National War Memorial, and the extension of the driveway system across the Champlain Bridge into the province of Quebec. In the twelve years from 1927 to 1939 the F.D.C. parks area was enlarged to 900 acres, and the length of the urban driveway extended to twenty-two miles. In 1934 the Commission was made responsible for landscape construction and maintenance of all federal properties in the capital area.

The abrupt end of the boom of the 1920's and the deep persistent depression of the thirties again discouraged ambitious and costly plans. The outbreak of war in 1939 further postponed the prosecution of a more vigorous program. Nevertheless, beginning in 1937, a series of events was in store destined to initiate a new and more active era in the history of Canada's capital. In that year the Gréber studies were begun. The prosecution of the war tremendously increased the burden on the national government. In four years the national budget skyrocketed to ten times its pre-war level: the national capital area was swollen by a great influx of military and civilian personnel connected with the war effort; departmental accommodation had to be rapidly and enormously increased.

Between 1918 and 1945, by construction, purchase, rental, and wartime construction of 'temporary' buildings, the total space occupied by the federal civil and military service was greatly expanded. Even a bare list of buildings tells an impressive story: the Hunter Building (1918); addition to the Printing Bureau, a new War Trophies Building, Administration Building, and Dairy Building, Central Experimental Farm (1920); Daly Building purchased (1921); Flower Building, Chemical Laboratory, Botanical Building, all at the Central Experimental Farm (1922-23); Fuel Testing Laboratory (1924); Fuel Testing and Ore Dressing Building (1927-29); Pyro-Metallurgical Laboratory (1925-29); Confederation Building (1928-31); Central Heating Plant (1929); National Research Council Laboratories and Administration Centre (1930); Justice Building (1934); Postal Terminal Building, Administration Building Central Experimental Farm (1935); Record Storage Building (1936); Industrial Minerals and Ceramics Building, Ore Testing Laboratory (1937); Supreme Court Building, and Post Office Building (1938). Between 1939-40 and the end of hostilities in 1945 no fewer than fourteen Temporary Buildings or additions to such, to house wartime staffs, were built in assorted locations stretching from Sussex Street to west Wellington Street, and as far southwest as Carling Avenue, on Experimental Farm property. Additions and annexes were also made during the wartime period to several of the older buildings. All readily available sites on government land were occupied, and several open spaces never intended for buildings were built upon before the war was over.

The heightened tempo of events fed by the furnace draft of a second global war accentuated the financial problems of the municipality of Ottawa in its relations with the federal government, and led directly to the Joint Inquiry held by the House of Commons and the Senate in the summer of 1944.

5

The Parliamentary Committee of 1944 was set up mainly to examine claims by the Corporation of the City of Ottawa for "better fiscal terms" from the federal government, in view of rapidly expanding tax-exempt government properties and the rising cost of providing municipal services for government buildings. Its terms of reference were however wide enough to embrace all the relationships between Crown and Town, including a recommendation for increased powers for a federal district body, if it thought such desirable.

Changes brought about by the Second World War were squeezing the city's financial position. The personnel of the civil and military service located in Ottawa rose from 12,000 to 33,500 in four years. The population of the city, mainly because of this factor, had meanwhile risen from 145,000 to 185,000. The erection of a series of temporary war buildings and the expropriation or rental of many older private buildings for war purposes had made heavy additional demands on municipal services. These exceptional war developments were superimposed on a steadily rising infringement and encroachment by federal government activities upon normal city operations, the corporation submitted in its brief to the Parliamentary Committee.

The city's case was that the annual grant of $100,000 a year plus payments for specific services did not begin to cover its costs and disabilities arising out of federal government functions.

It was, of course, conceded that there were *contra* items which might be set opposite such debits, in the form of substantial and growing benefits to the city of Ottawa from the presence of the federal government.

A simple formula of claim was advanced by the city. Mayor Stanley Lewis submitted figures showing that the total city assessment of both taxable and exempt properties was about $270 million in 1943, and that the property owned by the Crown represented over $65 million of this sum. (A further $3.7 million represented Federal District Commission property). Mayor Lewis suggested that a fair formula could be derived by assessing the Dominion Government on a basis equivalent to the ratio of government property to taxable property. This was about 27%, at the date of submitting the city brief. This, if calculated as a percentage of the city's current expenditure, would mean an annual federal government grant of just under $1,600,000. Such a grant, the city contended, would be a fair *quid pro quo* in lieu of taxation on government property. It was the proportion of city costs the government property would have borne, if, in fact, it had been taxable.

This was a formula which the federal government had heard before. As long ago as 1918 the then mayor of Ottawa, Harold Fisher, had contended that the federal government should submit itself to ordinary assessment in the same way as a private corporation, in which event, in 1918, the annual grant (or tax) payable to the City would have been $886,000.

The British North America Act exempts government property from any municipal taxation, however, and the government of the day in 1918 had not accepted Mayor Fisher's formula.

The case for the city of Ottawa in 1944 was presented by Mayor Stanley Lewis in an extensive brief, of which the following paragraph is one of the highlights:

"Mr. Chairman, our presentation is not for payment of taxation, but for payment of services with respect to government-owned property within the city limits. A glance at the map opposite shows just where the picture has been gradually changing over a period of years. The red area is increasing in the very highest assessed taxable part of our city. Not only has it taken taxes off the property, but off the business houses which were established in all those localities. As you can see, in a very short time our taxable property will be gone. That is why we base this brief wholly on the services rendered within that area. The City is just like a big house, so many rooms occupied by the Government, so many by the citizens, and every room in that house should bear its share of maintenance. You will see that in our brief we have shown the properties which have gradually been taken over by the federal authorities. Only yesterday we were notified that the Department of Mines has acquired practically two city blocks of an assessed value of over $17,000. This change is going on and on just like an ever-approaching glacier; that is, more and more properties are gradually being withdrawn from taxation."

The Ottawa Board of Trade, represented by Mr. C. E. Pickering, supported the city's submission. They too believed that the annual grant should bear the same ratio to the civic budget as the tax-exempt government properties bore to the taxable property within the city limits. They rejected the argument that the activities of the national government in the city fully compensated the city corporation for its increased service costs, by providing the citizens with parks, driveways and other aesthetic features of outstanding merit.

"This contention the Ottawa Board of Trade considers unsound. Every municipality must decide in its annual budget based on the municipal policy, the limit of parks, driveways etc. that are necessary and for which they can afford to levy taxation. We submit that in the case of the Capital City of Ottawa there is a dual and corresponding responsibility, that anything in excess of purely city parks, etc. is strictly a matter of Federal policy of beautifying the capital of Canada; and that the cost of all such schemes should be borne by the Federal Government.

"It is exceedingly unfair to ask the taxpayers of Ottawa to supply services necessitating large expenditures of money and suggest that this outlay should be offset by a park, a driveway or other developments that are considered by the Government proper for a Capital City. It is obvious that under ordinary municipal policies these extensive improvements would be uneconomical and considered a luxury."

The total effect of government expropriation of valuable commercial sites was examined. The city certainly lost the tax income on such expropriations, though it was argued by some parties that the business interests bought out or ejected normally removed to another site and began to pay municipal taxes on their new properties. But city spokesmen contended that such expropriations also blighted nearby areas. For example, Alderman L. L. Coulter said in his testimony:

"You have been told that those expropriations have amounted to a little over seven and a half million dollars in the past few years. That is a considerable sum of money. Take one instance on Bank Street with which I am familiar, for I have a business on that street. The Government expropriated the Jackson Building and land valued at nearly three quarters of a million dollars. That expropriation took away our business tax and the other taxes on that building, without any compensation whatever. At the same time in taking over this and other buildings and creating Government Departments, businesses in the neighbourhood are hurt. I am definite in that statement: such expropriations do hurt neighbouring businesses."

G. P. Gordon, commissioner of finance of the city, made a similar point:

"I might instance what happened after the last war, when the Dominion Government expropriated the buildings on the north side of Wellington Street. That part of the street was a very busy section at that time, several large commercial houses being located on the south side of the street. In a very short time those commercial houses were doing comparatively little business, just because of their proximity to those disused buildings."

Commissioner Gordon listed a number of additional costs which had been assumed by the city for traffic control, fire and police protection, and water supply, because of the wartime extension of the civil service and the proliferation of permanent and temporary office buildings all over the city.

Answering a query as to why Ottawa warranted special treatment for its government tax-exempt properties, Mr. Gordon said:

"Ottawa is unique — it is the national capital. It is there that the difference arises. There is a complex situation and a multiplicity of conditions, municipal and otherwise, so far as the Dominion Government and the City are concerned, which means, so to speak, that we are practically a twin city. I go further, it is what I may term a Siamese-twins city. That is, you cannot dissociate the municipality from the Dominion Government; and, conversely, you cannot dissociate the Dominion Government from the municipality. Certain services are given by the municipality to the Government for which, I submit, the municipality should receive reasonable remuneration. On the other hand, Ottawa is the national capital and, as such, there should be expenditures within the city which the Dominion Government should bear either wholly or at least in part if those expenditures are made by the municipality."

One awkward feature of Ottawa's request for an adequate *quid pro quo* for the transfer of valuable property to government title was that by this time there was hardly an urban community of any consequence in Canada which did not also contain Dominion Government buildings and properties; and it would obviously be politically impossible to make large grants to Ottawa without facing similar demands from right across the country. Hon. W. S. Fielding had managed to make out a case for exceptional treatment for the capital city in 1899, but the situation had changed materially in the meantime. The Parliamentary Committee of 1944 did not accept Mayor Stanley Lewis's contention that an annual payment of nearly $1,600,000 was needed to offset the city of Ottawa's loss of taxes from government tax-exempt property. It did, however, recommend to the government that for a period of five years the annual grant to Ottawa be raised from $100,000 to $300,000, with a review at the end of that period. And indeed the federal government found soon afterwards that other cities in Canada could not in equity be denied a general scheme of compensation for tax-exempt properties and for services to government buildings. The Municipal Grants Act of 1949 was the outcome. By 1955, Ottawa was receiving under that Act a sum from the federal government substantially in excess of the $1,600,000 asked for by Mayor Stanley Lewis in 1944.

6

The Joint Parliamentary Committee of 1944 devoted most of its attention to a financial adjustment with the corporation of the city of Ottawa. But it could not avoid some deliberations on divided jurisdiction also. As G. P. Gordon, commissioner of finance for the city, had stressed, Ottawa was a sort of 'Siamese-twins' city. All through the years since Confederation two separate entities had been growing up side by side and eventually intermingled. One was an Ontario industrial and mercantile city within a provincial urban municipality, within the control of the provincial ministry at Queen's Park, Toronto. It enjoyed local democratic government, and subject to the provincial law and regulation mentioned above, its voters and citizens and rate-payers were masters of its destiny. Its citizens, as municipal tax-payers, were interested in industrial and commercial expansion, and in the most satisfactory municipal services at the lowest cost. The other civic entity was the federal capital of a vast and growing nation. The Dominion Government was responsible to the Canadian people, not to Ottawa ratepayers only. A further complication arose with the creation of a crown agency, the Ottawa Improvement Commission, and its successor the Federal District Commission. By the time the 1944 inquiry was held the interested parties in the development of Ottawa included the city of Ottawa, parliament, the department of public works, the provincial government of Ontario, the provincial government of Quebec; and, increasingly, the suburban and rural municipalities of Ontario and Quebec adjacent to the national capital region. There was ample opportunity for the misunderstandings, resentments, liaison failures, neglect and overlapping activities which are generally to be found in areas of divided jurisdiction. When the provincial governments of Ontario and Quebec began the creation of special boards to deal with municipal planning, zoning regulations, water pollution and conservation, the need for better coordination or some kind of central authority grew still more urgent.

The kind of clash that could grow up even within the branches and agencies of a single government was illustrated during the 1944 parliamentary inquiry. The chairman of the Federal District Commission, F. E. Bronson, complained that he woke up one day to find that an addition was being made to the Royal Mint on Commission property without any one bothering to let him know. Nor had the City, which had donated part of the site to the F.D.C. earlier, been advised. The Federal District Commission also complained on another occasion about the erection of a far from aesthetic garage for the Printing Bureau, of which it had seen only the floor plan. The early Gréber plans, commissioned by the federal government, were made without F.D.C. participation.

There were two obvious ways of improving the unsatisfactory jurisdictional relations. One was by way of increased cooperation and coordination, the other by the creation of a central authority, with over-riding powers. The attitude of the several interested parties to these solutions varied greatly with their affiliations. Municipal voters feared the loss of the franchise and of direct control over their own local affairs. Provincial premiers like Mr. Duplessis could not be expected to initiate schemes to diminish their authority, still less to propose a permanent cession of a portion of their territory, either to the Ottawa government, or to a federal district agency of that government. From the viewpoint of the planners responsible for the future growth and appearance of the capital the attitude might vary from individual to individual, but the idea of a single central authority had the appeal that it would greatly simplify their operations.

The evidence of F. E. Bronson, chairman of the Federal District Commission, given before the 1944 parliamentary inquiry, indicates that he felt that a true "federal district" would be found to be inescapable and would in due course be established. In the course of his testimony in 1944, he said:

> "It seems it will be some time yet before a federal district is established."

In the meantime he suggested increasing the powers of the Federal District Commission.

> "The Federal District Commission has the power to carry out one feature only of the [Holt and Gréber] reports . . . . The Commission has no powers to deal with other important characteristics emphasized by Holt and Gréber that influence the orderly and systematic development of the general plan for the district of Ottawa . . . . It is suggested that the Federal District Commission be vested with these additional powers in order that the general plan for the Federal capital may be properly carried out."

When it came to make its recommendations to parliament, the joint committee expressed no opinion on the desirability or otherwise of a "federal district" in the administrative sense in which Mr. Bronson was using the words. But it did call attention to the growing complexity of the problem and the need for comprehensive planning and control, in this paragraph:

> "It is not the purpose of this Committee to make definite recommendations to the Government regarding the future character of a Federal District to embrace the park area and the municipalities on either side of the Ottawa River including the City of Ottawa. We are of the opinion, however, that this long-term project should be committed by the Government to a special commission of experts for investigation and report, involving as it would the possession of expert professional knowledge and the need for extended travel to study the plans and workings of federal capital districts in other countries. From the observations made by this Committee during its investigations, it is clear that with the growth of Canada and the corresponding expansion of its governmental activities, the administrative problems arising between the City of Ottawa and the Federal Government will become more complex and more difficult of settlement than they are now. As an indication of that prospect we would merely stress the inevitable difficulty that will arise in connection with the present reckless system of sewage disposal into the Ottawa River, the both banks of which within the most directly affected area, are the property of the Dominion of Canada."

Meantime, the Committee recommended "that the powers of the Federal District Commission be increased, and its personnel be enlarged to include, not only representation from the Ottawa area, but of the people of Canada as a whole. The name Federal District Commission might even be changed to include the idea of a National Capital."

7

One of the next major steps in planning the future of the national capital came about almost by chance. In 1936, Prime Minister Mackenzie King was in Paris, and while there he decided to look over the grounds of the 1937 Paris Exhibition, partly to make sure that Canada had been allocated a suitable site for its exhibit. It so happened that the director in charge of the Exhibition program spoke very little English, and so the Chief Architect, M. Jacques Gréber, was asked to accompany the Prime Minister of Canada on a tour of the proposed grounds. Mr. Mackenzie King was pleased to discover that the site for Canada's exhibit was a good one, situated next to that of Great Britain. In the course of his conversations with M. Gréber, he learned with interest that the noted architect and town-planner had designed one of the striking thoroughfares in the city of Philadelphia, with which Mr. Mackenzie King was familiar. Before the day's conversations were over, Mr. Mackenzie King had invited Jacques Gréber to come to Ottawa and help the government with the plans for Confederation Square, and the location in it of Canada's proposed War Memorial, which was to crown the northern terminus of a widened Elgin Street.

Jacques Gréber arrived in Ottawa in 1937. By this time Mr. Mackenzie King's enthusiasm for a more beautiful Ottawa had gained momentum, and he invited the French town-planner to make some studies of the entire national capital area. He was prepared to place M. Gréber in full charge of the future capital program, but the latter demurred: he felt that Canadian architects should do the planning, though he was keen to act as consultant. They had some discussions on the desirability of a federal district such as that at Washington, but the French adviser said that his own studies of such authorities in other parts of the world led him to believe that a federal district was not the answer. M. Gréber, incidentally, was opposed to placing the National War Memorial in Confederation Square, but the Canadian Prime Minister was adamant on this point. Later on, Mr. Mackenzie King conceded that he had probably been wrong in this decision. Because of traffic congestion some other site would have been preferable.

Some progress was made in 1937-39, and the National War Memorial in Confederation Square was ready for official dedication during the visit of Their Majesties King George and Queen Elizabeth in the late spring of 1939. The outbreak of war in September 1939 again halted action on extensive and costly plans for the national capital region. For six years the nation was otherwise committed.

The prospects of an early peace in the summer of 1945 revived the whole program. Immediately after V J Day, (on August 14, 1945), the first new steps were taken. On August 16, 1945, an area comprising some 900 square miles was defined as the National Capital District. On August 22nd, 1945, M. Gréber received a cablegram signed by Hon. Alphonse Fournier, Minister of Public Works, inviting him to come to Ottawa immediately and assume responsibility for "further development of Canada's national capital and its environment on both sides of the river". The cablegram mentioned the enlargement of the national capital area provided for in the Order-in-Council a few days earlier, and told him that it was proposed to make the whole national capital project a national memorial of the Second World War.

M. Gréber accepted the invitation and reached Ottawa on October 2nd. In a memorandum six weeks later he stressed the national character of the work entrusted to him. "To make its success sure and rapid," he suggested in an interim report, "I should like to act as Consultant to a National Capital Planning Committee, working in full co-operation with the Federal District Commission."

Such a committee was set up on March 8th, 1946. The By-Law of the Federal District Commission, creating it, stated that "the function of the

Committee shall be to draw up a master plan of the National Capital District." The Committee consisted of the Minister of Public Works of the Government of Canada, the Chairman of the Federal District Commission, two members appointed by the Corporation of the City of Ottawa, one member appointed by the Corporation of the City of Hull, and twelve members appointed by the Federal District Commission, of whom two were to represent The Engineering Institute of Canada, two The Royal Architectural Institute of Canada, one the County of Carleton, Ontario, one the County of Gatineau, Quebec. There were to be six others. "M. Jacques Gréber, Paris, France, shall act as consultant to the Committee," the by-law stated.

The Master Plan for the National Capital, published in 1950, and popularly known as the 'Gréber Report' is a submission to the National Capital Planning Committee by the National Capital Planning Service, Jacques Gréber as Consultant, John M. Kitchen and Edouard Fiset as Associates.

In a Foreword to the Master Plan dated November 18th, 1949, Prime Minister Mackenzie King said, in part:

"To be worthy of Canada's future greatness, its Capital must be planned with far-reaching foresight. This book presents to the Canadian people a remarkable review of what is believed will best serve this important end."

Some highlights of the Master Plan are presented in the next chapter.

CHAPTER TEN

The Gréber Master Plan

T he Master Plan for the National Capital was published in 1950. It was prepared by Jacques Gréber and his Canadian associates. It represents four years of intensive and skilful work. The book is an indispensible item in the story of Canada's capital. No summary can do it justice. It is couched in distinguished prose, and is illustrated by a magnificent series of photographs and plans. Students of the subject will find direct perusal of it indispensible. What is attempted here is a presentation of its essential outline, told so far as is possible in the original prose.

There are three basic elements of the Master Plan. One is *description* of the national capital area as Jacques Gréber and his associates saw it in 1945–49. The second is *analysis* of the principal deficiencies and problems. The third is a *prescription* for the kind of National Capital it can become; and in the opinion of the planners, should become and will become, if the plans please the Canadian public. This natural sequence of topics will be followed in the present outline.

2

"The National Capital Region, situated on both sides of the Ottawa River, is a harmonious blend of forests, farmlands and water, of which the Capital City is the centre," says the Report.

"The flat lands on the Ontario side and the nonchalant courses of its rivers make, with its pastoral scenery, striking contrast with the Quebec side, its undulated hills riddled with lakes, traversed by turbulent streams and covered by thick growths of trees.

"South of the Ottawa River, most of the land is occupied by farms and marshlands, interspersed by countless wooded areas, over which the pine and the elm tower majestically. The north fringe of the Ottawa River has the same characteristics, while the Gatineau Hills have a reverse proportion of forests and farmlands. All of this land of low lying hills, multiple lakes, streams and small valleys, in which farms rest between its wooded slopes, has a hospitable character of amenity and charm, most of which is still unspoiled. . . .

"The areas on each side of the Ottawa River, at the points where the Gatineau from the north, and the Rideau from the south reach its waters, are wonderfully endowed by nature. The strange horizontal stratas of grey rocks overhanging its south shore, its bushy banks, the foaming falls of the Rideau River, and the Gatineau rapids on the opposite shore, seem to conspire to make this nature spot an unforgettable composition, the rugged charm of which grips the onlooker and carries him back, in spite of the close proximity of the city, into a past seemingly filled with the calls of the early guides and the gleam of the campfires.

"The attraction of the Capital lies in this grim and strongly conjuring character, which has not yet been divested of the charm of its large wooded vistas, its picturesque canals and falls, the grandeur of its monuments and parks.

"The towers and gables of its public buildings give to it a picturesque and romantic outline. The natural charm of its surroundings are skilfully enhanced by the number and the gracefulness of its aged elms and blue-tinted evergreens, as well as by the exuberance of lawns and parks. A bird's eye view of the city leaves the impression that it is wrapped in green."

3

If the description had ceased at that point, there would have seemed to be little left for the city and regional planner to do. There was, however, a bleaker and more depressing aspect of the picture, which a more searching examination disclosed.

"Progress, through the exploitation of its natural forces, and the ill-considered use of the land, has somewhat begun to stifle and mar the scenery," the Report continued.

"Across the river from the stately buildings of the nation are piles of unsightly and disorderly industrial materials, factories, railway sidings, warehouses and chimney stacks spreading soot, smell and smoke. The beauty of the Chaudière Falls is hardly perceptible from portions of an antiquated bridge and roadway laboriously finding their way through this unsightly mass of structures. The hill and Parliament Buildings can only be seen occasionally through such environments.

"Within the city and the surrounding municipalities, there are many planted streets, which enhance the residential districts, but there are also too many streets which have been denuded of this natural element. Such streets, by comparison, offer depressing aspects. Buildings bordering on them, whatever be their particular architectural merits, seem to be disorderly, and clash with neighbouring structures. Houses often are too close to each other, and their individual designs, which may have merit when isolated, are shocking and unesthetical.

"Colours have been used without any relation to the shades of the neighbouring structures, and the perspective of a street is often inharmonious in forms and bulks, to which trees might have brought some degree of unity . . . .

"In commercial and semi-commercial streets particularly, utilities have encroached to such an extent that, in instances, the streets have become crowded to the limit by telephone, power, light and tram posts, and the sky can be seen only through a network of wires and transformers. Nothing is more depressing than the appearance of such streets, and nothing is so unworthy of the National Capital, particularly when this disorder is within a stone's throw of the Parliament Buildings.

"No architectural control having been enforced on commercial streets, their appearance is deplorable. If passers-by raise their eyes above the fallacious brilliance of the show-windows, they will see an unbelievable heap of volumes, forms and colours, which have arisen without any regard to adjoining structures.

"Lack of control has permitted the use of outdoor stairways and fire escapes, and incongruous commercial signs. Such conditions are common to most cities, but the Capital is the first city which should take appropriate action to stop those undesirable features.

"The nation is young and vigorous, its natural resources had to be exploited, its markets maintained and expanded, and it is only natural that some of the refining elements, which seem to have little to do with such materialistic aspirations, have been overlooked. But now Canada has reached its maturity and is becoming conscious and proud of its assets. Therefore, it is ready to revise and improve its ways of living and expanding, and in doing so is taking full cognizance of its intellectual and artistic culture."

4

What is the history of this degradation? How did some of the loveliest natural scenery in North America fall under such an industrial and commercial blight? In another passage the authors of the Gréber Report tell the story:

"The urban area which now includes Ottawa, Hull and their environs, owes *its birth* to its favourable location at the confluence of three large rivers. These waterways were the natural conveyors of lumber originating from the nearby forests.

"*Its early growth* was due largely to the construction of the Rideau Canal and, later, to the choice of Ottawa as the nation's Capital. . . . During the evolution of the city, the relative importance of these functions has been reversed. The present activity and prosperity of Ottawa are chiefly due to its status as the National Capital, in the life of which industry now forms a secondary part. . . .

"The introduction and expansion of railway lines within the growing community, while promoting its development, have become the major detriments to its rational and harmonious growth. The ever increasing encirclement of the city and the ruthless cutting through of its growing surface by railroads nullified the benefits brought by the latter and their satellite industries, to the detriment of the welfare and comfort of the citizens . . . The Chaudière Falls area has continued to develop industrially, expanding year after year, gradually encroaching with its plants, warehouses and railway sidings on residential zones, and congesting traffic on both sides of the river. The downtown area continues to expand commercially and semi-industrially, constantly encroaching on contiguous residential areas which thus become overcrowded . . . from the very outset, commercial, semi-commercial, industrial and semi-industrial areas have been allowed to expand to the detriment of adjacent residential districts. . . . The north end of Bronson Avenue, once the choice residential area, has had its properties converted into small apartments or replaced by flats. Metcalfe Street, where heavy traffic was formerly prohibited, has undergone a similar change. Sandy Hill undergoes the encroachment of commercial activities, despite the desire of its citizens to have it retain its residential character. . . .

"The search for space, the constant pressure from various activities together with the improvement of roads and public transportation, are factors which have fostered the expansion of suburban areas. As distances increased, outlying areas have shown a tendency to spread promiscuously, rather than to form outside nuclei. New and continuous developments occurring along the main lines of communication, have given to the latter the *twofold and irreconcilable character* of highways and commercial streets. . . .

"The city's expansion is now hampered by lack of proper communications As its development tends to follow along its westerly arteries, distances have become prohibitive, and those arteries have failed to meet the dual functions of shopping streets and through highways."

5

Like the authors of the Holt Report in 1915, the authors of the 1950 Master Plan saw the existing railway network as the crux of the traffic problem. However, since 1915, things had worsened in two ways. The network had become more extensive and more restrictive, and in the meantime the load of intra-city and external traffic had skyrocketed to levels the Holt Commission might have found incredible.

"The railroad lines were originally established on the outskirts of a limited urban area, without regard to future urban extensions and without provision for grade crossings.

"It is therefore obvious that the railroad facilities were organized strictly in keeping with the demands of railroad operations and their immediate economy, to the detriment of the normal growth and life of the community. Such locations of railroad rights-of-way failed to take into account their ultimate effects on land values and, consequently, on the financial equilibrium of the municipalities. This seeming lack of consideration for vital aspects of collective life is readily explained by the fact that the railroad was, then, the predominant factor in the prosperity of new settlements. Unfortunately, the disadvantages attached to such lack of foresight could not but be felt sooner or later, and finally have resulted in to-day's regrettable conditions.

"Eleven different lines traverse Ottawa and Hull, and segregate the whole in isolated parts. More than one hundred and fifty grade crossings obstruct circulation and constitute dangers within the urban area. More than one hundred streets lack outlets by reason of the railway-created obstacles. Residential developments are scattered in a framework of tracks, warehouses, factories and railway depots, with their concomitant noises, smoke and danger. Industries, naturally following railway facilities, add to the blight already caused by railway barriers, and both railway operations and industrial development are hampered by crowded surroundings, with no opportunity for expansion.

"Railway operations are complicated in consequence and result in loss of time, labor and money. Facilities are insufficient for the present volume of passengers and freight. Freight yards in the centre of the Capital, several single track lines, lack of space for new industrial sidings, slow shunting, distances of several miles from the station to the yards and round houses, in brief, it can be stated, that city expansion and building density is as much a detriment to railway operations and efficiency, as are the railways to the normal and economic life of the city and the safety of the inhabitants.

"A complete remodelling of railway facilities was highly justified in 1915. Its emergency is now a matter of *vital importance* for both railway and urban improvement."

6

In its condemnation of current conditions in 1950, the authors of the Master Plan did not overlook the fruits of the Ottawa Improvement Commission, the Federal District Commission, and other bodies or individuals who had made their contributions to the beauty and dignity of Canada's capital.

"We know, from precise and authentic documents what Ottawa was forty years ago, at the beginning of this century, and now we can see what has been accomplished through responsible institutions such as the Federal District Commission, despite two long and costly wars, followed by a serious financial crisis, and without juridical means adapted to the development of town planning. Therefore, we have no right to doubt that greater things can be accomplished in the forty or fifty years to come, particularly with the availability of a planning conception of the whole, which, if forcefully pursued, will avoid errors and waste."

This "planning conception of the whole" is presented everywhere throughout the fine large book of over 300 pages, with detailed plans and photographs and models. It is also presented in capsule form in pages 155 to 164 of the Master Plan, from which the following paragraphs are drawn:

The task before the Master Planners was, they point out, of a dual nature, "consisting of *two inseparable but differing programmes*, comprised of complementary elements.

"In the first instance, it was required to develop the physical framework of expansion for the *National Capital*, organizing its life for a period of at least two generations, without compromising the more remote future.

"A Capital is the *reflection*, the *symbol* of the whole nation. The Capital of Canada, as in all federated states, such as in the case of Washington, or Berne, has *special* importance: it is the city which, to every Canadian and to all foreigners, must be representative of all of the ten confederated provinces, without, however, prejudicing the attributes and prerogatives of their respective capitals.

"Chosen for this noble role by a far-seeing and wisely inspired Queen, the little Ontario town of Ottawa, the outgrowth of the pioneer village of Bytown, rapidly became a large city, and, with distances gradually losing their significance, blended itself with the neighbouring villages and localities around the beautiful Ottawa River, formerly a frontier but now a link between the two provinces of Ontario and Quebec, which are symbolic of Canadian greatness. . . .

"The planning of the Capital is therefore a *national undertaking, of which each Canadian can be proud* and through which national desires and aspirations can be expressed through material accomplishments.

"The first accomplishment, initiated by the Federal Government, will go down into history: it is the decision that the planning of the National Capital be *dedicated to the memory of Canadians who gave their lives to the nation in the second world war.*"

7

The first task, then, as summed up in the Master Plan, was:

"To give to the fundamental functions of the Capital elements essential to its expanding activities, parliamentary, governmental, diplomatic, social, and intellectual life, within a frame of dignity and hospitality as host to its innumerable guests, official dignitaries, delegations to national and inter-national conventions, and summer or winter tourists.

"The second imperative demand lay in the recognition of the territory of the Capital area as an already urbanized region, the place of living and of work of its citizens. . . . Two principal cities, Ottawa in Ontario and Hull in Quebec — mixed population, differing legislative and educational systems, — two provincial entities within which we must recognize their respective administrations, customs, language and aspirations; far from being a difficulty in our work, these conditions merely *intensified our interest* . . . "

"What then, briefly expressed, are the characteristics of our plan?

"The planning of the region of 900 square miles, which is the area of attraction incident to the Capital, involves, primarily, the establishment of a highway system through the improvement of existing roads and the creation of additional roads, to facilitate traffic movements throughout the region. . .

"In the centre, the urban region is delimited by a perimeter, intended to prohibit tentacular and linear extensions of constructions abutting upon highways. To that effect an area, zoned as a greenbelt, frames this perimeter and is subjected to regulations to protect the area comprised within the greenbelt against undesirable developments.

"Within the greenbelt and rural areas, sites having outstanding scenic value, and particularly those bordering lakes and rivers, are subjected to special regulation to ensure the preservation of their natural charms and rustic characters."

The fundamental problem within the green perimeter was, the Report affirmed,

"*The problem of existing railway conditions*", the solution of which provided "opportunity for the *reorganization of traffic circulation generally*"; railway rights-of-way which will be released will be utilized in the provision of a new system of main arteries and parkways. From this will result inestimable advantages in the amelioration and systemization of all traffic movements within the interior of and around the urban zone.

"Within the reorganized frame of circulatory arteries, the new *built-up areas* will be rationally distributed, and given the characters of complete self-contained groups rather than districts lacking the elements of community life, and suffering the detriment of necessitating interminable and superfluous daily traffic movements.

"In this organization of urban development, conceived with a nuclear tendency, and within which there have been taken into account existing conditions that cannot be disturbed but can be gradually improved, we define the limitation of urban expansions and tentacular developments by the establishment of a greenbelt. . .

"The life and the development of the National Capital and its neighbouring towns and municipalities necessitate the erection of public buildings in accordance with a studied programme of harmonious distribution and decentralization. . .

"With the view of suppressing the disorder and congestion resulting from the lack of a rational and functional system of public thoroughfares within the Capital Region, *the reorganization of traffic circulation necessitates the readjustment of transport generally* in keeping with physical developments and the relationships and needs of existing and developing communities, and taking advantage of new main traffic arteries.

"An essential complement to housing and to the complex activities of modern life is the *systematic organization of open spaces*, in order that they may best fulfil their regenerative function. Such open spaces should be predicated upon their functional relationship to the classes of population and their activities. They are as necessary to health and welfare as to rest and education, and constitute a capital element in social security.

"Recreation, in association with nature and tourism, completes the general system of methodical organization of leisure within the general frame of a natural site. Urban open spaces, wooded reserves and scenic drives are to be integrated in a general plan of *rational exploitation of all the elements of nature*, which it is important to develop and protect.

"If the protection and development of the gifts of nature in their totality have in the first place a utilitarian objective, favourable to the maintenance of health and to the physical enhancement and welfare of the inhabitants, as also to the pleasure of tourists and visitors, they can be equally justified on the grounds of aesthetics, because the preservation of the natural beauty of a site is an inestimable asset toward increased joy of living and general prosperity."

8

The principles outlined in the above summary were thereupon, in the Master Plan as published, developed in detail and applied to the several aspects of the National Capital Region: to the railway, transport and communication problem, the extension of the parkways system, the need for a number of new bridges, the expansion of the Gatineau Park areas, the 'greenbelt' proposal, and so on. In this impressive and indeed formidable array of changes, enhancements and acquisitions, it was, the Report suggested, vital to keep in mind the time-element and to plan a table of priorities. Some of the proposals demanded urgent and immediate action; others were long range operations, some were eventual operations to be executed only if financial resources became adequate.

The following list of intermediate and short range operations are interesting both because of the light they throw on the attitude of M. Jacques Gréber and his Canadian associates to the problem of the National Capital area in 1949–50, and because they serve as a benchmark against which the progress of the past decade can be currently tested.

Immediate and Short Range Operations

1. Construction of new bridge and approaches from Elgin to Waller Streets, between Confederation Place and Laurier Avenue.

2. Acquisition and zoning of land incidental to the adequate relocation of railway facilities; the equipment of new railway belt line, from its intersection with the C.P.R. Montreal south shore line, southerly to Chaudière junction, with the C.P.R. Prescott line; development and equipment of new industrial zones on appropriate grounds, contiguous to railway facilities.

3. Reservation of lands for Governmental buildings and public services.

4. Elimination of the Daly Building and of the buildings on the south side of Rideau Street east of and adjacent to the Union Station, as part of the completion of the approaches to Confederation Place; construction of a parking terrace on the site of the Daly Building, and of an additional covered parking area, directly connected with the Chateau Laurier.

5. Extension of Scott Street westerly to Highway No. 15.

6. Construction of parkway from Bayview Road to Island Park Drive.

7. Gradual elimination of the C.N.R. cross-town tracks and construction of the cross-town parkway on the vacated right-of-way.

8. Elimination of the Sussex Street C.P.R. line from Sussex Street to Hurdman's Bridge and construction of circular boulevard on the vacated right-of-way.

9. Gradual elimination of the freight yards at Union Station and their relocation on new freight terminal grounds east of Hurdman's Bridge.

10. Construction of new eastern approach from Montreal Road at a point west of Green Creek and linked with the MacArthur Road to Cumming's Bridge, Eastview.

11. Development and extension of industrial zones in Hull and Hull South.

12. Construction in Hull of new boulevard from Reboul Street to Montclair Boulevard, and connection to Mountain Road and Saint-Joseph Boulevard.

13. Partial improvement of Aylmer Road between Hull and the Ottawa Country Club (double drive and central boulevard). Diversion from Aylmer Road, west of the Country Club, by construction of a new driveway on rights-of-way of Hull Electric Railway, and of a direct by-pass highway north of the Aylmer Road and the Town of Aylmer, to relieve Aylmer Road approaching and within the town of Aylmer.

14. Construction of public buildings: — Printing Bureau; Department of Veterans Affairs Buildings; Headquarters for the Department of National Defence; Bureau of Statistics; National Film Board Building; Ottawa City Hall; Institute of Fine Arts; National Theatre; National Art Gallery; National Library; Public Works laboratories and workshops; Laboratories for Department of National Health and Welfare; National Stadium and Sports Centre.

15. Construction, in its first stage, of National Memorial Terrace on Gatineau Hills, dedicated to the Canadian fallen in the Second World War.

16. Construction of the Mountain parkway from the intersection of Brickyard Road and Mountain Road to Kingsmere.

17. In Hull, direct connections from Aylmer Road to (1) the Mountain Road, and (2) to the Mine Road, by the construction of two new boulevards on each side of Fairy Lake Park.

18. Widening of Laurier Avenue in Hull, north of Interprovincial Bridge, to Jacques-Cartier Park.

Among its "Long Range Operations" the Master Plan calls for the elimination of additional railway lines and the development of the vacated rights-of-way as traffic arteries, the construction of new bridges across the Ottawa River, the elimination of the present Union Station and its location on the belt line to the south, the extension of riverside parkways, the development of the east bank of the Rideau Canal as the railway facilities around the present Union Station are removed, new by-pass highways and the construction of new rapid transit highways leading from various parts of the city to the new Union Station and to the industrial areas. This part of the program calls for the construction of an esplanade on the western end of Parliament Hill and restoration of the Chaudière Falls industrial area. Among the new public buildings envisaged are a Civic Auditorium and Convention Hall, further government laboratories, a Botanical Garden, a Museum of Natural History and a Zoological Garden.

The outline of proposed developments concludes with the observation that "a town planning work is a continuous creation, comprised of progressively slow and flexible adaptations, as are all evolutions of nature, from which we should seek inspiration."

9

It is impracticable in such a summary as this to do much more than present the core of the recommendations. There are, however, a number of *obiter dicta* of great interest.

On the subject of *Trees*, the Master Plan is eloquent. "The Ottawa Valley is particularly endowed with a vigorous and exceptionally fine growth of trees. The various species of forestry in the region form a resplendent picture of vivid colours in the fall season, when elms, maples and birch trees compete with the sombre patches of conifers. One of the great charms of the Capital lies in its planted streets, and its parkway system. . .

"Trees, like architecture, are a definite factor in the enhancement of a modern city. They form the framework of buildings, the 'leit-motif' in street design, the aspect of which they may change entirely. They blend contrasting structures, and their removal from certain areas would be deplorable in the interests of the appearance of the streets. They are the luxury of the poor man's abode, and, in many instances, give charm to a modest house, which otherwise would be bare and desolate.

"Through lack of wisdom in planning, commercial streets are deprived of such environment, and, consequently, the trees are erroneously considered to be incompatible with the functions of commercial areas. On the contrary, nothing more than trees enhances commercial frontages, which, unless strictly controlled, cannot but express disorderly and chaotic aspects, by reason of their unrelated components and unrestricted publicity elements.

"Trees should not be the privilege solely of residential areas, parks and parkways. *They should be integrated in the design of industrial centres*, as well as of commercial areas. We see no valid reason why any street, whatever be its function, should be deprived of this element of beauty, charm and freshness.

"The development of a modern city is more beautiful and less conspicuous behind and under the shade of trees. The use of other natural elements in the enhancement of city developments is also very important, such as lawns, shrubs, flowers, rock-gardens, etc. The mania for the "megalopolis", the super-densely built self-contained block, is disappearing gradually, and the aspirations of the people are tending toward a more natural way of living. The principles of simplicity expressed by Sir Ebenezer Howard at the beginning of the present century are being confirmed. To ignore those basic principles, and man's deeper aspirations, of which aesthetics is one of the greater, tends toward ultimate social dissatisfaction and unrest."

10

Jacques Gréber and his associates stressed the human values which all town-planning was seeking to cherish. In their insistence on the need of zoning (what the Holt Report called 'district control'), they said:

"Such regulation is neither embarrassing nor prejudicial to the interests of individuals but on the contrary it protects them against encroachments, incongruous development and their resulting disorder. It is essential to realize and perpetuate the fundamental concept of the community."

And they used some of their strongest language to condemn the deplorable results in some parts of the national capital area arising out of failure to plan, and failure to enforce zoning:

"Throughout the area there is evidenced the effects of mushroom outgrowths, due to urgent needs, lack of previous planning and unrelated hasty subdivisions, with no provision for the essential human needs of community life. Any urban development is bound to degenerate if composed in the aggregate of successive groups of houses, in relation to which no space has been preserved for schools, churches, commercial centres, community halls, playgrounds and open spaces for rest and relaxation. Its inhabitants will necessarily have to seek elsewhere for these amenities, provide them through costly and wasteful displacements, or forego that concept of living of which these amenities are essentially the complements. . .

"Zoning must be flexible in its adaptations to the various classes of residential properties, in order to meet the needs and aspirations of various types of families. In so doing, the new community will not differ from the old village, from which inspiration can always be safely taken. There is a more urgent need for the fostering of community welfare in the town of the twentieth century, due to the complexities as well as the advantages which come with progress. A soul-less housing development, a mass of crowded tenement houses, may provide essential shelter, but lack the elements necessary for happy living. One of the merits of town planning is to protect mankind against this modern menace. The incidence of such wise policy on economics, and on social equilibrium, is obvious."

11

In at least two major matters, the Master Plan departed from the trend of its predecessors. One matter was physical, the other juridical. Earlier planners had regretted the failure of the authorities to reserve a wide avenue leading up to Parliament Hill from the south. (Frederick Cook, journalist and one-time mayor of Ottawa once recalled that he had asked Sir John A. Macdonald in the 1880's why the blocks between Metcalfe Street and O'Connor Street for several streets back had not been cleared and reserved for such an imposing vista of the Parliament Buildings. Sir John A. had replied that he personally had been in favor of such an action, but his colleagues in the cabinet, aghast at the total bill for the buildings and grounds, were opposed to incurring the necessary additional outlay). Jacques Gréber, too, was at first attracted by the idea that even at that late date it might be better to face the cost of opening up such a majestic approach. The Master Plan explains in detail why this feature was not incorporated in the completed proposals:

"At the commencement of our studies in 1938, we had envisioned the creation of a main artery extending southerly from Wellington Street and facing the Houses of Parliament, by utilizing and widening Metcalfe Street, the easterly facade of which would have remained intact while its westerly facade would have been set back symmetrically in relation to the central axis of the Peace Tower, a monumental street, implying, from its width, a street opening rather than a widening. Such a proposal at first hand seems desirable and logical and has been repeatedly drawn to our attention. It does not lack attraction and we have examined it in all its aspects, but have not retained it for the following reasons:

"1. The widening of Elgin Street was in course of construction to provide a north-south traffic collector from the streets entering upon it, while its northerly extremity, likewise under construction, terminated at a large area now partly completed.

2. The profile of Metcalfe Street would have required to be retained and it is such that the resulting perspective would not have been satisfactory, or would have required costly revisions.

3. At its northerly termination with Wellington Street it would have been necessary to provide an enlarged intersection of dimensions similar to that of Confederation Place, in order to ensure adequate space for all traffic movements.

4. Expropriations essential in the construction of such an enlarged intersection and street widening . . . would have been prohibitive, due to the structures involved, i.e., the Rideau Club, United States Embassy, Birks Building, Royal Bank Building, churches, Carnegie Library, Medical Arts Building and others.

5. From the point of view of traffic circulation, Metcalfe Street even when widened would not have been as efficacious as Elgin Street, due to the position of its extremities.

6. But the principal reason for its rejection was on the grounds of aesthetics. The architectural characteristics of the Parliament Buildings are basically Gothic, adapted to the Victorian mode. Even if the East and West Blocks were subjected to architectural modifications in the future, the whole would retain its picturesque character and any development of its silhouette would gain by not being observed symmetrically but angle-wise, which would ameliorate the volume of the Peace Tower, the elongation of which, when seen from the front, is emphasized.

"For this reason, in addition to those already outlined, we abandoned the projected widening of Metcalfe Street in favour of the oblique perspective of the Parliament Buildings from the future main entrance to the City paralleling the east side of the Rideau Canal and extending southerly to Hurdman's Bridge, which will not lack in grandeur and monumental effect. From this area, even though through present chaotic conditions, the view of the Parliament Buildings is already very imposing."

12

The other matter in which the Master Plan advocates a policy rather different from what might be forecast on theoretical grounds concerns jurisdiction. We might suppose, in the light of all the frustrations of numerous and divided jurisdictions, authorities, autonomies and rights, that a town planner would inevitably gravitate toward the idea of a single supreme authority. Jacques Gréber and his colleagues did not allow themselves to be lured into this simple, logical, but possibly undemocratic solution. The Master Plan does not call for a "Federal District" in the Washington sense. As early as June 7th, 1939, in a preliminary report to the Prime Minister, Jacques Gréber had carefully refrained from endorsing such a drastic political step, and, by drawing on examples from other parts of the world, left the inference that the objectives for a greater National Capital in Canada could be achieved through the use of cooperation and coordination between the many interested jurisdictions.

"I understand," M. Gréber wrote in 1939, "that the question may be considered of eventually creating a District Capital for the Dominion of Canada, along the principle of the District of Columbia in the United States.

"As I have no qualifications for discussing the need for a Federal District Capital from the political or general administration viewpoint, I beg to submit to you the following remarks, limited to the *purely city planning problem*.

"Several examples of regional planning and comprehensive by-laws on city development, in Europe and in America, show that this particular problem, even when it affects a large number of municipalities, may be *successfully studied and solved without deeply changing their respective administrations*, but by organizing, only for the purpose of their *better co-ordinated planning and common zoning and building legislation, a central Planning Board*, specially appointed to elaborate and to control the execution of the plans and the enforcement of the by-laws."

After describing the sort of Planning Board which could be set up in Canada, and which, as a matter of fact, was set up after the war, M. Gréber drew encouragement from the experience in France and the United States. The *Comité Supérieur de l'Aménagement de la Région Parisienne*, for example, included "the whole agglomeration of more than six hundred cities, townships and villages directly connected with the city of Paris, within a radius of approximately twenty miles from the centre of the city, and depending upon several different *départements* or prefectoral administrations.

"Other regional plans in France," he added, "are being prepared along similar principles for all important urban centres.

"The New York Regional Plan, the Philadelphia Tri-State Planning Corporation (Pennsylvania, New Jersey and Delaware), are other examples of similar central authorities, entrusted with a *purely technical work, without interfering with the existing Town or State administrations.*" In the 1950 Master Plan Report it is even asserted that "far from interfering with, or lessening the autonomy of any one of the components of the urban group, the unity of conception in all plans and by-laws related to zoning, building and development, has the effect of strengthening the authority of each municipality in its particular territory."

(Further studies, however, of the baffling problems of divided jurisdiction in the Canadian national capital region subsequently modified M. Gréber's original expectations that the conflicting interests could be easily reconciled.)

CHAPTER ELEVEN

Problems and Progress

The Gréber Master Plan for the National Capital Region was the fourth comprehensive scheme to be drawn up in half a century. Earlier plans, in the main, remained blue prints. The Gréber Plan was more fortunate in its timing. There were still the old jurisdictional frustrations, but the Canadian people were now in a mood to authorize action, and the national economy was at the most buoyant level in Canadian history.

Ten years from the publication of the Gréber Master Plan it was possible to report that "all the major proposals . . . were *in process* of realization."

The Master Plan proposed a series of sweeping and even fundamental changes in Canada's capital region. They have been fully summarized in the previous chapter and will not be repeated here.

The agency to carry out the new plans was designated shortly after Jacques Gréber and his Canadian associates began work on the vast planning program. In 1946, by new legislation, the federal government confirmed the Federal District Commission as that agency. Its membership was enlarged from ten to twenty, including a representative from each province, and it was given additional powers commensurate with its new responsibilities, as far as the authority of the federal government went in conveying such powers.

Realization of the Master Plan, even under ideal circumstances, would have been an engineering and town-planning project of great magnitude.

As it happened, the progress of the years 1946-61 had to be made in the face of a welter of divided and sometimes clashing authorities. It is a situation peculiar to the Canadian federal system. Something of its complexity can be seen in the fact that the present area within the National Capital region (1,800 square miles) takes in all or part of 66 municipalities, some in Quebec, some in Ontario. Neither the federal government nor its agencies possess any direct authority over any of these municipalities. They are exclusively subject to their own provincial governments, under Section 92 of the British North America Act. When work began on the Master Plan not a single one of the municipalities in the capital region had "land use plans" or effective zoning plans. Vis-à-vis the local authorities, the Federal District Commission possessed only the power to advise and persuade. Lacking direct control, the Commission had to seek to attain its objectives by oblique and indirect means.

It was clear from the outset that the radical changes proposed in the Gréber

Master Plan could not be realized without reconciling or overcoming extensive private and municipal interests, some of which seemed likely to be adversely affected by the proposed national capital works and projects. The chain of democratic influence led from the individual property-owner and taxpayer through his municipal council to the provincial capital. The federal government and its crown agency the Federal District Commission was in a sense insulated from direct dealings with the property and the people of the national capital, by the provincial governments at Toronto and Quebec City. Yet a certain amount of direct and unquestionable authority had to be achieved in some way.

Administrative machinery under such circumstances was likely to be complex and at times baffling. A considerable part of the history of the first fifteen years of the National Capital Plan is concerned with constitutional problems. Something of the tests and triumphs of those years will become apparent, it is hoped, in the following pages.

2

The fact that the National Capital Plan was presented to the federal government on the eve of the greatest era of economic expansion in our history was in one sense a stroke of good fortune. But it also meant that the Plan had to be realized amid the dynamic swirl and inflationary impact of a period of unprecedented urban growth, which led to sprawl in the national capital region, as elsewhere. The tempo of the decade following the completion of the Gréber report lent an air of urgency to all the activities of the Federal District Commission. It was clear in many areas of planning that if immediate action were not taken, future progress would be far more difficult, and perhaps even too costly to contemplate.

The metropolitan area of the national capital has been the scene of unprecedented urban growth since the outbreak of the Second World War. To some extent Ottawa and Hull have merely shared in the general growth of Canadian cities. But much of the capital's expansion has reflected the special dynamic factors in federal government growth described in Chapter 2. Canada entered the post-war period on a high level of forced draft stoked by wartime demand, and a slump was expected, on the analogy of the First World War aftermath. This failed to appear. A brief period of readjustment and reconstruction was followed by a series of inflationary and provocative events: the outbreak of the Cold War, the Berlin Blockade, the Korean War. The prodigious back-log of consumer and capital demand in Canada and in other parts of the world sent Canadian production figures soaring to new records.

About this time a dramatic upswing in Canada's birthrate and renewed activity in immigration added to the buoyant mood of the times. In 1949,

Newfoundland entered the federal union, bringing vast new resources,— 155,000 square miles of territory, 400,000 people, some of the most sturdy and spirited people in the world. Such an accession materially enhanced the importance of the national capital at a single stroke. The national budget, which had stood at $500 millions in 1939 had climbed to $6 billions by 1960; after allowance for the change in the value of the dollar this is still six times as great. The 280 civil servants found adequate to serve a nation of $3\frac{1}{2}$ million people in 1867 had to be multiplied 150 times to serve the 18 million people of 1960.

The effect of these and other forces on the growth of Ottawa, Hull and environs, was dramatic. A population of 238,000 in 1945 rose to over 400,000 in 1960. In December of the latter year, the Industrial Commissioner of Ottawa, Robert Bullock, was claiming for his city the title of "Fastest Growing City in Eastern Canada". The number of motor vehicles in the area had multiplied three times in fifteen years. New buildings valued at over $600 millions were erected in the Ottawa area between 1947 and 1960. The number of churches doubled between 1945 and 1960. The number of individual houses nearly tripled, and the number of apartment buildings rose from 930 to nearly 1,700. The educational plant of the city had to cope with an increase in school population from 25,000 in 1945 to 60,000 in 1960. The number of primary and secondary schools was doubled in the 15 years. The University of Ottawa was working on a plan which would eventually cover an area now occupied by twenty city blocks; Carleton University, after a modest beginning, was working on a Master Plan of about thirty buildings located on a magnificent site of 130 acres between the Rideau River and the Rideau Canal.

Such facts and figures suggest the surging spirit of the times. While Ottawa and Hull and the adjoining municipalities were feeling the drive and spur of urban expansion they were increasingly conscious of the presence of the federal government, and the scope and consequence of the national capital plans being geared for rapid realization. Ottawa had always been conscious of the fact that it was also the seat of the federal government, but in the early years — as we have seen — the influence was modest. The interaction accelerated, especially after the establishment of the Ottawa Improvement Commission and the Federal District Commission. Still, up to 1927, with the crown agency still essentially a parks commission, the national impact was short of being decisive. When the Federal District Commission began expropriating property in the heart of commercial Ottawa for Confederation Place, a new phase was begun. This was emphasized a bit further in 1937 with the appointment of M. Jacques Gréber. The war intervened and deferred for a time the full effect of national planning, but in 1945 the fortunes of Ottawa, and to a lesser extent of Hull and of all the adjacent municipalities, were at last caught up irrevocably and extensively into the new National Capital Plan. From 1945 onward the steps which were being taken to create a national capital of beauty and significance bore more and more extensively on the plans and budgets of the affected municipalities. So the story from 1945 onward is largely a chronicle of action and re-action, challenge and response, between the planning body set up by the federal government, and the corporation of the City of Ottawa and of adjacent municipalities. As each grew, as each took action, the affairs of the other were changed and complicated thereby.

3

In earlier chapters it has been stressed that because Ottawa, Hull and their environs grew up without benefit of town-planning and in the great railway building phase of the industrial revolution, many undesirable conditions were shackled upon the growing national capital. The national capital plan had to be developed in the light of these adverse conditions. Vast sums of money had to be spent in correcting the mistakes of the past. Parts of the plan could be realized without serious interference with the life of the city; but a major program of urban rehabilitation would obviously be necessary in the long run. It would be impossible to make omelettes without breaking eggs. If the Gréber Plan was to be fulfilled there would need to be sweeping alterations in several essential aspects of Ottawa city and in the adjoining municipalities. Some private and corporation interests would have to give way to the master plan if the dream of a great national capital was ever to be realized. The federal government had the plan, the funds, the accepted responsibility, and in the final analysis, the weapon of expropriation; but the municipal governments, through the provincial rights inherent in Section 92 of the British North America Act, were in a strategic position to resist some of the forces conjured up by the exploding capital. While the record shows on both sides a commendable degree of consideration and cooperation, there were from time to time frank expressions both of frustration and of concern. The National Capital Plan at times seemed to be threatened with deadlock; some citizens of the municipalities and some private owners of property at other times saw their own personal interests and sentiments having to yield in the name of the public and national good.

All these relationships came out vividly in the joint parliamentary committee of 1956, which was instructed to review and report upon the work of the Federal District Commission in carrying out the National Capital Plan.

The committee sat for several months: its evidence and briefs ran to 1,056 pages of verbatim report. Its proceedings are a prime source for anyone investigating the history of the federal capital.

To illustrate some of the general statements on jurisdiction, and the difficulties which the Federal District Commission had to grapple with, I have quoted below a few typical passages from the evidence.

This is how the situation in 1956 looked from the more local viewpoints:

From an association of builders and contractors: "A subdivider in this city finds that a great deal of his work is hampered by the many public bodies with whom he must deal and to a certain extent he must work in the dark whenever he attempts to register a sub-division, whether it is in the city proper or one of the townships.

"He must first of all submit a sub-division plan to the Ontario Department of Planning and Development and from there this plan is submitted to the municipality. When the City of Ottawa is involved, the plan must go to the Technical Advisory Committee, which reports to the Ottawa Planning Area Board. On the Ottawa Planning Area Board are representatives of the City of Ottawa, the township of Gloucester, the township of Nepean and the Federal District Commission. A subdivider is not allowed to be present at these meetings and his business is discussed and dealt with by four different public bodies and he is asked to conform to different requirements which are not always realistic."

The subdivider might be turned down by the Ottawa Planning Area Board but there was an appeal to Queen's Park, and this might succeed: "In cases where subdivisions are proposed far in advance of normal development the Ottawa Planning Area Board has refused to recommend approval. In these cases an appeal to the Ontario Municipal Board is open to the developer," the then Mayor of Ottawa (Dr. Charlotte Whitton) told the parliamentary committee, "and, unfortunately, most of the appeals which have been taken have succeeded and the Ontario Municipal Board has recommended to the Minister of Planning and Development the approval of the plan of subdivision notwithstanding the opposition of the Ottawa Planning Board. This is a result which the City deplores but which it is powerless to prevent. . .

"The Ottawa Planning Area Board has, with four exceptions, three of which were insignificant, consistently refused to approve of urban type subdivisions in the area designated as a rural-urban zone (greenbelt) by the Ottawa Planning Area Board. Here again appeals have been taken by developers to the Ontario Municipal Board, and that Board, refusing to recognize the rural-urban zone as having any special character, has on several occasions approved of large urban type subdivisions in this transition area."

Some owners of property in the "greenbelt" area, including farm families with a long history in the community, were inhibited by the planning of a restricted "greenbelt", and through the reeves of their municipality they voiced strong objection to any interference with their freedom to sell their property on the open market or to hold it for higher prices.

"Unlike a zoning by-law, which is for the general benefit of persons within the zoned area, a Greenbelt, if it has any benefit, is for the benefit of those outside the zoned area, is for purposes wholly dissociated with the enhancement of the value of the ratepayers' property," the Reeve of the Corporation of the Township of Nepean told the parliamentary committee. "A municipal council is only the instrument of its ratepayers and it is wholly beyond the realm of practicability to expect any municipal council so to act in direct opposition to the interests of its ratepayers.

"If some overall national policy requires a Greenbelt, with which suggestion Nepean does not agree, then the national government must adequately compensate the Nepean ratepayers. Certainly it must not expect the Nepean council under the phony excuse of "zoning" to deprive its ratepayers of the present values of lands which they and their forefathers have held for generations." The Reeve of Nepean (Mr. D. Aubrey Moodie) added: "The Council of Nepean believes that conditions should be made attractive and desirable for development in concentric circles, but it has too much reading of history to believe that Canadians of pioneer stock will tolerate being ordered by any government at any level where they shall establish their homes. The tyranny of the Greenbelt is more than Nepean citizens are prepared to tolerate."

Citizen reaction to national planning within the urban area of Ottawa was expressed by the Mayor of Ottawa in the following strong terms:

"Possibly because the Federal District Commission and the National Capital Plan . . . had their origin in the Ottawa Improvement Commission, any inquiry or discussion of these relationships to the municipal government of Ottawa has emphasized — and somewhat necessarily so — the actual physical setting and development of the community.

"But this cannot be done — especially to the degree of emphasis of the Gréber report — to the disregard of the overriding responsibility of the municipal authority and the living of the community, that is the capital. The fact of Ottawa, the city, a community, almost half a century older than Confederation and fully a century older than 'The National Capital Plan', cannot be set aside.

"The zones of its business and commerce, its residential areas — luxury, average, mediocre and substandard — cannot be ruthlessly dealt with on the lines of a blueprint or an overall plan or sudden sweeping zoning and rezoning.

"The reality of living, the rights of ownership, the relationship of the homes, the churches, the schools, the stores and services, the community's recreation resources, both commercial and otherwise, their eating places, in short all the pattern of their living must be seen through the 'overlay' as it were of what the planners may dream, may desire, may work towards, but only in justice and consideration of what is, as well as what may be. It can all be very frustrating but it is important to distinguish whether it is the slower, surer, safer processes of a self-governing democracy at the level of its people's local government or a culpable indifference or non-cooperation which explains the gradualness of development and change among the municipalities which are practically all no less anxious than any especially constituted mechanism of the national government to justify and realize their dignity as part of the national capital area."

4

As reported above, the dynamic upsurge of Canada as a whole, reflected particularly in the growth of the national capital between 1945 and 1960, was driving the federal government and the corporation of the city of Ottawa and adjacent municipalities into a state of compulsive and intimate partnership. The federal government was overflowing all its old physical boundaries, extending its federal properties, influencing and altering traffic flow, the pattern of residential and office occupation, making heavier demands on municipal services, sometimes getting in the way of civic proposals.

The citizens and ratepayers of Ottawa could not fail to be thrilled at the successive announcements of glorious new proposals for the beautification and enhancement of the national capital, but the nagging question as to who would be expected to pay for all these improvements and dislocations in the normal civic life constantly haunted the local taxpayer. It appeared certain that the whole face of the national capital region was to be gradually transformed by costly throughways, parkways, new bridges, new street plans, new clusters of government buildings, new monuments and memorials, a colossal new sewerage system leading to a sewage disposal plant—but how much of all this was to be added to the debenture load of the city of Ottawa?

The brief of the city of Ottawa presented to the Parliamentary Committee in 1956 by Her Worship Mayor Charlotte Whitton documented the situation at length and with persuasive detail. Here were described the headaches and growing pains imposed on the key municipality in the national capital area, by the dynamic growth during the post-war years of the national government.

Early in 1947 the Ottawa City Council had taken steps to establish an Ottawa Planning Area Board, the city's brief reported. With the approval of the Ontario Minister of Planning and Development, the joint planning area had been designated as: the City of Ottawa, the Town of Eastview, the village of Rockcliffe Park, and the Townships of Nepean, Gloucester, March, Torbolton and Fitzroy. The City of Ottawa became the "designated municipality" to direct the planning. One of the first tasks undertaken by the new board was a study of the problem of unified administrative control for the urban area of the national capital. This effort was designed to cooperate with the National Capital Planning Committee set up in the previous year.

In December 1947, the Ottawa Planning Area Board submitted a report which emphasized the desirability of unified control of land uses, control of types and standards of building construction and all other phases of community planning, fire and police protection, water supply and distribution, sewers and sewage disposal, sanitation, transformer stations and distributions of electricity, transit, design of other public works, health and welfare, education and assessment.

The report defined the area over which unified control should be established, consisting of the municipalities and townships listed above.

No definite recommendation was made on the manner in which unified control was to be established, but two alternatives were suggested, namely, annexation or the establishment of an interurban administrative area. The City Council decided that annexation was the better solution.

At that time Ottawa occupied an area of about 6,100 acres. When annexation was first contemplated, the City had in mind an additional area of about 6,000 acres which would, it was calculated, provide for a doubling of the population as it then was, and thus provide for about 25 years of expansion at current rates. The idea was that an area of that size could be planned and integrated economically and conveniently by systematic, fairly compact, developments from the centre outward without placing too great a financial strain upon the City, or too heavily mortgaging its future.

"It was early realized, however, that Ottawa is not an ordinary municipality free to follow the most economical course," the Ottawa brief related, "but has a unique position and a unique responsibility as the key municipality within the National Capital area. As well as being a muncipality in the Province of Ontario it is the Capital of Canada, and, as such, a partner in the plans of the Federal Government, as expressed through the medium of the Federal District Commission and its various agencies."

With this in mind the City of Ottawa decided to acquire, by process of annexation, more than 24,000 acres of adjacent territory, so that it could be properly planned and developed within the framework of the master plan of the National Capital planning authority. Thus, while Ottawa in 1944 had a population slightly under 164,000 in an area of 6,100 acres, Ottawa in 1955 had a population of about 223,600 in an area of more than 30,000 acres; and by the end of 1960 the population had further risen to 260,000.

The new boundaries were chosen having in mind the probable limit for urban development as indicated in the studies of the National Capital Planning Committee and the extent to which it was feasible and economical to extend the water and sewage facilities of the City. The latter had been delineated in a report of a firm of engineers, Gore & Storrie of Toronto, engaged in 1948.

Application to the Ontario Municipal Board for authority to annex part of the Township of Nepean met opposition from the County of Carleton and the Township itself. The size of the original area asked for was somewhat reduced and the effective date of the annexation was deferred to January 1st, 1950, but otherwise the City of Ottawa's application was successful. In 1949 a further application was made to the Municipal Board for a portion of the Township of Gloucester and this, after a hearing, was also granted, effective in January 1950. Though the Town of Eastview and the Village of Rockcliffe were entirely within the new annexed area their inclusion in the enlarged boundaries of the City of Ottawa was not deemed essential to the achievement of the principal objectives which had been laid down to the development of the national capital.

5

The enlargement of the City of Ottawa in 1950 to an area nearly five times its size in 1949 created, of course, immediate and massive problems of urban development, and the whole period was crowded with events. In August, 1948 the City acquired the franchise and physical assets of the Ottawa Electric Railway Company, and set up the Ottawa Transportation Commission to operate the system. After annexation took place in 1950 the Commission acquired all the independent bus companies which were operating transportation systems within the annexed areas. In December 1949 the City acquired the franchise and the electrical business of the Ottawa Light, Heat and Power Company Limited, and these assets were placed under the existing Hydro Electric Commission of the City of Ottawa.

In August, 1948, the engineering firm of Gore & Storrie of Toronto had begun an extensive study of water supply and sewage disposal for the entire area within the limits of greater Ottawa. Their aims also included the prevention of contamination of the raw water supply and provision of adequate drainage facilities for storm water. Two-thirds of the cost of the survey was shared by the City of Ottawa and the Federal District Commission, and the remainder was assumed by Gloucester and Nepean Townships, Eastview and Rockcliffe Park.

Among the engineers' recommendations, made in July, 1949, the following were of major importance:

A unified control over all water supply and sewage disposal for the City of Ottawa and urban areas is essential.

The existing water works system should be protected against pollution up-stream.

The engineering firm recommended additions to the water works system at an estimated cost of nearly $6 millions; and two stages of construction for sewage disposal, at a total additional cost of nearly $19 millions. The system recommended was meant to serve a maximum population of about 350,000 residing within the Ontario Urban Zone as defined in the National Capital Plan.

In 1950 land development showed signs of becoming a major problem and a series of by-laws was passed to provide for adequate sub-division control.

When the area of the city was multiplied five times by the annexation of 1950, there were large areas in the new parts—as also in the older city—which were not protected by zoning by-laws. Some limited zoning took place in 1950, 1951, 1952 and 1953, and a more extensive program of zoning was begun in 1954.

The Master Plan of the National Capital Planning Committee meanwhile recommended a transition zone between the urban areas of Ottawa and the outside rural area, a zone which acquired the popular name of the "Green Belt". This proposal was strongly supported by the City in 1956 "not only on the ground that municipal water and sewer services cannot be extended into this zone, but also on the larger ground that the maintenance of this zone is essential for the preservation of the national capital as it has been planned. If urban development is permitted to straggle continually outwards creating fringe after fringe, the concept of those who have planned the capital and the millions of dollars that have already been spent in developing the plan will undoubtedly be lost."

Following earlier traffic studies, the City of Ottawa, in association with the Ottawa Transportation Commission, the Federal District Commission, and a group of Ottawa merchants, engaged in 1954 the services of Wilbur Smith and Associates of New Haven, Conn. to study the overall parking and traffic problems of the area. In 1955, a Department of Traffic Engineering Services was set up with a qualified Traffic Engineer as Director; and in 1956 a Parking Authority was created. Steps were taken by the Ottawa Transportation Commission to eliminate street cars on all routes, replacing them with modern buses. Original plans had called for the conversion to be complete by 1967, but subsequently this programme was considerably advanced, and the street car made its last official run on Ottawa tram lines on June 29, 1959.

These and other inevitable investments and expenditures by the City soon confronted the Council with staggering debenture debt and debt charges. At December 31st, 1955 the debt of the City amounted to just over $37 millions, of which $17.6 millions represented utilities debt to be financed out of earnings

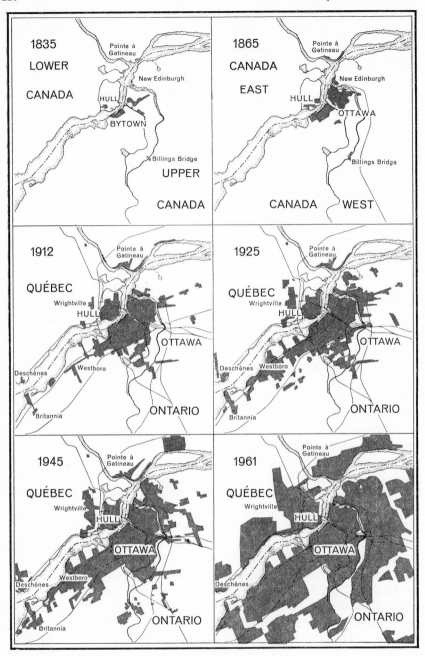

The Growth of the Ottawa-Hull Urban Region

of enterprises. The forecast of capital needs during the next decade (1955–65) then indicated that the City of Ottawa would be faced with debenture borrowings of $97.6 millions between 1956 and the end of 1960, and a further $94.4 millions in the following five years. (A check of the figures made at the end of 1960 showed that this estimate was probably not far off the mark).

Meantime the Ontario and Quebec Governments were dealing with related issues and problems. Ontario in 1946 enacted The Planning Act, and under it, in the following year, the Ottawa Planning Area Board was set up. Water testing of pollution in the Ottawa river was begun by the Ontario Department of Health in 1951 and continued for four years. A Water Resources Commission for the province was authorized, and the first appointments were made to it in May 1956.

A Provincial Town Planning Branch was set up in the province of Quebec under the Department of Municipal Affairs. Sections of the Cities and Towns Act and of the Municipal Code were also applicable to the problem of municipal planning on that side of the Ottawa River.

6

The City of Hull did not escape the influence of the rapidly expanding national government activities after the war. Perhaps the word 'escape' is misleading, because the results of the influence were in many ways highly beneficial. Downtown Hull lies, as can be seen on the map, close to the centre of the political heart of Canada: its southern boundary is not much more than an arrow's flight from the Parliament Buildings. If the Ottawa River had not stood there as an effective barrier, had the bridge connections between the cities of Ottawa and Hull been more numerous and satisfactory, had the political relations between Quebec City and federal Ottawa been at times more cordial . . . I suspect that in such a case governmental Ottawa would have overflowed Parliament Hill to the north (as well as to the south, west and east) long before it did. As it was, Hull remained largely outside the physical influence of the expanding capital for over sixty years. It was only in 1928 that the Federal District Commission began to acquire lands on the Hull side of the river for parks and parkways, and not until after the Second World War that the first important federal government building, the Printing Bureau, was built on adjacent Quebec soil.

The effect of national capital activities on the City corporation of Hull was traced in 1956 by His Worship Mayor Thomas Moncion, appearing before the Parliamentary Committee. Federal acquisitions of land within the Hull city limits had by that time added up to more than a quarter of the total area, and some expensive adjustments had been necessary. New industrial sites had to be developed to provide for those displaced by the Federal District Commission in its parks programme. Some areas had had to be annexed for residential purposes. In his brief to the Committee, Mayor Moncion listed a number of activities and expenditures which had been undertaken because Hull was in the national capital area, — outlays which would in all likelihood have been deferred or been found unnecessary in other circumstances. On the grave and growing problem of sewage disposal in the Ottawa River, the Hull municipal authorities testified that the financial resources of the city were quite inadequate to permit them to engage in any single-handed attack on a solution.

The beneficial changes in Hull and its environs made by the Federal District Commission were freely acknowledged. "In the past few years, the Federal District Commission set up, on the banks of the Ottawa River, a park extending from the Interprovincial bridge to the Gatineau River. Jacques Cartier park provides a magnificent view of Parliament Hill. The demolition of houses which formerly existed there brought great improvement to that sector of the city, especially when it is recalled that the area was also spotted with gas tanks a few years ago.

"The Federal District Commission also set up in our City other parks of smaller area, namely, the Fontaine, Ste. Marie and Brébeuf parks, which contribute to enhance the appearance of the Laurier, Frontenac and Tetreault wards.

"Moreover, by the building of two new parkways, namely, the Gatineau Parkway and Lac des Fées parkway, the Federal District Commission brought special development to another sector of our City, which formerly had not been developed to its full value because of numerous expenditures that such a development involved.

"The recent elimination of streetcar tracks from the Chaudière Bridge, as well as the building of a new traffic lane on the same bridge, did improve the appearance of that area as well as traffic itself."

The Hull City authorities stressed on that occasion their awareness of the strategic location of Hull within the national capital area, and, indeed, contended that "more than any other municipality, the City of Hull has given very tangible evidence of its co-operation with the federal authorities in the implementation of the Gréber Plan." The early history of Hull emphasized its commercial and industrial nature, but by 1956, when these representations were being made, it was asserted that between five and six thousand federal civil servants were living in the City of Hull, and that half of the population of Hull depended on the federal government for its income.

7

Other municipalities within the National Capital area were further away from the core of federal activities, and, in general, were not so profoundly affected by them. Special note should, perhaps, be made of the position of the two municipalities of Nepean and Gloucester, as a result of Ottawa's annexation policy.

The Township of Nepean had a population approaching 25,000 in 1949. The City of Ottawa annexed 7,400 acres, representing 85 per cent of the assessment. When the annexation was complete Nepean was left with an almost exclusively rural population of only 2,500. Yet in the next five years the outflow from the City of Ottawa again raised the population to 8,000, largely urban. The annexation of January 1st, 1950, left Nepean "without any municipal staff or municipal buildings, except the township hall. It had no fire hall, no police station, no township garage, no health unit—all had been taken away. It had no clerk, no fire department, no road department, no assessment department, no municipal staff of any kind." The municipality had, in fact, to be virtually recreated. But as the result of the influx of population after the annexation the population rose from 2,508 in 1950 to 8,167 in 1956, and the assessment from $2,763,900 to $8,412,550 in the same period.

Gloucester Township was similarly though not so severely affected. Its population was cut from 10,000 to 5,000 overnight, in 1950, and the annexation by Ottawa of 14,605 acres left it with 63,000 acres of assessable land. As with Nepean, the population jumped back again quickly, and by 1956 it stood at 11,450.

8

The headaches of divided authority having been so numerous and painful, it is not surprising that radical reforms have been proposed from time to time, including the decisive one of a wholly federal territory embracing the entire national capital region. The advocates of such a step in the past have included John Hamilton Gray, W. S. Fielding and Mackenzie King. The 'solution' of a federal district was certain to come up again in the hearings of the parliamentary inquiry of 1956. Some of the comments on the jurisdictional problem voiced on that occasion are still of live interest. The Federal District Commission, in its official brief, suggested minor amendments in the direction of enlarging its powers, but nothing of such a fundamental nature.

Some members of parliament, serving on the committee, were more outspoken in their views.

Senator John J. Connolly, for example:

"The ideal situation, if the Federal District Commission is to accomplish the purpose for which it is established, would be to have an area there in which the jurisdiction over all these things would be in the hands of the F.D.C. That is the Washington arrangement, but I take it the municipalities in the area resist the idea of divesting themselves of their autonomy."

Senator Norman Lambert, later on in the inquiry, recognizing the constitutional difficulties, pleaded for progress by means of cooperation. The F.D.C., he said, were the first people to admit that they were bound by jurisdictional limitations, "but that does not preclude development by cooperation, and I think that is the nub of this whole thing."

One impulsive comment by a member of the committee stood out from much patient examination of the constitutional problem. It came from M. J. Coldwell, a distinguished Canadian parliamentarian, and one not at all given to authoritarian solutions. After listening to Major General Howard Kennedy, then chairman of the Federal District Commission, and several of his staff, testifying on the fragmented division of authority, Mr. Coldwell noted "a sense of frustration regarding the centre of Ottawa" and then burst out as follows:

"It seems to me that the F.D.C. has been caught in an impossible position here, with all these various authorities with whom you have to negotiate, so much so that the plan cannot be carried out. It seems to me that unless there is one authority it cannot be done. I think that public opinion should be informed of this and perhaps some time public opinion will ask for a federal district here with authority to do the kind of thing that should be done in planning this national capital . . . .

"I have listened to the discussion since we began . . . I felt that this was a most frustrating job both for the commission and for this committee and that there was no real authority anywhere. The negotiations you attempt do not seem to bring results where we expect them to bring results, which is right in the central area of the capital."

During the inquiry, in the course of a personal brief, Mayor Charlotte Whitton of Ottawa took exception to the name 'Federal District Commission', on grounds that it smacked of centralization and suggested the possibility of non-democratic use of power. This drew a spirited reply from the Chairman of the Federal District Commission, Major General Howard Kennedy:

"The idea seems to have been implanted that the F.D.C. is not averse to the creation of a federal district along the Washington pattern. In reply to this, I want to make it abundantly clear that I know of no member of F.D.C. who harbours such ambitions, least of all the chairman. I, personally, could not be induced to serve on a body with powers and responsibilities such as those applying to the group, or groups, administering Washington.

"I do not believe that such a body can, or will, be created here and would consider it a disaster for F.D.C. to take over such matters as police, education, health, fire protection or even in broad outline the engineering services of any or all of the municipalities in the national capital area . . . I hope this will clear F.D.C. of some of the taint of wishing to become an autocratic body."

Another interesting suggestion about relationships was made by Watson Sellar, then Auditor General of Canada. He stressed the constitutional point that the ultimate seat of power within such Ontario municipalities as Ottawa was Queen's Park, and the provincial Minister of Planning and Development was the key man in all municipal planning. The following quotation from the evidence gets at the core of the matter:

Senator Connolly (Ottawa West): "Officially, under the law that prevails in these areas here, the Federal District Commission has no official status?"

Mr. Sellar: "None whatsoever."

Senator Connolly: "And, really, to give whatever is to be done here official status, the cooperation and active assistance of the authorities which administer the Planning Act is essential."

Mr. Sellar: "Yes. My feeling is this, sir, that it is desirable that this Act — and I am now speaking of the Federal District Commission Act — should be broadened so that there is authority for the Federal District Commission to act not only for the government of Canada but also for the province.

Senator Connolly: "With a province?"

Mr. Sellar: "For a province. They can do both. So that if the Minister of Planning and Development, under the Planning Act, decides to set up a new type of planning area board for this district, he could ask that the government of Canada authorize the Federal District Commission to play a legal role in administering and developing that plan."

The discussion that followed indicated that the constitutional aspects of any such delegation of powers by the province to a federal agency would have to be explored further, but the idea attracted the members of the committee, and it interested the chairman of the Federal District Commission. On the following day Major General Howard Kennedy analysed the relationships of the F.D.C. in the following terms:

"The most serious limitations of the present F.D.C.," he said, "are created through its lack of status *vis-à-vis* provincial and municipal governing bodies." A method was needed "for resolving the nebulous situation arising from the ineffective Ottawa Planning Area Board and its relations with the department of planning and development and of municipal affairs as well as with the adjoining municipalities."

"I am convinced," he went on, "that the solution of F.D.C. difficulties lies ... as Mr. Sellar suggested yesterday, in a working arrangement between the two senior governments on either side of the Ottawa river, between federal government and Ontario government in Ontario and between federal government and Quebec government in Quebec and that dealings with separate municipalities could then be carried out by the provincial departments delegated to work with F.D.C. Meantime F.D.C. can continue to develop the overall plan for the area conscious that it has no jurisdiction over the municipalities concerned, but also conscious that its planning can serve as a guide and aid to them along sensible lines in their planning."

9

The parliamentary committee was not specifically instructed to do more than "review and report upon the progress and the programs" of the Federal District Commission, but it is clear from the evidence in a number of places that some municipal officers within the capital area were apprehensive that out of the inquiry recommendations might go forward to the federal government advocating greater powers for the Federal District Commission or even an approach toward the Washington type of Federal District.

For example, the Reeve of Nepean Township (Mr. Moodie) said: "We do not believe that the ratepayers of this area should be called upon to forfeit their municipal administrations." The Mayor of Hull (Mr. Moncion) said: "Citizens of Hull in particular are proud of their municipal system, and under no condition would they relinquish the autonomy they have been granted. As Mayor," Mr. Moncion emphasized, "I take advantage of this opportunity to reiterate the feelings of the population, who are strongly opposed to any political integration or to any change in the administrative system of the National Capital."

In this he was holding fast to earlier sentiments from the same source. In the 1927 debate in the House of Commons on the Federal District Commission, Joseph E. Fontaine, Liberal member from Hull, said that he was "absolutely opposed" to any idea of a federal district, "because it would despoil us of our most cherished rights."

The brief of the City of Ottawa presented to the parliamentary committee in 1956 acknowledged the need of more effective machinery of cooperation between municipal and federal authorities. It reminded the committee that the Federal District Commission was not the only link with the national government:

"The F.D.C., its origin and development, is primarily an agency for the beautification—the 'improvement' originally—of the National Capital. Gradually, it has become a planning agency, but still, primarily, a physical planning agency, essentially engineering and architectural in its administrative arm, generally advisory to the Government within its terms of statutory reference and with its executive powers and responsibilities accordingly relevant.

"Other essential statutory and executive powers and duties are properly exercised, even within that part of the National Capital area that is the City of Ottawa, and even within this area of physical development, by various other authorities—Parliament itself, the Dominion Department of Public Works, the Dominion Department of Transport, the Dominion Department of Agriculture, the R.C.M.P. and the Department of Justice; and—very important for the City—the Municipal Grants Act Branch of the Department of Finance, the Province of Ontario and the County of Carleton. The Crown Corporation, Central Mortgage and Housing, deals almost daily with the City in most vital matters as does the Veterans' Land Act Administration.

"In the rapid change and accretion of the activities of government, the F.D.C. has assumed (or had assigned, in the absence of any other agency 'ready to hand') negotiations and, indeed, decisions, in respect to City of Ottawa matters, in which fundamentally not only government policy but Parliamentary authority are properly involved.

"The F.D.C., under present or projected powers, has been drawn into most extensive public works, highways, parks, real estate holdings and operations of all types of properties, into business as the lessor of concessions, into matters basic to assessment, taxation and similar obligations and decisions ordinarily exercised through Parliament or the Government, and finally into policies and programs which can not only affect but determine the basic civil rights and living of individuals and communities today and for all future time.

"The City enjoys all the general powers delegated to such a municipality by the legislation of the Province: it may require other and special permissive powers to play with full effectiveness its part as the most vital municipality in the partnership of the Dominion in the development of the Capital. Such special powers may only be made available under special supervision of the Province.

"An analysis of the problems before this Parliamentary Committee would seem to bring out fairly clearly that the F.D.C. and the City of Ottawa alike must face, impartially, some realignment of procedures and possibly definite readjustments in their relationships *vis-à-vis* the Dominion Government, and in the evolution of some special relationships of the City under the powers of the Province of Ontario."

10

The report of the parliamentary committee, dated July 30th, 1956, took note of the conflicting viewpoints. The pertinent paragraphs are quoted below:

"A series of jurisdictional problems arise. The proposed National Capital area includes portions of the Provinces of Ontario and Quebec. It is superimposed upon certain municipal organizations within each province. As the Plan is brought to fruition, works must be undertaken which affect the sphere of provincial or municipal responsibility. But because they are conceived as part of a scheme for the creation of a national rather than a provincial or a municipal development, these works may be more elaborate than would be required for provincial or municipal purposes. Again, since they are to be installed within populous municipalities, they have a bearing upon the works required by these municipalities for their own development. Sometimes, as in the case of driveways and parks, they add improvement which the municipality would not instal, or if it were installed it would be installed upon a more modest scale. At other times the creation of the work of the National Capital imposes upon the municipality concerned the burden of additional services or the building of works of greater magnitude than the municipality alone might undertake.

"For the resolution of these conflicts, cooperation between the three levels of jurisdiction is essential. Hitherto, the emphasis is upon cooperation between the Federal District Commission and the municipalities concerned. A greater measure of integration of planning with the provincial authorities should emerge. . .

"The Committee is of the opinion that the over-all plan of the National Capital should be submitted to both the Ontario Minister of Planning and the Quebec Minister of Municipal Affairs. This, if agreement is possible, should be regarded as the background against which all individual cases should be dealt with as they arise. At the same time we think that an appropriate representative of the government of Canada should consult with the above provincial authorities in view of determining ways and means of implementing the plan, and we feel that this could be achieved in such a way that it would be fair to all concerned."

Prospect

The early work of the Ottawa Improvement
Commission consisted mainly of improving the
banks of the Rideau Canal and the construction
of a Driveway alongside. This picture is from the
annual report of the Ottawa Improvement
Commission, 1904, and is entitled "Rideau
Canal Driveway, A Pagoda at Somerset Street."

The Langevin Block on Wellington at Elgin, completed in 1888, was the first of a long series of "Departmental" buildings.

From the Ottawa Improvement Commission Annual Report, 1904, "Rideau Canal Driveway, Pagoda West of Bank Street." The Ontario Association of Architects were critical of this work: "The association would respectfully point out that in many cases the fundamental principles of the disposition of masses and of consideration for natural features, have given place to a striving after effect by overelaboration of detail and the use of a quantity of meretricious ornament quite devoid of artistic quality."

Left:

The Russell House, centre of Ottawa social life for 40 years, demolished in 1927 by the Federal District Commission to provide part of the open space now popularly known as Confederation Square.

Below left:

The Sappers Bridge to left and Dufferin Bridge to right, with steps leading down to the station platform. This area was reconstructed in 1911-27 to become Confederation Square.

Below:

One of the last of the great squared timber rafts, that of R. M. Hurdman, on its way down the Ottawa River to Montreal, about 1908.

The original Center Block, designed by Thomas Fuller, was destroyed by fire on February 3rd, 1916. The present Parliament Building was constructed in the years 1916-27. Duncan

Campbell Scott the Canadian poet wrote, that the fire "was terrible and tragic, it was the most terrifying and beautiful sight I have ever seen."

*A painting done in 1911 for the Grand Trunk
Railway Company, for publicity purposes,
showing the newly-constructed Chateau Laurier
and Union Station.*

The Victoria Memorial Museum on Argyle Avenue, which housed Parliament during 1916-1920.

The Connaught Building on Mackenzie Avenue.

The Public Archives on Sussex Drive.

The Royal Canadian Mint.

The Confederation Building on Wellington Street.

*The buildings on these pages, with the
exception of the Confederation Building,
were erected before 1918. Periods of great
expansion in the population and industry of
Canada have always been reflected in enhanced
demands for space to house and accommodate
the civil and military service of Canada. These
requirements continue as Canada's growth
soars. To ensure a harmonious and efficient
expansion of the governmental buildings and
open areas, the Government has requested the
National Capital Commission "to co-ordinate
the development of public lands in the
National Capital Region."*

*Vincent Massey Park, located beside the
Rideau River, near Hog's Back Falls, provides a
75-acre setting for picnic groups, large and small.*

The fixtures and structures in the urban parks
maintained by the National Capital Commission
are functional, pleasing in appearance, and often
a little daring. This refreshment pavilion in
Vincent Massey Park illustrates this type of
facility.

Lac Lapêche, one of the larger lakes in Gatineau Park. This lake and others like it are being developed to provide visitors to the Capital with an ideal place for outdoor recreation and enjoyment.

In 1903 Landscape Architect Frederick G. Todd said in his report to the Ottawa Improvement Commission: "The Dominion of Canada is famous the world over for the extent and beauty of her forests, and for this reason it would seem appropriate that there should be reserved in close proximity to the Capital good examples of the forests which once covered a great portion of the country." Gatineau Park, a 75,000-acre area, of which 62,000 have been acquired, has been the Government of Canada's answer. Skiers can drive to the snow-clad hills within half an hour from the Parliament Buildings, across the Ottawa River.

▲

The Gatineau Parkway, a paved, limited access road, is being constructed through the park to allow the many features to be enjoyed. Along this road may be observed a variety of fur-bearing animals, deer, bear and even moose. The Park is a protected area for wild life, including many species of birds, animals and flowers. Visitors are able to experience in Gatineau Park a typical section of Canadian landscape, untouched forest, ancient rocks and placid lakes, contained and preserved for future generations, within the Capital Region.

*The headquarters for Canada's Postal Depart-
ment, from the rear, revealing the large areas
that must be provided to park motor vehicles.*

Far left:
The Sir Charles Tupper Building at Confederation Heights, headquarters of the Department of Public Works, largest public building in Canada.

A determined and successful effort has been made to decentralize the new government buildings to areas outside the central business district. Large integrated building groups like the laboratories of the National Research Council on the Montreal Road now exist. Close to residential areas, linked together by present or planned future Parkways, they have met the need for a rapid increase in space requirements, with a maximum of efficiency and economy.

Confederation Heights, Government building group, three miles from the City center.

The Thomson-Cole House, Ottawa, completed in 1834, owned by the National Capital Commission. Its generous proportions, fine dressed stone work and simple fanlight door, still mark it as a handsome house.

The Joseph Tesky House, Appleton, Ontario, built in 1835. The National Capital Commission has made an inventory of the buildings of historic or architectural importance in the National Capital Region and is co-operating with all the local municipalities toward their preservation. The Ottawa Valley still has many of these stone houses, constructed by masons discharged upon completion of the Rideau Canal. Essentially Georgian in design, they are fit to be ranked among the classic buildings in Canada.

The Queensway—Alta Vista interchange in the Hurdman's Bridge area of Ottawa, near the construction site of the relocated Union Station. This traffic interchange is typical of the many required where main city streets intersect the Queensway. An east-west throughway, 17 miles long, Queensway construction was made possible by the abandonment of the tracks of the Canadian National Railway, part of the railway relocation work of the National Capital Commission.

The City Hall of the Corporation of the City of Ottawa. As the statutory Capital of Canada, the corporation of Ottawa is inexorably influenced by the Federal Government building programme in the area, and by the plans and work of the National Capital Commission. Co-operation in planning, financing and execution of many projects of mutual concern to the Crown and the Town is continually undertaken by the two disparate jurisdictions with varying success.

The chief industry of the National Capital
Region, apart from government, is the
production of paper from pulp. The E. B. Eddy
Company with 1,250 sq. miles of timber limits on
the Gatineau River, is deeply rooted physically
and economically across the river from
Parliament Hill. The company, which started
operations on this site in 1851, controls over a
mile of Ottawa River shoreline.

Some people find the presence of a sulphite mill
only a few hundred yards from the open windows
of Parliament anomalous. Others see it
symbolic of Canada's industrial might. The
present Capital Planners have agreed that the
problem will not be solved in their generation.

The great Chaudière Falls, which offered
explorers and fur traders an obstacle to
navigation of the Ottawa River, were partially
stilled by construction of stonedams in 1826-27.
The hydro-electric power thus developed, has
attracted and sustained industry within the area.
The National Capital Commission, however,
hopes to redeem a portion of this beautiful
historic ground by reclaiming and restoring
Victoria Island and Richmond Landing.

The south shore of the Ottawa River, for approximately 8 miles west and 4 miles east of this location, is owned by the National Capital Commission. The river, long polluted with sewage, is to be rendered clean by the construction of a giant sewage disposal plant six miles downstream. The Macdonald-Cartier Bridge, joining Ottawa and Hull, will be built one mile downstream to replace the Alexandra Bridge, constructed in 1900, shown here.

The Union Station is to be demolished.

The Cenotaph, and Elgin Street.

The oblique approach to Parliament Hill.

Nepean Bay and the LeBreton Flats area of Ottawa, showing existing roundhouse and railroad trackage.

A scale model built in 1950 of the same area, shows the more desirable land use that could be achieved.

Jacques Gréber's Master Plan of 1950 is
gradually being realized. All the major proposals
are being undertaken and some of them are
completed. The removal of all the rail lines but
one, from the central area; the decentralization
of the majority of new government buildings
and provision of land for future construction;
the acquisition of a Greenbelt; the provision of
open space in the urban area; Gatineau Park.
The National Capital Commission may now
turn to refinements of the plan and to carrying
out worthy projects on the land acquired.

CHAPTER TWELVE

Foundations of the Capital Plan

The Gordian knot of divided authority could conceivably have been severed after the war by the establishment of a federal district subject to federal authority. But the national government possessed no powers of coercion over the two provinces primarily concerned, to make them cede the necessary area; and the voluntary cooperation of Ontario and Quebec in such a venture was unlikely, to say the least. There would have remained in any event the determined opposition of many voters within the affected municipalities, expressed through their elected councils. Formidable administrative innovations and adjustments would have been required. Negotiations would have certainly been lengthy and difficult at best. Meantime the Master Plan for the National Capital might have gone down the drain, through inaction, land speculation, rising land values, and largescale haphazard private construction and enterprise.

The National Government did not even throw out feelers looking toward the creation of a "federal district" of the Washington type. It was not, however, without resources of its own. There were other devices, other approaches, available to it.

It could materially strengthen its crown agency, the Federal District Commission.

It could provide that agency with much more substantial funds.

It could give the Federal District Commission authority over the site and architecture of federal buildings and projects in the national capital area.

All of these steps were actually taken between 1945 and 1950. For the record, the main events of the period are related here, as they pertain to the realization of the Gréber Master Plan.

The amendments made to the Federal District Commission Act at the end of the Second World War were designed to speed up the development of the national area. The Commission, in the words of Senator Norman Lambert (in the 1956 inquiry) was thus given "plenary powers" to deal with the affected municipalities. "That is why the Act was revised at that time. I certainly know that it was Mr. Mackenzie King's idea that he was giving the F.D.C. just about all the power that the federal government could give it to proceed with its work," Senator Lambert said.

The membership of the Commission was enlarged and its representation made nation-wide.

In 1946 the National Capital Planning Committee was formed.

In 1948 Parliament established the National Capital Fund, which provided a total of $25 million, payable in ten annual grants. Further revisions to the Act outlined new terms of reference and gave additional powers. The Commission was made responsible for co-ordinating federal construction and development within the national capital area. As a result, the location, architecture and general nature of proposed federal works in the area were first submitted to the Federal District Commission for approval. A similar approval had to be obtained by any builders on land owned, leased or otherwise controlled by the federal government. The City of Ottawa was granted by statute authority to control the appearance of buildings on lands facing public property or streets, and the F.D.C. was requested to advise the City in the administration of this Act.

Following the 1956 parliamentary inquiry further changes were made in the legislation.

A new National Capital Act was enacted, and the name of the Federal District Commission was changed to the National Capital Commission. This was established on February 6, 1959. The National Capital Region was enlarged from 900 square miles to approximately 1,800. One advantage of this was that it took in the whole of several important watersheds of rivers flowing into the Ottawa.

The financial resources of the Commission were greatly enlarged by provision of government loans for the acquisition of lands.

As a result of the more generous financial support in the post-war years, a sum of just over $50 million was spent by the Commission for improvements alone during the period April 1st, 1947 to March 31, 1960.

2

With the legislative powers and financial resources recited above, the Federal District Commission and its successor, the National Capital Commission, were able to make giant strides toward the realization of the Gréber Master Plan. Many of the details are reported in this and the next chapter.

The key to the creation of these extensive capital works and projects was, under the circumstances, the land acquisition program. The federal government and its agent, the Commission, lacked direct authority over the municipal governments, and there were no effective municipal zoning plans. The solution lay in speedy acquisition of strategically located lands within the national capital area, on both sides of the Ottawa River.

In this land acquisition program the federal government's powers of expropriation were available if all other means failed. With this latent power, and with the funds readily available, the F.D.C. and the N.C.C. have been able to act quickly and decisively in especially sensitive areas. For example they acquired property on Wellington Street threatened by undesirable private development, which in the absence of effective zoning laws within the municipality could not have been otherwise prevented.

The rapid and extensive purchase of property over the 15 year period placed the crown agency in the position of ensuring the ultimate realization of the Gréber Master Plan (as originally conceived, and as amended from time to time in the light of new internal and external influences).

From 1946 to the end of 1960, the Commission acquired some 1800 properties, extending to approximately 6,250 acres, exclusive of Gatineau Park. The land so acquired will permit the further development of the Ottawa River Parkway, the Rideau River Parkway, the Western and Eastern Parkways, and many other important projects. Further acquisitions comprising 589 properties totalling 24,300 acres account for the major part of the Greenbelt in Ontario (not finally secured until drastic action was begun in 1958), and embrace a substantial reserve area for future government building sites. The importance of this last factor is seen in the statement that in spite of a building program exceeding $111 million in the decade 1950–60, the federal government has in sight or on the drawing boards extensive future projects which will require thousands of acres of land for their fulfilment.

The land acquisition program had cost to the end of 1960 about $39 million. This may appear a very substantial chunk of the taxpayer's money, but it needs to be seen in perspective. Much of the land was acquired before the recent soaring inflation of land values, for as little as a tenth or a twentieth of current prices. And as a yardstick to test the reasonableness of the outlay of $39 million it can be mentioned that the property required for the widening of *one* street in Montreal—Dorchester—cost $20 million.

Despite the spectacular enlargement of Gatineau Park, with its vast acreage, it is within the City of Ottawa, and within the townships of Nepean and Gloucester, that the land purchase program has been most influential, making possible the realization of key elements in the Master Plan for the National Capital. Without such purchases, the basic project of railway relocation, the new industrial areas, the Greenbelt, the Queensway and the extensive new system of parkways could not have been achieved.

A note on the ways in which these properties were acquired will be of interest.

Expropriation by the Department of Public Works on behalf of the Commission was employed in acquiring the property needed for the Gloucester industrial areas and for the Rideau River and Ottawa River Parkways. There were 550 property owners involved. About 50 per cent of the settlements were completed in the first two years after expropriation began in 1947, and about ten per cent per year afterwards. While disagreement about price held up many settlements, others were delayed because titles were confused and it was difficult to find persons authorized to negotiate for the property.

A second method was the use of private appraisers. Properties required were surveyed and local real estate appraisers were asked for a report on values. If survey and title were satisfactory, offers were made to the owners in writing. If the offers were refused an expropriation notice was registered. At the same time a real estate agent was authorized to try to settle the amount with the owner. Lands for the Queensway and the Eastern and Western Parkways were acquired in this way.

A third method was direct purchase by negotiation with the owners. The Commission's own staff was augmented especially for this purpose in 1959, and it proved to be the most effective of the three methods, about 80% of the settlements being completed in the first year of its operation. The Commission's negotiators were instructed to be patient, to go to a great deal of trouble to reach an agreement satisfactory to the owner.

In the course of acquiring the properties necessary for the National Capital Plan, the Commission found it possible to achieve another desirable objective at the same time. Considerable areas of urban blight and sub-standard housing were cleared in the course of property acquisition. Slum areas were cleared and replaced by projects fitting into the National Capital Plan. This kind of dual gain was most evident in the Nordic Circle area, beside Leamy Lake, Lazy Bay to Tunney's Pasture, in Westboro and certain sections of the waterfront at Woodroffe, Junction and McCullough Streets, Mackenzie King bridge area, the Hog's Back area, and the Rideau River front, particularly in the Hurdman's Bridge section. These projects led to the removal of 658 dwellings, housing approximately 2,000 people.

3

The Holt Commission (1913–1915) regarded railway relocation as the *sine qua non* of the achievement of a national capital worthy of the Canadian people. The Federal District Commission and its successor fully agreed with this, and took radical steps toward its realization. At the same time they were faced in 1945 with a condition which had grown up in the years since 1915. The sprawling uncontrolled extension of the urban area of the capital in an age of mass ownership of automobiles and trucks threatened the whole concept of the national capital plan, in the opinion of the Commission. It believed that one of the most dramatic and foresighted proposals of the Gréber Plan was the establishment of a Greenbelt around the entire metropolitan area. "A necklace for the National Capital," Jacques Gréber called it. The "exploding metropolis"—so characteristic of all 20th century urban expansion in North

America threatened the basic concept. There was violent criticism of the Greenbelt idea, however, and between 1945 and 1958 very slow progress was made toward its realization.

The Greenbelt was intended to circumscribe an area large enough for the accommodation of some 500,000 persons. The inner limit was chosen by considering what area could be economically provided with municipal services. It was intended that the Greenbelt would encompass within its own boundaries areas of great natural beauty. As well as limiting urban sprawl, it would provide sites for buildings, especially but not exclusively government buildings.

Typically, any city core, faced by costly service extensions, tries to promote concentric, nucleated development. Typically, too, the abutting municipalities seek to attract development at all costs, even though this usually takes the form of individual houses on large lots with septic tanks and wells. Such development is, of course, a financial burden on the municipalities, difficult to service, unsightly; and requiring schools, fire and police protection, without compensating industrial assessment.

From 1947 to 1958 the Commission grappled with the problem and tried a number of approaches, all without much success. One of these was comprehensive land use planning, but this failed because the affected municipalities did not possess comprehensive land use plans or comprehensive zoning by-laws. In 1956 the federal government stepped in, through its agency Central Mortgage and Housing, and at least held up residential construction in the proposed Greenbelt area by withholding loan insurance on proposed homes within the area.

The possibility of acquiring development rights in the Greenbelt was thoroughly examined but proved difficult and expensive. Early in 1958, by land use controls and zoning methods, an attempt was made to secure the belt on the Ontario side through the Ottawa Planning Area Board, but despite the strenuous efforts of the City of Ottawa and the Federal District Commission, the attempt failed.

In June, 1958, the federal government authorized the Federal District Commission to establish *by purchase* a 37,500 acre Greenbelt, an action subsequently described by the Washington (D.C.) *Star* as "meeting the problem of urban sprawl head on."

Objections to the formation of a Greenbelt were lodged by the municipalities of Nepean and Gloucester, as was related in the previous chapter. The Reeve of Nepean Township attacked the concept in vigorous language. "It is discriminatory and confiscatory," he contended before the 1956 inquiry. "The Greenbelt is merely a repressive measure to take care of the short-comings of planning for services, the failure to assemble land, and to offset the positive imposition of obstacles in the way of the genuine subdividers." He submitted that the Greenbelt, unlike urban zoning, was not for the benefit of any of the ratepayers within its boundaries. "On the contrary, it is to their grave detriment, since there can be no doubt that it would deprive the owners of the established present values of their lands."

The brief of the Township of Gloucester presented to the same committee said that the township "was extremely critical of the Greenbelt proposals," which, they said, incorporated and continued 'a false and impractical theory' in the proposed Gréber perimeter. "Urban development in concentric circles," the Gloucester brief continued, "has the beauty of symmetry and abstract logic. But the motor car, population growth, the freeway and our very culture makes this European concept largely inapplicable to North American conditions."

The argument that tentacular or de-centralized growth should be discouraged because of the high cost of extending central water and sewerage services to the outlying areas was also attacked by the Gloucester brief as being an outmoded idea. "Modern technology has greatly modified the importance of this concept. Whole cities in the United States of America and we believe numerous cities and towns in Ontario supply water from community or municipal deep wells." Separate sewage disposal plants were, they contended, also practicable. Gloucester township also objected that some of the finest residential land in the area surrounding the capital would be removed from development by the Greenbelt proposal. (These Nepean and Gloucester arguments were, incidentally, sharply challenged during the 1956 hearings by the F.D.C. and other authorities).

The opposition of many farmers, landowners and speculators in the area can be readily understood. The wave of building expansion was likely in due course to engulf them all and make it necessary to sell, or to move, but the operations of the free market, if left alone, held out the prospect that when the time came the owners would be richly rewarded. The intervention by the Crown, while it guaranteed a fair current return for their property, denied them the right to hold out for a higher increment if they so wished.

Though criticism of the Greenbelt was not entirely stilled by the decisive action of the federal government in 1958, the official view of the National Capital Commission was then and is that it constitutes a vital and integral part of the whole master scheme, and that the establishment of such a Greenbelt will be completely vindicated by the passage of time. It paved the way for realization of the total concept of the Master Plan "and the creation in the Canadian capital of Ebenezer Howard's classic regional system— metropolis, greenbelt and satellite."

Within a short time, the Commission reported, there was a striking increase in the density of land use within the urban area after the establishment of the

Greenbelt, contrasting sharply with the uneconomic use of land prior to this time. Two of the most dramatic examples are in the downtown section where a number of new building projects have commenced or are in the planning stage, and in the newer suburbs where much greater densities are contemplated together with a highly desirable diversity of building types.

The Greenbelt surrounding the national capital on the Ontario side is about $2\frac{1}{2}$ miles wide and when purchases are complete will occupy an area of about 65 square miles. Within that area there was, at the end of 1960, a total of 25,775 acres of farm land, 5,930 acres of federal government holdings, 7,300 acres of wooded and waste lands, 875 acres of stream and bottom lands, 560 acres in residential and commercial use and 945 acres in use for railways and in roads.

The plans of the National Capital Commission for the future use of the Greenbelt may be summarized as follows:

The predominatingly open space character of the area must be preserved. As the area is limited in size, only uses which can make a positive contribution to the development of the National Capital can be permitted.

Where the nucleus of a sound, balanced community already exists, as at Bells Corners, it is proposed that a self-contained village or hamlet be encouraged to grow. Commission staff sees an ultimate population of 12,000 at Bells Corners. Another hamlet of up to 10,000 may be possible at Blackburn when the necessary services can be provided.

Government establishments within the Greenbelt early in 1961 included Uplands Airport, Connaught Ranges and National Telecommunications Research. An area of 300 acres to the north and west of Bells Corners is allocated to the Mines Branch of the Department of Mines and Technical Surveys. The Animal Research Institute of the Department of Agriculture will occupy 4,000 acres in Nepean township in the southwest corner of the Greenbelt.

Two large parks and two smaller ones are to be developed within the Greenbelt. In the east a large natural park is proposed for the Green's Creek Valley, extending from Innes Road to the Ottawa River. A park of 900 acres is planned in the westerly portion of the Greenbelt adjacent to the Shirley's Bay establishment of the Department of National Defence and the research centre of the Northern Electric Company. It will front on the Ottawa River and will be developed for bathing and boating. Two smaller parks on either side of the Rideau River will have a combined area of several hundred acres and will provide bathing and boating facilities. Parts of the Greenbelt will be used for reforestation projects, and limited recreational facilities may be developed therein.

The Holt Commission singled out railway relocation as basic to any major improvement in the traffic pattern of the capital city. It analysed the problem thoroughly, and made clear-cut and forthright proposals for the permanent solution. No progress, however, was made. The growth in the city's population, and the relatively much greater increase in the number of trucks, buses and private automobiles, turned what was a serious annoyance in 1915 into a traffic engineer's nightmare forty years later.

The National Capital Planning Committee (created 1946) quickly went into action on the railway and highway problem. It appointed a sub-committee for each aspect; and on June 2nd, 1947, interim reports were laid before the federal government. These recommended the immediate acquisition of suitable lands for new railway freight terminals and yards, and for new industrial sites. Before existing rail facilities could be re-located, new sites had to be readied to receive them. On October 1st of the same year, the Minister of Public Works was authorized to expropriate four areas, of about 6,600 acres all told, for such purposes. Meantime a plan providing for the ultimate removal of the many railway lines that criss-crossed the cities of Ottawa and Hull was approved in principle, and referred to the railway companies for study.

This key project was pursued with vigor, and by 1950 the first stage of what was originally planned as a three-stage program to re-locate the whole railway system serving the national capital area was well under way.

The first relocation project to be grappled with was the elimination of the "cross town" tracks of the Canadian National Railways. As long ago as 1924 there had been an opportunity to remove this stubborn barrier to north-south road traffic, but the proposal met defeat in a City of Ottawa referendum. In 1950, there was an additional incentive to remove the tracks, since the released right of way (with substantial augmentation) provided a rare opportunity to construct a limited access express-way through the very heart of the capital region. Satisfactory negotiations with the provincial government and the adjacent municipalities permitted construction to begin on an urban thoroughfare linked at each end with provincial highway 17, the Trans Canada Highway. When completed, The Queensway will greatly facilitate through traffic, will provide some of the finest urban views in Canada, and will, when connected with other planned links of the urban traffic system, materially ease the congestion in the nucleus of the city.

An arrangement with the C.N.R. provided that the Federal District Commission would create alternative rail facilities bypassing the main urban area to the south of the city. Such replacement rail facilities were begun in 1950. A connection was made between the C.N.R. Renfrew and Beachburg subdivisions near South March; and five-and-a-half miles of main line track, bypassing the central area, was constructed, extending from just east of the Rideau River crossing to Hawthorne. In November 1953, the first benefits were seen when the through freights from Montreal to Winnipeg and back began to use the bypass to the south instead of travelling through the heart of the city. Freight yards were built in the new railway belt acquired near the Walkley Road, with the intention that they would ultimately serve as terminal yards for *all* railway systems serving the capital area. Construction was begun of nine miles of yard tracks, a yard office, freight car repair and auxiliary facilities, including a signal control system. By August, 1955, the C.N.R. was able to transfer its freight marshalling and car repair and maintenance operations away from the heart of the city to the new Walkley Road site. This ended seventy-five percent of the previous freight operations along the crosstown tracks in the city. In 1960 the final steps were taken to end the remainder of the operations on the crosstown tracks and make the entire right-of-way available for the extending operations of construction of the Queensway.

Stage One was thus complete by 1958. The Federal District Commission had installed the new facilities at a total cost, including property, of about $3,600,000; and in exchange had received valuable railway-owned property in the central area available for the new limited-access highway. Stage One eliminated twelve miles of trackage in the capital area and eleven level crossings.

5

The Gréber Master Plan had originally proposed the elimination of *all* tracks from the entire central area, the building of a new railway bridge across the Ottawa River at Duck Island, and the removal of the Union Station to a site four and a half miles away, in the Walkley Road area.

The reason why this sweeping solution was unacceptable to the railway companies in certain respects was explained to the parliamentary committee in 1956 by Major General Howard Kennedy:

"After new studies and discussions with the railway companies, it has been determined that the Duck Island crossing would result in uneconomical rail operations and is therefore completely unsatisfactory to both the C.P.R. and the C.N.R. Thus, the present connection to Hull by the Prince of Wales Bridge (C.P.R.) just west of the Chaudière Falls, and the tracks leading to this bridge, the C.P.R. Ottawa-Prescott lines, which parallel Preston Street on the west side, will have to be retained."

At that time, the Chairman of the F.D.C. saw serious complications ahead:

"The new station in south Ottawa to replace the Union Station will not be constructed in the foreseeable future," he believed, "and as a result it became necessary to design all other elements of the Master Plan in such a manner that they will function satisfactorily with both the interim and ultimate railway schemes. As the existing station will be retained for many years, the solution of projects requiring immediate attention has become exceedingly complex, especially in the Pretoria Bridge, Hurdman's Bridge and Union Station triangle."

Happily, a solution to General Kennedy's complex problem was found much earlier than appeared likely when he spoke. On October 31st, 1959, Prime Minister John Diefenbaker announced that authority had been given to the National Capital Commission to proceed with the final stages of the railway relocation program which the Commission had recommended in the Ottawa area. This included the construction of a new passenger terminal in the Hurdman's Bridge area; and though it did not eliminate quite all the crosstown trackage in the way the Gréber plan had originally proposed, it did open up the way for a solution of nearly all of the major relocation problems, many years sooner than had appeared likely.

In its 1959-60 Annual Report, the National Capital Commission called the Prime Minister's 1959 announcement "one of the most important milestones in the fulfilment of the National Capital Plan."

The decision to proceed at an early date with the construction of a new Union Station in the Hurdman area permitted the second and third stages of the railway relocation program to be combined. The following major operations were scheduled to get under way at an early date:

Removal of (a) the C.P.R. main line from Nepean Bay to Bells Corners; (b) the C.P.R. Ottawa-Hull connection via the Interprovincial Bridge; (c) the C.P.R. Sussex Street spur; (d) the C.N.R. connection to the Chaudière area via the crosstown tracks; (e) the C.P.R. Broad Street yards and local freight terminal; and (f) the C.N.R. Nicholas Street and Ottawa East round-house facilities.

"The C.P.R. yard operations and local freight terminal will be relocated on space reserved for them in the permanent new railway sites already developed for the C.N.R. in the Walkley Road and Hurdman areas," the Report explained.

"The most significant development of Stage Two will be the construction of a new station in the Hurdman area to replace the present Union Station. The removal of the railway station from the centre of the City will substantially reduce the ultimate costs of the railway relocations, make possible an early rehabilitation of the central area of the Capital, and greatly advance the progress of the National Capital Plan."

Construction projects under Stage Two also include various track connections between the C.P.R. and the C.N.R. to permit joint operation, a new freight switching yard at Walkley Road for the C.P.R., new diesel locomotive shops, trackage in the new industrial areas, and the extension of the railway signal systems.

The retention of the C.P.R. Prescott line into the Chaudière region and across the Ottawa River on the Prince of Wales railway bridge still leaves one set of railway obstructions to city road traffic, which the planning body had originally hoped to eliminate entirely. To reduce the inconvenience of this line to a minimum, grade separations will be achieved by excavation and the depressing of the railway tracks below the grade levels employed for street traffic.

The value of the railway relocation program is brought out by the key statistics. When completed it will have removed 35 miles of trackage from the metropolitan area, will have eliminated 70 level crossings, and will have made available for desirable redevelopment a total of about 440 acres of railway-occupied lands. Most of this acreage is located in or adjacent to the central area of the capital region.

In particular, the relocation of the present Union Station will free an area of about 16 acres in the very heart of the national capital. The way has thus been opened up for some dramatic and interesting developments affecting the whole central axis from the west end of Wellington Street to the Lower Town business district, and the traffic links with the new Queensway thoroughfare. Preliminary proposals include a permanent pedestrian shopping Mall, a Parkway or Drive leading to the Queensway along the east bank of the Rideau Canal, extensive new parking areas, both underground and multi-storey, and a major relief for the traffic flow along Rideau Street eastward, in the form of a right-hand loop for north-bound motorists. Sites will be available for a complex of new office and public buildings on the present site of the railway depot and yards. It will be possible to complete the environment of Confederation Square in an aesthetic and monumental fashion, and to realize the dream of a highly impressive approach to Parliament Hill from the south-east.

CHAPTER THIRTEEN

A Dream Emerging?

The accelerated growth of the national capital since 1945 has added in fifteen years a population equal to the whole city of 1911, and an area many times greater. Many parts of the old city have been changed beyond recognition. Only those citizens whose duties take them methodically around and about the 30,000 acres within the Ottawa city limits can keep up with all current developments. There have been radical changes in public transport, in the highway systems, in parks and parkways. The accumulated total of government building between 1945 and 1960 surpasses all the earlier public building since Confederation. The number of motor vehicles has multiplied several times. The density of traffic steadily increases, and the parking problem frustrates the engineers.

Many of the changes between 1945 and 1960 have been imaginative and aesthetic, constructive and ennobling. Others are regressive. Some are planned and controlled, elements of form and color in a master mosaic: others represent individual whim and self-centred interest.

The new Ottawa can be seen to good advantage along the northeastern end of Sussex Drive, and on Colonel By Drive, and across the new Bronson Bridge, and on the completed section of the Queensway, and along Carling Avenue. It can be seen in some of the new sub-divisions, and in Tunney's Pasture, and on Confederation Heights. Its promise is visible in the west end of Wellington Street, and in modern suburban factories, and in imposing office buildings in the heart of town. The environs of the National Capital Region begin to prophesy the future in extended parkways, beside the Lac Des Fées, at Leamy Park, and along the Ottawa River, and in the incomparable gateway to the Laurentian Mountains, via the new Gatineau Parkway. It can be seen timidly and experimentally in attempts to convert Sparks Street into a leisurely and gracious Mall, and in plans to give a new complexion to Rideau Street.

But the new Ottawa cannot mask the shortcomings of the old Ottawa, which still obtrude everywhere. Elements of a shabby provincial shopping town of late Victorian inspiration still rub shoulders with national symbols of soaring significance. The motor age turns the noble spaces of Parliament Hill into vast parking lots: congests the narrow commercial lanes in the heart of the city: fills the air with foul exhaust gases. The 'Grand' River of the voyageurs is still treated like a common sewer (though with partial remedy in sight at last). Government 'temporary' buildings still encroach on citizens' parks and playgrounds, twenty years after their erection. Much suburban development fails lamentably to foster true community life. Some of the grandest natural river scenery in North America is still serving for factory sites and yard space for big business. Culturally, the national capital still lacks facilities found even in some impoverished towns of central Europe; and perhaps it also still lacks enough enthusiastic patrons to fill the theatre, opera house or concert hall, even if such were there. While we celebrate the progress, we must be conscious of the long way still to go.

The developments which have been singled out in the present chapter cannot be ascribed to any single agency. They are federal, provincial, municipal and private in their total and cumulative effect. They are the result of much give and take, much accommodation of conflicting interests, as well as of overall planning.

In her testimony before the Parliamentary committee of 1956, Mayor Charlotte Whitton said, a bit optimistically perhaps: "Personally, I feel that this mighty nation that is to be can afford in the first century of its existence *one dream city*." In some respects we are witnessing the early stages of such a dream. The growth of the national capital has always been the result of a complex of combined forces, institutional and individual, and will always be so. But in the years following the Second World War, there has been a new sense of drive, imaginative execution, and long-range vision. Many of the developments described in the remainder of this chapter are directly due to the decision to draw up a Master Plan in the period 1946-49. They came about because the Federal District Commission and its successor the National Capital Commission have been given by parliamentary action the necessary funds and the resources to make progress with it.

2

While the railway relocation program was being worked out between 1947 and 1960, some of the more urgent street and highway traffic problems were also being tackled. Among the more impressive achievements in these fields were the construction of the Mackenzie King Bridge over the Rideau Canal and the existing railway installations, opened to traffic in 1951, the Sussex Drive and Bytown Bridges project, completed in 1954, the improvement in the Hull approaches to the Chaudière Bridges, opened to traffic in 1955, the Dunbar Bridge over the Rideau River, also opened to traffic in 1955, the widening of Carling Avenue, of which the first stage was completed in 1957, and the construction of the bridge over the Rideau Canal at Bronson Avenue, completed in 1960. By the latter date substantial progress had been made in the major Queensway project, and the official opening of one of its links took place in November 1960.

These improvements, coupled with the elimination of street cars and the replacement by modern motor buses, the introduction of one-way streets and a modern traffic lights system went a long way in facilitating vehicle flow, though meanwhile the traffic density grew vigorously and created the impression of a race in which there was no assurance that the forces seeking to free and speed up the flow of traffic would win out in the end.

Most of the major construction programs were joint enterprises, with the cities, the provinces, and the national government—or one of its agencies— sharing the cost.

The Mackenzie King Bridge was built by the Federal District Commission in cooperation with the Department of Public Works, and with the City of Ottawa contributing about 14 per cent of the cost. The project was given priority in the postwar Master Plan. It was designed to relieve traffic congestion through Confederation Square by opening up a new traffic artery, linking Albert and Slater Streets to the west of the Canal with Stewart and Wilbrod Streets to the east; and to divert truck traffic from Wellington Street.

The new Sussex Drive and Bytown Bridges project was built to provide a direct and impressive route between Government House and Parliament Hill. It required the construction of two new bridges over the Rideau River at Green Island and the improvement and widening of the Drive from George Street to the entrance to Rideau Hall. The Federal District Commission assumed two-thirds of the cost of this work.

The widening and improvement of the approaches to the Chaudière Bridges was needed to relieve the congestion in the flow of traffic between the two cities and the two provinces at this point. Street car tracks were removed, a steel trestle bridge was constructed to provide separate north and south traffic lanes, and the remainder of the roadway was widened from 24 to 46 feet. The whole cost of this project was provided from the National Capital Fund, administered by the Federal District Commission.

The Dunbar and Bronson Avenue bridges were part of a joint project aimed at creating a new entrance into the city from the south, and relieving Bank Street of some of its traffic congestion. The route was also meant to serve patrons of the Ottawa Airport. At the time these projects were planned a large new government site had been located on Rideau Heights and these new bridges and the connecting highway would be essential by the time the new government buildings were occupied. The Dunbar bridge was constructed by the City of Ottawa, and the Federal District Commission contributed about one-sixth of the cost.

The Bronson Avenue Canal Bridge was also a city project. The National

Capital Commission contributed forty per cent toward its cost and undertook the landscaping and the maintenance of the landscaping adjacent to the bridge and its approaches.

The widening of Carling Avenue was necessary to facilitate the flow of traffic to and from the western area of the capital region. The first stage of this City of Ottawa project was completed, as far as Kirkwood Avenue, in 1957. The Federal District Commission and the Department of Agriculture contributed most of the land required in the widening.

The Queensway was dedicated by Her Majesty Queen Elizabeth II on October 15, 1957. This is the most ambitious traffic project in the development of the national capital. It will require seven years to complete, and will cost upwards of $31 million. As it is, in effect, a section of the Trans Canada Highway (No. 17) re-routed through the heart of the national capital, its cost is being shared by the Province of Ontario, the City of Ottawa, the federal Department of Public Works and the National Capital Commission. Construction began in 1958. The first segments to be undertaken were beside Mann Avenue, east of the Rideau River, and between Carling Avenue and the city limits. By 1959 motorists were using the Mann Avenue and Alta Vista traffic interchanges. The first stage to be completed was that lying between Hurdman's Bridge and Green's Creek, linking up this portion of the city traffic with Highway 17 to the East. The next stage links the Kirkwood interchange with the Richmond Road (Highway 15) to the west and is ready for use in the autumn of 1961. Work also began in 1960 on the section between Kirkwood Avenue and Loretta Avenue. The completion of arrangements between the two railways released the right-of-way east of Loretta Avenue in 1960 and will permit the development of the Loretta Avenue to O'Connor Street section to begin in the early future.

In addition to the provision of new interurban arteries, several parkways were begun or extended between 1945 and 1960 which also contributed somewhat to the easier flow of traffic, although commercial vehicles are in general denied the use of such routes. These included extensions to the Rockcliffe Park driveway system, the building of a new Parkway by Fairy Lake in Hull (Promenade du Lac des Fées) the conversion of the old 'Canal Road' from Bronson Avenue to the Falls at Hog's Back into 'Colonel By Drive', and the commencement of a section of the Eastern Parkway system to serve traffic from the National Research Council's laboratories on the Montreal Road and the offices of the Central Mortgage and Housing Corporation. The Eastern and Western Parkways will eventually provide a belt driveway encircling the national capital area on the Ontario side linking up with the Lady Alexander section of Rockcliffe Park Driveway on the east, and Britannia to the west.

NATIONAL CAPITAL COMMISSION

EXPENDITURES FOR DEVELOPMENTS AND IMPROVEMENTS
WITHIN THE NATIONAL CAPITAL REGION

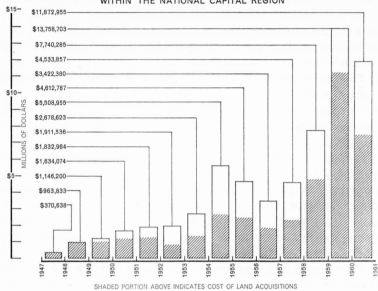

$15—

$11,872,955———
$13,758,703———
$7,740,285———
$4,533,857———
$3,422,380———

$10—

$4,612,787———
$5,508,955———
$2,678,623———
$1,911,536———
$1,832,964———
$1,634,074———

$5—

$1,146,200———
$963,833———
$370,638———

MILLIONS OF DOLLARS

1947 1948 1949 1950 1951 1952 1953 1954 1955 1956 1957 1958 1959 1960 1961

SHADED PORTION ABOVE INDICATES COST OF LAND ACQUISITIONS

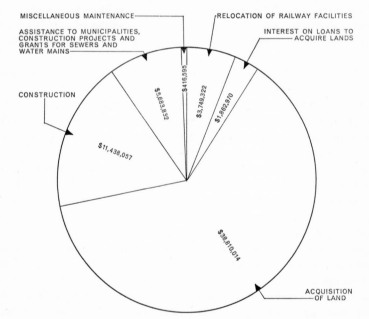

MISCELLANEOUS MAINTENANCE

RELOCATION OF RAILWAY FACILITIES

ASSISTANCE TO MUNICIPALITIES,
CONSTRUCTION PROJECTS AND
GRANTS FOR SEWERS AND
WATER MAINS

INTEREST ON LOANS TO
ACQUIRE LANDS

CONSTRUCTION

$416,595

$5,683,832

$3,749,322

$1,862,970

$11,438,057

$38,810,014

ACQUISITION
OF LAND

CUMULATIVE TOTAL OF EXPENDITURE: $61,960,790

On both sides of the Ottawa River, extensive additions have been made to the Parks of the National Capital area since the end of World War Two. The Gatineau Park and Parkways are of such magnitude and special interest that they are dealt with in a separate section below.

The most impressive addition to the urban park system in the past fifteen years has been Hog's Back Park and adjacent Vincent Massey Park between the Rideau River and the Bowesville Road. The need for this was seen in the late 1940's when Rockcliffe Park became seriously overcrowded. In 1954 development of the Hog's Back area began. A great open space was created, and examples of principle and design provided for other Canadian cities. Three years later a fifty acre park and seventy-five acres of fully-equipped picnic fields were ready for public use, especially for government departments. Proposals for further development in this area include a combination band-shell and open air theatre. These parks have already come to rival Rockcliffe Park in popularity, though the 'atmosphere' of the two areas is quite distinct. Hog's Back Park and Vincent Massey Park offer at close hand views of the tranquil sweep of the Rideau River, a turbulent waterfall over picturesque tilted cliffs in a setting rich in historical lore, going back to the first settlers and the pioneer engineering of Colonel By's day, as well as some beautiful views of the Rideau River valley, the Rideau Canal, the Experimental Farm, Carleton University, the Peace Tower and the Laurentian Hills on the northern horizon.

In the same period development began of a 125 acre park for the Hull area between Leamy Lake and the Gatineau River. By 1960 an access road from Fournier Boulevard had been provided, and two overlooks constructed, with parking facilities nearby. One of these overlooks faces east and gives visitors a close-at-hand view of log-sorting operations on this busy river, and the other faces north and provides a striking view upstream toward the hills out of which the Gatineau River flows. The City of Hull is taking advantage of the natural advantages of the site to develop a bathing beach on Leamy Lake.

From Frederick Todd onward, all architects and town planners have looked with some dismay at the potentially magnificent spot where the Rideau River tumbles over limestone ledges into the Ottawa River, which early in the history of the region was taken over by Thomas MacKay and other industrial pioneers for mill and manufacturing sites. Later on, the Bureau of Statistics and the National Film Board moved into the evacuated mill and factory buildings. The time came at last, in the 1950's, when the ancient and potential grandeur of the region could be fully restored. The old lumber mill buildings on Green Island were removed, as were those of the Film Board on John

Street, as soon as other quarters (in Tunney's Pasture and at Montreal) were available. The old building foundations, roads and walks were removed, and heavy grading, sodding and planting were begun. In conjunction with the complete reconstruction of Sussex Street (into Sussex Drive) the area was transformed almost beyond recognition. Such fine buildings as the French Embassy, the National Research Council's headquarters building, and the modern Ottawa City Hall were given a setting worthy of their aesthetics, and the visitor and citizen once more had close access to the wonder of the twin curtain-like waterfalls which had attracted the admiring attention of Samuel de Champlain in 1613.

To any one devoted to early Canadian history the little park on the river at Val Tetreau is in the nature of sacred ground, for it was here that illustrious explorers and pioneer missionaries and martyrs made their portage around the Little Chaudière Rapids. A monument to Jean de Brébeuf, the Jesuit martyr, was erected there in the 1920's. A motor road led to the monument and around it, but for years there were inadequate facilities for parking or for leisurely exploration of the whole site. The Federal District Commission was able to report in 1958 that the setting of the Brébeuf monument had been completely reconstructed, the circular motor road removed, and replaced by a paved terrace for pedestrian use. The park was then extended by two acres and it now commands a grand view of the Ottawa River east to the Parliament Buildings and west to the Remic Rapids and the Champlain Bridge. A parking area makes it convenient for residents and tourists to visit this memorable historic site.

One of the finest views of Parliament Hill is from across the Ottawa River on the Hull side. All national capital planners of recent years have deplored the encroachments of industrial and commercial properties which for a time curtained off nearly all the fine vistas of Parliament Hill and its environs from the north and northwest. The principal industrial plant directly across from Parliament Hill represents a major capital investment and is not likely to be disturbed in our own day, but east of the Interprovincial Bridge the dreams of the planners have been gradually realized. Industrial properties were acquired, the land cleared and planted to grass and shrubbery, and a historic old stone house was saved for a museum. As a result a fine river park was gradually provided for the City of Hull, from which the impressive skyline from the Prime Minister's residence as far southwest as the Supreme Court can be seen to great advantage. It had the additional benefit of enhancing the beauty and dignity of the view from the northern shore of the Ottawa River as seen from Rockcliffe, Rideau Falls Park, Nepean Point and Parliament Hill. In the early 1950's the E.B. Eddy Company approached the Federal District Commission to discuss improvements which might be made in the appearance of its plant as seen from Parliament Hill. A program of screen-planting the shore line with tall trees was begun, and the company did considerable re-building, re-painting and general tidying of the plant and its environs. The erection of a large "promotion" sign was received with less enthusiasm.

4

The floral displays of the National Capital area were greatly expanded after the Second World War, until by 1957 the Ottawa-Hull region was reputed to offer "the largest public display of flowers in North America." Of course from the beginning of the activities of the Ottawa Improvement Commission (in 1899) there had been numerous floral beds and clusters, but the manner of displaying them, and the choice of floral material took on a radically new and far more striking character in the fifteen years after the Second World War. Early in the century the fashion was to dot Ottawa's parks with many small floral designs in the form of stars, crescents, circles and crowns, and there was extensive use of foliage plants. The earliest driveways were narrow and more suitable for horse drawn vehicles than for motor traffic and the flower beds were such as to merit close and studied attention. The era of the automobile and the greatly enhanced speed of motor traffic along the newly designed driveways called for a more simple and solid treatment. Freely flowering varieties with bright colors were banked in great masses of uniform color which even a passing motorist and his passengers could view and appreciate at a glance.

An incident of the war itself, by a happy accident rather than by design, led toward the mammoth displays of spring bulbs for which the National Capital region has become famous.

In the autumn of 1945, a total of 142,000 tulip bulbs were planted. Of these, 100,000 had been a gift to the City of Ottawa from the people of Holland, in recognition of the part played by Canadian soldiers in freeing Holland from Nazi occupation. In the following year, Her Royal Highness the Princess Juliana of the Netherlands (later Her Majesty Queen Juliana) arranged the first of a series of annual gifts of tulip bulbs (from 15,000 to 20,000) in grateful memory of the birth of a royal princess at the Ottawa Civic Hospital during the Second World War. Her Majesty was particularly anxious that the many kindnesses shown her by the Hospital should be remembered by plantings in and about the grounds.

The number and variety of bulbs planted by the Federal District Commission in its parks and bordering its parkways have grown rapidly. By 1949 the number was 183,000, and a decade later the three spring shows of bulbs exceeded three million blooms. There were no fewer than 200 varieties of tulips, as well as great numbers of daffodils and crocuses. Gifts from other donors, including the Associated Bulb Growers of Holland, the Canadian Girl Guides, and a generous Ottawa seed house swelled the total display. In 1951 an Annual Tulip Festival was inaugurated. In the following year displays of tuberous begonias were increased, until in several years they became one of the most popular features of the parkways. In the hope that the Flowering Crab Apple might in time become associated with spring—as the Japanese cherry is at Washington—in the Canadian capital, hundreds of specially bred hybrids developed at the Central Experimental Farm were set out along the principal routes. In 1958, 15,000 tulip bulbs given to the Commission by the Associated Bulb Growers of Holland were planted in Major's Hill Park, following a ceremony in which Miss Helena Quant, the Dutch Tulip Queen, made the formal presentation. Each spring the Annual Canadian Tulip Festival is formally opened by a distinguished public figure.

5

The parliamentary committee of 1956 regarded as "a project of basic importance" the elimination of the causes of pollution in the Ottawa River. "It seems to your committee that the purpose of the beautification of a capital district would be frustrated if the pollution of this great water resource were allowed to continue unabated," their report asserted. "Raw sewage and industrial wastes are dumped into the stream without control and with alarming results."

So far as the Ottawa side of the river was concerned the remedy lay in the construction of a great interceptor sewer picking up all the wastes hitherto dumped raw into the river, and terminating in a sewage disposal plant downstream. The cost will be upwards of $20 million. Engineering surveys and cost estimates by the city of Ottawa were completed in 1958. The sum of $5 million was allocated by the Federal Government through the National Capital Commission toward these works, in addition to the assistance provided by loans. The prospect as this book goes to press is that the dumping of raw sewage from the city of Ottawa into the Ottawa River will have been terminated by the middle 1960's.

6

The spectacular increase in the numbers of the civil and military service with headquarters at Ottawa not only led during the Second World War to the hurried erection of twelve large temporary buildings and several smaller ones, but also to an unparalleled building program in the first fifteen years after the end of hostilities. Well over $100 million was invested in new permanent structures during that period; and yet nearly all the space in the temporary buildings was still occupied in 1960, waiting for the completion of additional permanent buildings. In 1960, the federal government was also renting in Ottawa and vicinity a total of nearly 2 million square feet in 84 different buildings.

The earliest policy on the grouping of government buildings was to locate them on or near Parliament Hill, for reasons of convenience. A radical change was introduced with many of the buildings erected after 1945. According to the brief of the Federal District Commission presented to the Parliamentary Committee in 1956, "decentralization was recommended as a means of avoiding downtown congestion and of permitting civil servants to live in residential areas near their offices, as well as for obvious civil defence reasons."

There was, in the event, both decentralization and further centralization. On the one hand steps were taken to fill out the western end of Wellington Street by the erection of two very large office buildings for the Departments of Veterans Affairs and Trade and Commerce. A third large structure, the National Library, is planned for this area, and awaits the demolition of Number 1 Temporary Building. Another large structure built not far from Parliament Hill during the period was the Lorne Building on Elgin Street, to house the National Gallery until such time as a permanent Gallery is built.

The decentralizing policy up to 1960 had led to the erection of three somewhat distant groups of government buildings, and had greatly increased the existing accommodation in two others.

About $15 million had been invested in nine new buildings at Tunney's Pasture by the autumn of 1960, with major additions in prospect at an early date, including a "high rise" administration building for the Department of National Health and Welfare, which, when complete, will be the loftiest building in the whole national capital region.

In the Booth Street area, where modest Mines laboratories were originally constructed in the 1920's, a cluster of seventeen buildings had been erected by the end of 1960 at a total cost not far short of $25 million.

The completion of the Dunbar Bridge across the Rideau River in 1955 opened up a convenient new area (Confederation Heights) for government buildings. The first of these to be occupied was the $7½ million dollar Sir Charles Tupper Building, in the summer of 1960. Three large Post Office buildings in the same area were completed during 1961, and other large departmental buildings are planned in the same area.

Extensive building on the land of the Central Experimental Farm was undertaken during the period 1945–60. By the autumn of 1960 an official list of the Department of Public Works showed 71 structures large and small in that area and more were proposed, although there was growing opposition in some quarters to any further encroachment on the Central Farm for such purposes. About $7 million was spent in government buildings on the Farm site in the post-war period to 1961.

Other major additions to government buildings included the purchase of a Seminary Building on Tremblay Road for the R.C.M.P., the building of a Forest Products Laboratory on the Montreal Road, the addition of a number of laboratories to the National Research Council's Montreal Road cluster, the Department of National Defence Hospital on Alta Vista Drive, and the Defence Research Board establishment at Shirley's Bay. The impact of such a mammoth government building program on the economic and physical development of the Ottawa area was stressed in the 1956 parliamentary inquiry. It was, of course, apart from and in addition to the unusually high investment by corporations and individuals. The decentralization of government offices has solved some problems of administration, and has created some new problems of communication and staff morale.

7

A wedge of the Precambrian Shield points its granite finger directly at the heart of the national capital, its finger nail descending to the alluvial Aylmer Plain only three miles away from the Peace Tower. The escarpment of the Lower Laurentian mountains commands a fine view of the Ottawa River and its broad valley, the summits reaching altitudes of 1300 feet in places, thus rising a thousand feet above the farm lands along the base. The Precambrian 'complex', as it exists on the border of the Ottawa–St. Lawrence Lowland, is described by Dr. Alice E. Wilson as consisting of "crystalline limestones, gneisses, and quartzites, intruded, deformed and metamorphosed by bodies of granite, syenite and other igneous rocks." This rich variety of colored rocks and minerals adds to the interest of the geologist and to the pleasure of the spectator. The Precambrian ridges are lightly forested with hardwoods and evergreens, interspersed here and there with small meadows and beaver dams, alluvial valleys and stony pastures. Like all the Canadian Shield it is jewelled with lakes and gay with tumbling cascades. It is of limited economic value, but ideal for the vacationist, the nature-lover, the skier and the bird-watcher. From the earliest days of settlement the people of Ottawa and its environs have found sanctuary there. Though never of much attraction to the farmer, the miner or the wood-cutter, it was in danger of being despoiled of its thin stands of fuel and pulpwood; and all early planners, Frederick Todd in 1903 in particular, urged the preservation of large tracts of woodlands before it was too late.

Three decades after the Todd report, nevertheless, no tracts had been acquired. Only in the 1930's did the government begin to be concerned about the rapid way in which the light cover of forest on the Gatineau Hills was being ruthlessly stripped; and an extensive survey was authorized. The result was "The Lower Gatineau Woodland Report", which spurred immediate action. By the outbreak of hostilities in 1939, a total of 16,000 acres had been purchased, in what was then planned to become eventually a park of about 50,000 acres. The intention was "to preserve the area in its natural state of wooded hills, valleys, lakes and streams as a public park, recreational area and wild life sanctuary." A small staff of rangers and firewardens was engaged to conserve the resources of the area. The war slowed down the program of extending the park area, but by 1947 some 22,000 acres had been acquired, and this total steadily grew,—to 26,000 acres by 1950, and to 50,000 acres by 1955. By this time the revised objective was a total area of 75,000 acres, of which about four-fifths had been secured at the end of 1960. The attractions of the area soon became evident: the estimated attendance in the year 1947 was 200,000, ranking it first of any federal natural park in Canada.

The records of Gatineau Park show a vigorous expansion and steady development of its resources. In 1949, the Federal District Commission acquired substantial holdings on the shores of Lake Lapêche. Ski facilities were developed, many trails, bathing beaches, shelters and camp facilities were gradually added. In 1950, the extensive holdings (about 600 acres) of the late Prime Minister W. L. Mackenzie King, including the residence "Moorside", were turned over to the Commission as trustee for the people of Canada. In the same year, a road was constructed from Dunlop's on the Meach Lake to Camp Fortune, in time for the Dominion Ski Championships of 1951. In the latter year, the Edwards-Herridge property of 4,500 acres surrounding Harrington (Mousseau) Lake was purchased. In 1952, a sub-committee of the Federal District Commission prepared a long-range Master Plan for the development of the area. The essential recommendation was that it should be developed as a 'wilderness Area' with the works of man hidden or subordinated throughout. At this stage the main need was a means of access to the heart of the new parklands, and in 1952 approval was secured for the construction of the Gatineau Parkway. This was to begin at Val Tetreau. The first survey work for the Parkway reached Old Chelsea in 1952, and clearing of trees and underbrushing began in the two mile stretch between Taché Boulevard and the Mountain Road. In order that the best current practices in mountain parkway construction could be incorporated into the Gatineau project, a sub-committee of the Federal District Commission visited the Shenandoah Valley of Virginia and the Great Smoky Mountains of Tennessee.

Another gift of inestimable value to the Park was made by F. E. Bronson, for many years chairman of the Federal District Commission. It consisted of about 330 acres north of Luskville, and among other attractions contained what was described as "a most beautiful stream".

The boundaries of the Park by 1954 embraced four large lakes and about forty smaller ones. Ninety per cent of the total area was forest, mostly decid-uous trees, with maple predominating, but including also stands and scatter-ings of pine, spruce, balsam fir, hemlock, larch and juniper. The wildlife of the park included deer, bear, fox, beaver, mink, and raccoon.

8

Since 1955, rapid progress has been made in building the first links of the Gatineau Parkway, which is planned eventually to give access to the whole area. In 1956 the Fortune Lake section of it was officially opened by the Rt. Hon. Louis S. St. Laurent, then Prime Minister. This connected with the Meach Lake Road, and provided a fine highway to the Champlain Lookout, highest point accessible by road in the Park. On October 2nd, 1959, the Pink's Lake and Kingsmere Sections were officially opened by the Prime Minister, Rt. Hon. John G. Diefenbaker. This new section offered motorists a fourteen mile scenic drive outstandingly beautiful in many respects, including numerous rock-cuts, showing multicolored faces of Precambrian granites.

The Gatineau country has inspired a flow of eloquent and poetic language from many devotees. In the 1956 parliamentary inquiry the brief of the Ottawa Ski Club, presented by Mr. Herbert Marshall, opened in this vein:

"The easy accessibility of this magnificent natural area to Ottawa and Hull is an asset of great value not only to the inhabitants of this region but to visitors from far and near. Its wild, natural beauty, variety of flora and fauna, picturesque lookouts, lakes and streams, mountainous terrain, make it a par-adise for hiker, camper, skier, swimmer and all who love the unspoiled face of nature and respond to the need for the healing quiet and beauty of the Canadian woods. Here at the door of the Capital City can be seen at its best the renewal of spring, the abundance of life in bird, flower, animal and tree in summer, the glory of fall coloring in autumn, the clean whiteness and the invigorating crispness of the winter scene."

Even more rhapsodic was the tribute paid by Mr. R. Percy Sparks, a man whose ancestral roots in the Ottawa area pre-dated the arrival of Colonel By. He was testifying in his capacity as Chairman of the Gatineau Park Advisory Committee:

"The fifty mile parkway which is now being planned may be developed as the most interesting and beautiful fifty mile drive in the whole of Canada. In ten minutes, after leaving the Parliament Buildings, the visitor will cross the Ottawa River close to the exact spot at which Philemon Wright, the first white settler, established his colony in 1801. Here they will plunge into a wilderness of 80,000 acres of wooded mountains, lakes and streams, teeming with wild life, and not much different from what it was when Wright first saw it.

"They will pass through pine woods which will remind the visitor of the early days of Canada when the white pine of the Ottawa Valley laid the foundation of the great lumber industry for which this valley became famous. On the higher slopes the scene will be varied, particularly in the fall, by the foliage of the hardwoods, maple predominating, which clothes the hills now, as then. They will travel through these hills and valleys which form part of the Precambrian Shield, said to be the oldest exposed rocks on the face of the earth.

"The Parkway will take them to many overlooks, providing vast panoramic views of lakes and wooded hills. They will reach the top of an escarpment which falls almost perpendicularly for more than a thousand feet. This escarpment follows the Ottawa River for 15 or 20 miles, and is mentioned by Champlain in the report of his trip up the Ottawa River in 1613.

"Below them they will see another aspect of Canadian life. A magnificent pastoral scene on the flat, of fine agricultural land, between the escarpment and the river, dotted with farm homesteads and surrounded by fields and woodlots.

"On their return to the City, from some of the higher hills, they will see in the distance the smokestacks of the great pulp-and-paper mills, and other industries, in Ottawa, Hull and Gatineau Mills, recalling to their minds Canada's great industrial development.

"This Parkway will make it possible to remind the visitor of Canada's great mining industry. This area has long been noted for the variety and beauty of its minerals and rocks. Samples of more than 20 varieties of minerals have already been collected from the park area. At open cuts along the parkway where any of these minerals occur, signs will be erected telling the story of the particular mineral formation shown, and of the Precambrian Shield generally.

"Throughout the Parkway there will be many points of interest. Although not immediately on it, but accessible by short loop roads, there will be picnic grounds and other places of recreation, houses and other structures showing the life and work of the pioneers, nature trails and nature museums illustrating the natural phenomena of Gatineau Park in its many aspects, handicrafts and folk art and many other points of interest concerning the history, the arts, culture and life in Canada.

"Here, in a two hour drive, the visitor can glimpse, in miniature, the whole Canadian scene."

CHAPTER FOURTEEN

Of Things to Come

It would be pleasant to give this book an unqualified 'happy ending', with a fairy tale prophecy of a dream capital finally realized: a rhapsody or dithyramb of a queen city renowned throughout all the world for its majesty, its haunting beauty of natural setting, and the handiwork of man.

Such a treatment, however, would merely establish the failure of the author to come to grips with sober realities, including the complex problems of urban expansion in the middle decades of the twentieth century.

Greater Ottawa suffers from the travail and growing pains characteristic of all metropolitan areas in North America. "The Exploding Metropolis" creates headaches here as elsewhere.

If one could ignore for a moment the incidental (but of course decisive) fact that Ottawa is the national capital of Canada, its history and problems might be sketched in a few simple paragraphs which would also apply to all other Canadian cities.

Ottawa, like all cities, has been moulded by its physical setting, and its successive stages have been determined by the changing technology and political thinking of the time. It came into being in an age of canals and waterways, at a time when ten miles an hour was about the maximum speed attainable by man, and when the urban interests of most citizens were limited to the distance of an easy walk.

The railway and telegraph era invaded the Ottawa Valley in the 1850's and 1860's, and for half a century the railway dominated the growth and change of the city of Ottawa.

Beginning early in the 20th century the railway age was challenged and in time largely overtaken by the age of the motor vehicle and the highway.

Increasingly after 1930 earlier modes of transport were supplemented by propellor-driven aircraft, and after 1950 by jets.

The hey-day of individualism gave way somewhat grudgingly to new concepts of collectivism and government planning.

Our political and social institutions in general have been much slower in evolving than the technological framework of the society. As one discouraged writer has put it: "The twentieth-century is more than half gone while we still grapple with nineteenth-century problems using a nineteenth-century outlook."

When the first federal government agency was created in 1899 to improve the appearance of the capital, the urban settlements on the Ottawa River were a typical product of nineteenth century Canadian industry and architecture.

The early capital "planners" could dream and hint and gently suggest modest changes in the pattern of growth: they possessed some very limited areas of jurisdiction: they could serve as civic gardeners and tree planters, and lay out attractive drives, and design some desirable parks. But "downtown" Ottawa kept on spreading without much regard for the dreams of the early planners.

To become a capital worthy of Canada's growing stature as a nation, more than palliatives or sylvan fringes were called for. Nothing less than a radical transformation of the civic pattern of Ottawa would do it. This would have needed unchallenged authority and ample funds. Neither of these essentials was available in the earlier period.

In the past fifteen years, as described in some detail in the last two chapters, significant progress has been made.

Moreover, some of the basic requisites for further advances have been secured, — notable achievements considering the conflicts of interests and authorities.

The jurisdiction is still divided, progress still hinges on cooperation, conciliation, compromise, bargaining, financial baits, democratic pressures. It also depends on the willingness of Canadians to provide the necessary funds.

Under these circumstances, swift, dramatic, forthright recreation of the urban heart of Ottawa is idle to look for.

This may frustrate some of the planners and dreamers, but it seems to be the way the Canadian people want it; and a compromise is maintained between swift action and individual freedom. Defenders of the right to make individual choices, sworn enemies of centralized planning and of sweeping authority, may deliberately choose 'freedom in chaos' over arbitrary aesthetics. However, as technology continues to transform the old social environment, the philosophical liberal faces harder choices.

The problem of urban life, in the opinion of a great English liberal weekly, now transcends party politics and traditional ideology. *Laissez-faire* has been buried deep. "No rational man," *The Observer* contended in June, 1960, "would now deny the need for some planning in this country. Not even the most passionate *laissez-faire* liberal, taken to see the South Coast fenced with bungalows or Oxford choked in a river of motor cars or the desolate urban sprawl which devastates the countryside for miles around our great cities, could honestly say: 'Well, it's a pity; but I would rather this happened than that any local, regional or national authority had the power to stop it.'" As the editor went on to remark, if everyone has a car, and no room to drive it, no one can enjoy a car. If everyone has a house in the country, there will be no country.

Canada still has ample space, but what is happening in Britain today is a portent of what will happen in Canada tomorrow, if there is no planning here. For the liberal the problem is no longer how to stop planning, but how to achieve a maximum of individual freedom in a new age of planning.

Some readers may feel that the themes of deadlock and frustration arising out of divided jurisdictions and the inevitable clashes between public and private interests have been overworked in this book. But they are, to my mind, of the very essence of the story; and they are still at the heart of the problem of creating a more magnificent national capital. The technical and financial resources are within reach. The obstacles are, at heart, political and jurisdictional. The problem of authority, of political relations, is not, of course, peculiar to Ottawa. Every expanding metropolis faces it. Stewart Bates, President of Central Mortgage and Housing Corporation, thinks that no issue of the 1960's exceeds this problem in size and complexity. New kinds, perhaps dramatically different new kinds, of administrative forms may be needed. "To serve the present and future city interests," Dr. Bates told a meeting of international mayors in the spring of 1960, "calls for political finesse of the highest order, perhaps even political genius in the evolution of suitable forms of government."

As compared with Mortreal or Toronto, Ottawa's metropolitan problems may seem relatively simple, but there is in the situation here a unique complication, not faced elsewhere in Canada: the dominance of federal interests, the need to make Ottawa a worthy symbol of an emerging nation, the problem of achieving national objectives without bankrupting local ratepayers and paralysing local democracy.

2

Early in 1961, the future program of the National Capital Commission was examined by its administrative staff, and there was general agreement that there were three fundamental aspects or problems. At that date, the following estimates and forecasts seemed realistic:

1. *The future program of the National Capital Commission:* By 1970, the National Capital Commission will have largely completed its contribution to the National Capital Development on the basis of land acquisition and construction of projects beyond the capabilities of the municipalities to do themselves within a reasonable time. The major elements:

   (*a*) *Land acquisition.* This program was pursued vigorously from the beginning and most of the land required for the major elements of the plan was acquired by 1961. This program could be regarded as fairly well completed with the exception of the greenbelt in Quebec.

(b) *Parks and Parkways.* Most of the parks and parkways set forth on the National Capital Plan should be completed within ten years.

(c) *Gatineau Park.* The major developments in Gatineau Park will probably have been completed in the next ten years.

(d) *Railway relocation.* This major program will have been completed by mid-1965, on the Ontario side of the river.

(e) *Roads, bridges and streets.* The Commission's contribution has been the provision of the rights-of-way and a portion of the costs of construction. Most of the land has now been acquired for the major roads, and these include limited access connections to other urban communities. These last connect to the north, east and west and two to the south.

(f) *Greenbelt.* The balance of the Ontario greenbelt land will have been acquired by 1964. Its effect on the downtown area of Ottawa seems to be substantial, as indications grow of an awakening interest by the public and private investors in the heart of the National Capital. The greenbelt represents a conscious and forceful effort to plan the growth of a metropolitan region. The program will not be complete until there is a greenbelt in Quebec, and this project should be started as soon as possible.

(g) *Historical program.* The acquisition and preservation of historic buildings is under way. If the government so decides, it will gain momentum in the next decade, following which this program may sharply taper off.

The progress of the above projects has reached a point where it has become possible for the Commission to concentrate on urban renewal and rehabilitation, especially of the central areas. Also, if the present boundaries of the National Capital Region are maintained as the area of responsibility for the National Capital Commission, the formation of satellite communities must be encouraged, and their growth guided along high standards of development.

The problem of urban redevelopment in the centre of the national capital is bound to assume increasing magnitude and importance in the forthcoming decade. Its solution will obviously require cooperation between all of the interested parties. Most of the property affected is privately owned, and is likely to continue so. Some of it is crown property, and in critical areas it may be necessary for the Crown to extend its present ownership by purchase or expropriation. The corporation and the taxpayers of Ottawa are intimately interested in the core of the capital. The people of Canada, through the federal government, have a large stake in its aesthetic future. The National Capital Commission will be able to make a major contribution by the provision of ideas and technical services. Working as a harmonious team, the several interests can make the sort of transformation necessary if it is to become the beautiful and impressive city the Canadian people are likely to desire.

2. *The boundaries of the National Capital:* These have been greatly extended in recent years. Whether they are now at the optimum limits or whether still further extension will be needed as the population of the national capital region soars, it is difficult to forecast.

The influence of the National Capital planning program over future developments is not uniform throughout the whole area. In respect to crown property and government buildings its advice may be decisive. Within the whole urban core of the national capital region its influence is bound to be considerable, since the requirements of good national capital planning and of good metropolitan development are likely to run in parallel paths. The situation is less satisfactory in the suburban areas, where the local interests of the residents may be diametrically opposed to the pattern the National Capital Commission would like to see adopted.

On request, the National Capital Commission has frequently given advice to suburban communities, but in many instances only that part of the recommendation is followed which agrees with the local view. Such piecemeal acceptance of sound planning advice and methods is frequently worse than if no advice had been tendered.

The public tends to blame the Commission for the bad planning in suburban districts, unaware of the limitations on the Commission's authority. Moreover, the Commission has sometimes been criticised by municipal councils for decisions unpalatable to their ratepayers, when in fact the National Capital Commission had nothing to do with the decision.

3. *The National Capital Commission and local government:* An inconsistency in the present position arises from the fact that while the federal government through the Municipal Grants Act contributes continually increasing sums to the maintenance of services and costs of the municipalities within the area, especially to the corporation of the city of Ottawa, it has no direct voice in municipal policy. By statute the federal government is deprived of any vote in the spending of such funds, its advice is not sought and in general is not wanted in such spending.

There are at least three possible solutions to this anomaly:

(*a*) By the creation of a metropolitan government with a council in both the Ontario and Quebec portions of the National Capital. On these councils the federal government might be given representation equivalent to one-fifth of the council, this being roughly equivalent to the percentage of municipal revenues contributed by the federal government. In a council of say ten members the federal government would be represented by two members. If such a step were taken the Ontario and Quebec members would maintain close liaison informally between themselves, the respective provincial authorities, and the federal government. Such metropolitan governments would have control over and be responsible for the collection of taxes for sewer and water services, education, streets and roads. They would have control over land development, zoning, and the aesthetics of civic design.

(b) By the establishment of one municipal council in Ontario and one in Quebec, between them governing all the area within the outer limits of the greenbelt. This could be accomplished by the cities of Ottawa and Hull annexing up to the outer limits of the greenbelt within their respective provinces. The federal government could be given appropriate representation within the two councils.

(c) The creation of a true *federal* district would now, as always, appear to offer the prospect of the most *efficient* form of government. It may not be a feasible proposal because of political and democratic objections, at any rate in the immediate future.

3

The swift and accelerating nature of the changes in urban growth, and the evolving concept of the role of government, have made it necessary for the National Capital Commission and all other parties interested in the future of Ottawa and region to adopt a fluid and flexible approach to the problem. Time tends to make all plans obsolescent, in detail at least. Planning a 20th century city is a never-ending process. The National Capital Plan laid down basic principles, and much of it has been realized. The Commission has adopted a program of regular review of the basic plan at five year intervals. It is engaged in a continuous analysis of the changing scene.

The Commission expects that the next fifty years will see changes and developments in transport at least as dramatic as the last fifty, during which road and highway traffic have largely replaced the historic nineteenth century railway networks. Moreover, as Ottawa becomes a more mature city, many new activities will be drawn here. Recent events at Washington may give some clue as to the nature of these new activities. There will be the establishment of new national and international bodies. The presence of the research facilities of the federal government and its emanations should continue to attract research plants of large corporations, of which the Northern Electric Research and Development centre in the Greenbelt is a forerunner.

All plans for the future must take into account the forecast by the Royal Commission on Canada's Economic Prospects, that the size of Canadian cities will continue to grow, and that by 1980 as much as 80 per cent of Canada's total population may be living in urban areas. The interdependence of the parts of the city region will also increase, because with modern modes of transportation it has become quite feasible for people to work at distances 20, 40 and even 60 miles away from their homes, commuting daily to their jobs. The aim of a planning agency should be to seek the maximum economic development and with it the enjoyment of civic liberties assured within the framework of an acceptable environment. A measure of control cannot be avoided if these aims are to be realized.

In making plans for the city region of Ottawa-Hull, it is necessary to recognize that the area has many functions which overlap and are both complementary and in conflict. The National Capital is at one and the same time several different entities:

(a) A regional market and distribution centre serving the Ottawa Valley from Pembroke to the St. Lawrence.

(b) A moderately-sized industrial center – pulp and forest products, printing and sundry light industries.

(c) An important center for research and development.

(d) A transit center.

(e) The federal capital of Canada.

This last function has become the most important and significant one. This dominance must be expressed in the shape and impact of the city. Indeed, as is frequently noted, the whole region is frequently now symbolized by one part of one building, the Peace Tower. At the same time, however, it is important to realize that the federal government is a working organization. The government is *part of* the city and will not function either as a business activity or as a symbol of nationhood unless the city itself is healthy. To apply cosmetics to the decayed body of a disorganized city will not achieve the purpose for which the Commission exists.

The principles of land use and orderly urban development which the National Capital Commission keeps in mind are as follows:

Definition of the city and region by preservation of suitable open space and by a greenbelt, so that growth may be accommodated without producing an amorphous and congested mass of inefficient building.

Designation of areas of fairly close-knit and integrated residential development, each of them served by suitable community and social facilities and commercial areas.

Preservation of the vigor and interest of the 'downtown' area and an increase so far as possible in the diversity of entertainment, shopping and commercial enterprise within that area.

Improvement and clarification of the communications system including the removal of railways and their ancillary industries from central areas.

Creation of a number of areas offering a suitable *milieu* for efficient and creative work for the government service.

Raising of the standard of civic design especially in the downtown area. The crux of this work will be the proper development of the Union Station site, the completing of a center for the performing arts and related works.

Provision of open space on an appropriate scale, and by the reservation of suitable land to provide for the future growth of such new activities as may reasonably develop in a great national capital.

Some of the objectives will be difficult to attain so long as many sectors in the National Capital Area are unzoned. Progress in several areas must await the preparation, adoption and execution of adequate municipal plans. It is apparent from the narrative that continuously since 1945 the development of the National Capital has had the benefit of advice from a number of distinguished architects, town planners and landscape architects. For a number of years the Architectural Committee of the Federal District Commission complemented and enriched the services of the permanent staff of the Commission; and the Design Committee of the present National Capital Commission, also consisting of outstanding authorities in these field, has been even more active in seeking to ensure that the architecture and the urban design of the National Capital measure up to the best standards available and practicable. However, this has not meant universal approval of the design of all the new buildings, projects, and basic plans for the region. Indeed, it is to be expected that among the experts and authorities there will always be sharp divergences of opinion. A. S. Mathers, F.R.A.I.C., Toronto, when chairman of the Architectural Committee of the Federal District Commission, recalled (in 1955) that in its earlier days the Committee had been criticized by certain elements in the profession for its approval of certain projects which had not been designed in accordance with the aesthetic theories of those critics. The Architectural Committee, he wrote on that occasion, was well aware of the sharp and sincere differences of opinion on these matters of design. The Committee believed in artistic freedom, he said, and asked only that the architect chosen to design government buildings, whether "a Georgian or a classicist on the one hand or a free wheeling disciple of Le Corbusier on the other" should give his best in his own *métier*. Existing buildings might exercise an influence on buildings erected nearby, but when new areas were allocated for new groups of buildings and when no prior occupancy of the area exerted an influence, "the Committee expects and requires only that the architects involved produce buildings that are aesthetically satisfying and in harmony with each other."

In any event, outside criticism is voiced from time to time. It may take the form of a general indictment from such an authority as Alan Jarvis, former

Director of the National Gallery, who finds many recently constructed federal buildings, both in Ottawa and elsewhere, to be ugly. "At any rate", he summed up in his column in the Ottawa *Journal* on March 12th, 1960, "it cannot be said that we are creating public buildings in Canada which characterize a youthful, robust and prosperous nation. (Correction: most Federal buildings do look expensive)". It may be a challenge of the very basis of the Greenbelt conception as developed by Jacques Gréber, on the ground that his is a European concept, already somewhat outmoded by the new technologies. The criticism may run completely counter to the common opinion, as in an editorial which appeared earlier this year in one of the Ottawa papers, deploring the neo-Gothic architecture of Parliament Hill, and extolling the lofty slabs of glass and steel so popular in office and apartment buildings to day.

The Canadian Architect of Toronto, whose editor is James A. Murray M.R.A.I.C., and whose editorial board includes a staff of professional architects, devoted a large part of its May, 1960 issue to the National Capital Plan. In "A Comment By the Editors", the underlying principles of the Capital Plan were considered. The chief points in this generally favorable analysis may be summarized as follows:

1. The arguments advanced in support of the Greenbelt inspire counterarguments. So far in history limitations upon a city's physical size have proved impossible. The city tends to jump the barrier. In that event a greenbelt tends to become a sort of circular city park, a green ring in the city. Or the circle may be left undeveloped. In either case, the ring requires the extension of transport routes and municipal services to the rest of the city on the other side, which increases the cost of services. A greenbelt of itself cannot control sprawl immediately outside. If satellites are established there, they too must be controlled, since each one will tend to enlarge itself.

2. The Greenbelt concept at best will be only one half of a team unless the "contained city" within it is zoned so as to attain the desirable character. The editors felt that this condition was still a long way from being achieved.

3. Ottawa still lacks the metropolitan population needed to support cultural activities on a scale and of a quality worthy of a great national capital. Under these circumstances, the editors wondered whether the planners should "be satisfied with manipulating the government components symbolically, and leave the culture alone."

4. On the issue of centralization versus decentralization of government buildings, the editors agreed that whichever plan was adopted, there would be critics. Should an attempt have been made to create one large central urban core, impressively and excitingly grouped and defined, flanked by areas of largely residential character; or is it better to aim at a city of many neighborhoods of different social character? The editors, after weighing the gains and

losses of decentralization of government buildings, thought that the decision to create massive groups at a considerable distance from Parliament Hill was a wise one.

5. On the Commission's 'open space' policy, embracing Gatineau Park, the parkways, the waterfront spaces, the Greenbelt and other recreational facilities, the editors of *The Canadian Architect* offered unqualified praise and congratulation.

To provide still another point of view, the author of this book invited Humphrey Carver, well known Canadian authority on housing, and keen student of urban sociology, to elaborate on some frank views he had earlier expressed before an Ottawa chapter of architects.

On the idea of Ottawa as the National Symbol, Mr. Carver felt that we have not yet clarified what it is we wish to symbolize here. It is usually claimed in the tourist literature, he says, that the Peace Tower is the central symbol of Canada, particularly in the War Memorial Chamber. While agreeing with the idea that it was in two world wars that Canada achieved full nationhood, he questioned whether these were the truly nation-making events of Canada's history. Perhaps we should reconsider exactly what it is we are trying to symbolize in the national capital, and in that way we may be able to advance with greater assurance toward a goal.

Humphrey Carver has doubts also about the current policy of decentralizing the government buildings. If we had wanted to make a strong impact in expressing the scale of the capital's function, he suggests, there would have been nothing more effective than a sheer massing of the Government buildings. Size itself, he says, is the most dramatic fact about building in a city. The decision to decentralize may have removed such a possibility. He believes that with modern traffic management it would have been possible to give the centre of Ottawa the kind of dramatic concentration which otherwise only occurs in much larger cities.

Mr. Carver thinks that much more could be made of Ottawa as an international city, as a "gateway to the rest of the world and as a place where people from many different nations meet Canada". As a great world trader, as a 'middle power' often called upon for mediation, we should make more of this aspect. One way of giving physical recognition to it, he suggests, might be some kind of major square at the centre of the city which might be surrounded by the offices and trading posts of other countries — a kind of international bazaar.

Like many other observers, he is depressed by the present appearance of the central business district, and does not feel that attempts to "make some amenities on Sparks Street" by experimenting with a Mall are much more than pathetic nibbling at a problem which calls for drastic reconstruction.

The suburbs of Ottawa he regards as generally deplorable. There has been
no system and no pattern for putting together the essential community features
which have been scattered in the "explosion" of the metropolis, he says. This
is a key problem of all modern cities, but very little has been done about it in
Ottawa. He wonders whether the policy of the federal government in decentralizing its offices has not actually expedited the suburban expansion, giving
it volatility and increasing the problem, but without offering a solution to the
inadequacy of the suburban community.

Humphrey Carver regards the acquisition of the greenbelt as an extraordinary enterprise, but expresses grave doubts about its value. He feels that
since the time when the 'greenbelt' conception was first elaborated by Sir
Ebenezer Howard in 1898 it has been rendered largely obsolete by the
automobile.

Like the editors of *The Canadian Architect*, Humphrey Carver expressed
great admiration for the driveways, parkways and parks of the national capital
region, which he feels have undoubtedly contributed wonderful qualities to
the Ottawa environment.

It is not surprising that such honest differences of opinion on some of the
basic policies in the planning of the national capital should have emerged. It
is a healthy and constructive thing that they should continue to be expressed.
Very few major issues find unanimity anywhere. The choices of architectural
styles and city patterns may not even lend themselves to rational debate,
because they rest to some extent on individual taste and intuition rather than
on objective criteria. Decisions must often be made in the knowledge that
much can be said on both sides. Public debate in advance is useful and so is
the frank searching comment of specialists in the several fields.

5

In a time of swift change all estimates of the future are likely to be soon
outdated or outmoded. But the plans actually on the drawing board and the
statistics of growth make it safe to venture a few broad predictions about the
national capital region. The curve of rising population has been exceeding all
earlier expectations, but the sharp definition of the greenbelt may tend to
stabilize the population within the ring at a figure approaching 600,000. The
city of Ottawa itself is currently growing at the rate of about 10,000 persons a
year. This by the centenary of Confederation would give it a population of
330,000; and a similar rate of growth in the whole capital region on both
sides of the river would give greater Ottawa-Hull a population not far short
of half a million by that time.

The main physical changes of the next decade are already adumbrated in
the plans and principles outlined above. The business heart of Ottawa will be

gradually transformed by the erection of what are now called 'high rise' buildings. The removal of the Union Station to the Hurdman's Bridge location will set the stage for a dramatic new urban centre within the large cleared area thus created. The 'temporary' buildings of the Second World War will revert to open spaces, or will provide sites for such government structures as the permanent Art Gallery and the National Library. The cluster of government buildings on what was called Rideau Heights — and was re-named Confederation Heights — will be greatly enhanced by several large and lofty departmental structures. The Tunney's Pasture site will soon be fully occupied, stopping short only at any encroachment on river parkland. The Canadian Broadcasting Corporation's headquarters building will be realized, presumably on a site south of the Rideau River. The 'Pentagon' problem, a massive headquarters for National Defence activities, will be settled. A series of new bridges, over the Ottawa, over the Rideau, over the Canal, are already in the plans and will be imperative soon. The Queensway and its feeders and approaches will be in operation well before the anniversary of Confederation. The West Block will be completely reconstructed without impairing its original charm. The old site of Richmond Landing will have been recreated as a park of great historic interest. A new War Memorial may rise on Nepean Point. Sussex Drive will be further developed into the impressive boulevard which Frederick Todd once envisaged, a scenic and historic route of endless appeal and peerless setting.

Physical changes of this sort can be confidently expected. The nature of the transformations in the social and cultural composition of the national capital cannot be so easily predicted. Technology is still thrusting revolution upon the social life of the Canadian people. The next stage may be a great advance in the 'hovering' type of aircraft, such as the helicopter. That would make the 'air age' more pervasive than ever, solving the problem of short haul and the exasperating time delays between the heart of any metropolis and its distant airport. If not, then other types of extremely rapid interurban transit may come to the rescue of the commuter. Traffic congestion and the parking problem seem likely to tax the ingenuity of engineers for a long while.

A continuation of present trends will certainly emphasize the international flavour of Canada's capital. As world interdependence grows, more and more of the world will come to be reflected and represented in the great world capitals. The number of national organizations will continue to soar. There is little sign that the role of government in Canadian affairs will decline. The reverse is indicated. The Department of Public Works can never pause in its plans for future accommodation. It has to run fast even to stand still. The educational apparatus of the national capital will perforce respond vigorously to greater challenges. More and more, Ottawa will become the repository of indispensible resources for research and development.

6

In the sixteen years since the end of the Second World War exciting strides have been taken toward a beautiful and impressive national capital. The reasons for the progress can be easily enumerated, and they indicate what is needed for further advances. The ingredients of success in this project may be cited as intelligent planning, the cooperation of the affected parties, the support of the Canadian people, and the leadership of the interested governments. So far as the federal government is concerned, the interest taken by the Rt. Hon. W. L. Mackenzie King and his colleagues has already been reported in some detail. The government of Rt. Hon. L. S. St. Laurent carried on the Mackenzie King tradition. The present prime minister, the Rt. Hon. John G. Diefenbaker, and his cabinet, have manifested their interest and concern about the beautification of the national capital in a number of practical and concrete ways. It was under the leadership of Mr. Diefenbaker that the government decided to act swiftly and decisively to acquire the Greenbelt lands; and to make a major 'breakthrough' in the railway relocation program by the decision to move the Union Station. The very substantial sums made available to the National Capital Commission in grants and loans over the past three years constitute further dramatic evidence of the determination and sincerity of the present government. This national project, indeed, enjoys the support of all political parties. This in turn reflects a general willingness on the part of the Canadian people to bring into being a national capital of enduring beauty and grace.

7

All capital cities come to be eloquent of the land and the people they serve, even when they grow up Topsy-like, without conscious plan. What we are witnessing at Ottawa is progress toward the attainment of a master design. In this respect it is unique in Canadian city-building. The task is a challenge of great magnitude and demands the finest resources of knowledge, imagination and taste that the country can provide. It requires an intimate knowledge of Canada and its history. To plan a symbolic capital for "The *Unknown Country*" would be a frustrating exercise. If Ottawa is to be a true and vital symbol of Canada and its people, no pains can be spared in searching out and symbolizing the essential spirit of the land, from sea to sea, and from Pelee Island to Arctic Cape Columbia. In the past half century the revolution in communications and in transportation have made it possible for a transcontinental society to knit together into an effective federal nation. Revolutionary forces know no political boundaries, and are at the same time busy building a world society. No generation in history ever faced more profound and testing forces than the Canadians of today. The capital of Canada must sensitively reflect and symbolize the surging spirit of its people. But it must also increasingly take note of "the endless pageantry of the world". The years since the end of the Second World War have seen vast changes in Canada and in the Canadian capital, but unless all the signs fail we are only on the threshold of a still more exciting age.

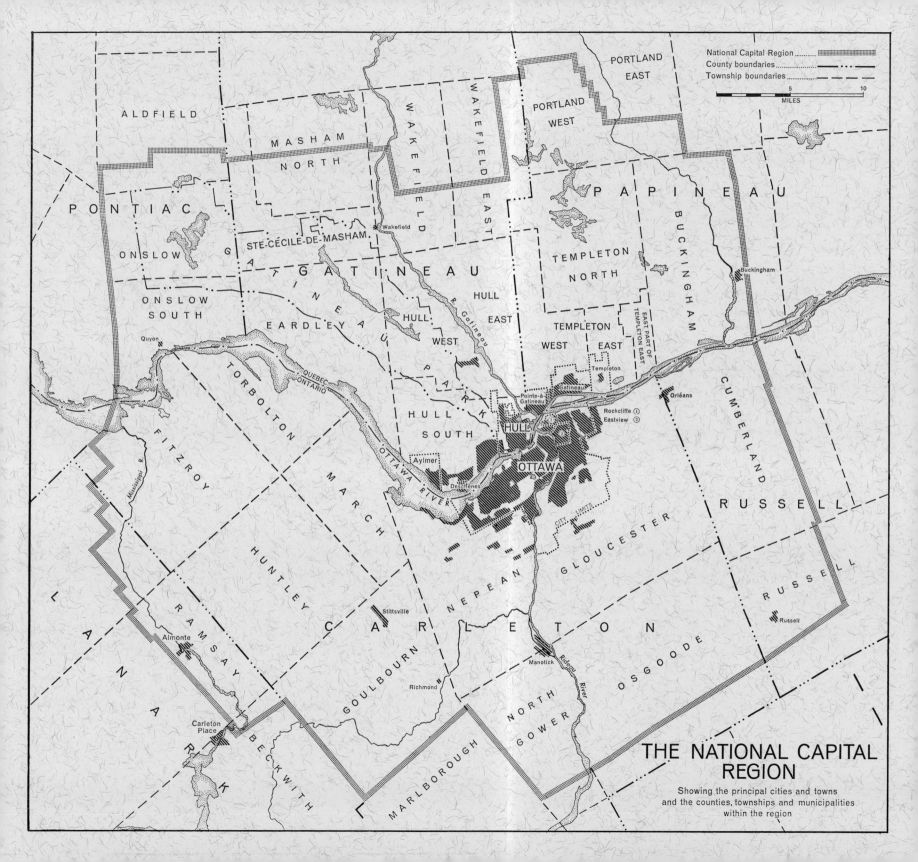

THE NATIONAL CAPITAL
REGION

Showing the principal cities and towns
and the counties, townships and municipalities
within the region

DUCK ISLAND

QUEBEC
ONTARIO

HIGHWAY NO.17

HULL

SUSSEX ST. SPUR

INTERPROVINCIAL
BRIDGE

UNION
STATION

NICHOLAS ST
YARDS

HURDMAN'S
BRIDGE

C.P.R.

BROAD ST
YARDS

PRETORIA
BRIDGE

ROUNDHOUSE

Nepean Bay

ROUNDHOUSE

HIGHWAY NO.8

O·T·T·A·W·A · R·I·V·E·R

C.P.R.

C.N.R.

O T T A W A

C.N.R.

C.P.R.

RIDEAU R.

WALKLEY ROAD
FREIGHT YARDS

RENFREW SUBDIVISION

HIGHWAY NO.17

TO SOUTH MARCH

HIGHWAY NO.15

HIGHWAY NO.31

OTTAWA-PRESCOTT LINE C.P.R.

RAILROADS—1961

Railroads removed since 1945 ....
New construction ....

C.N.R. BEACHBURG SUBDIVISION

Bells
Corners

ULTIMATE
RAILROAD REVISIONS

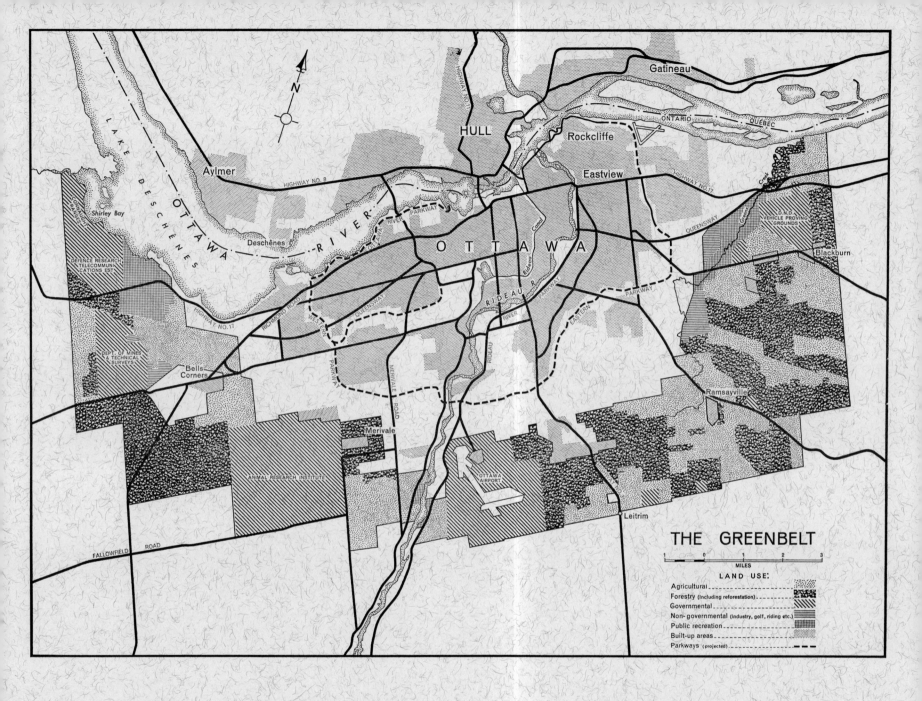

THE GREENBELT

MILES
1 0 1 2 3

LAND USE:

Agricultural ....
Forestry (Including reforestation) ....
Governmental ....
Non-governmental (industry, golf, riding etc.) .
Public recreation ....
Built-up areas ....
Parkways (projected) ....

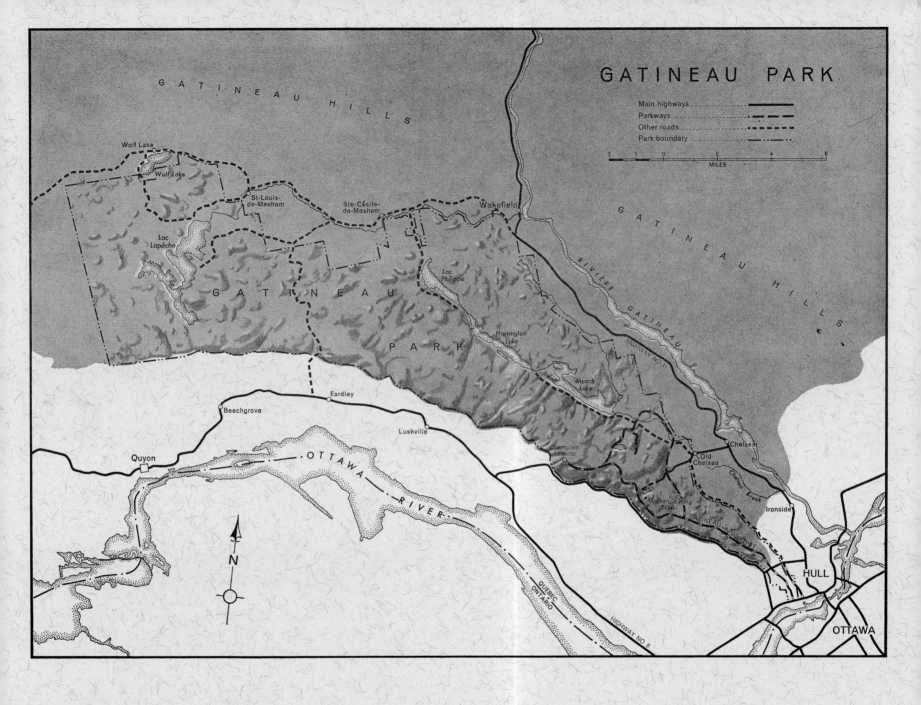

GATINEAU PARK

Main highways	———————
Parkways	—— —— ——
Other roads	‑‑‑‑‑‑‑‑
Park boundary	—·—·—·—

2 1 0   2   4   6
MILES

GATINEAU HILLS

GATINEAU HILLS

Wolf Lake
Wolf Lake
St-Louis-de-Masham
Ste-Cécile-de-Masham
Wakefield
Lac Lapêche
Lac Philippe
GATINEAU
Harrington Lake
PARK
Meach Lake
RIVIÈRE GATINEAU
HIGHWAY NO. 11
Eardley
Beechgrove
Luskville
Champlain Lookout
Old Chelsea
Chelsea
Chelsea Brook
Quyon
OTTAWA — RIVER
Mackenzie King Estate
Ironside
GATINEAU PARKWAY
QUEBEC
ONTARIO
N
HULL
HIGHWAY NO. 8
OTTAWA

Frederick G. Todd *"You may ask, Is it
reasonable to look so far ahead as one hundred years or
more, and to make plans for generations in the distant
future? We have only to study the history of the older
cities, and note at what enormous cost they have overcome the lack of provision for their growth, to realize
that the future prosperity and beauty of the city depends
in a great measure upon the ability to look ahead, and
the power to grasp the needs and requirements of the
great population it is destined to have."*

—from the Todd Report of 1903

Acknowledgements

I am conscious of my indebtedness to many persons, living and dead, in the preparation of this history. I learned a great deal from the writings of the late Dr. Arthur Beauchesne, from the works of Dr. Lucien Brault, Blodwen Davies, Sir James D. Edgar, J. L. Gourlay, Anson A. Gard, J. H. Gray, the Hon. Andrew Haydon, H. P. Hill, J. E. Hodgetts, Hon. Francis Robert Latchford, Robert Legget, A. R. M. Lower, Francis Parkman, A. H. D. Ross, Harry J. Walker, Dr. Charlotte Whitton and Dr. Alice E. Wilson. I read with interest what Fred Cook and Carleton J. Ketchum have written about federal districts. I am grateful for the invaluable assistance of staff members of the National Capital Commission, in particular, of Peter H. Aykroyd, Douglas McDonald and Alan Tate. My conversations with Jacques Gréber, with Haldane Cram, (a former secretary of the Federal District Commission), Alan H. Armstrong, Humphrey Carver and Dr. R. H. Hubbard yielded some fresh insights and much acceptable material. Dr. Lucien Brault, author of *Ottawa Old and New*, has kindly read and corrected the chapters on early Ottawa history, with which he is so thoroughly familiar. I wish to thank Miss Hilda Gifford, Librarian of Carleton University, Miss M. J. Creighton, Librarian of the Department of Public Works, and T. E. Monette of the Parliamentary Library for their unfailing courtesy and patience in unearthing useful sources. For research assistance I am indebted to Joseph Scanlon, Miss Norah Story and Miss Viviane Matte. To my colleague Dr. James A. Gibson I am especially grateful for the light he was able to throw on the choice of Ottawa as the capital of Canada. Dr. Arthur Bourinot kindly gave me permission to quote from the Duncan Campbell Scott correspondence. I thank Dr. James Wreford Watson, Rt. Hon. Malcolm MacDonald, J. M. S. Careless and Bruce Hutchison for the quotations from their published works. Walter B. Herbert, Director of The Canada Foundation, shared, as always, his rich resources of printed material and of creative ideas. My wife, Magdelana, greatly lightened the task of preparing the manuscript for the printers. If there are other substantial contributors whom I have failed to mention, I extend my thanks and apologies here.

Before closing a note of acknowledgements I should voice a conviction that grew on me as I wrote this book: that all the great works of man owe an inextinguishable debt to the unrecognized and unrenowned army of obscure workers who make them possible. It is in the nature of things that while thousands build, one or two men or women are prominent at the unveiling or the ribbon-cutting ceremony. All through the history of Ottawa and the building of the national capital, there have been these unsung heroes and builders, without whom nothing much could have been accomplished. If dedications were in fashion, I would have dedicated this book to the obscure army of men and women who have created the living capital of today. I wish it had been possible to make more careful citation of numerous personal links as the chronicle unfolded, but many vital contributions were not generally known, even at the time, and are now irrevocably forgotten. In an account of the growth of the federal capital, it would be anomalous not even to list the names of the chairmen of the Ottawa Improvement Commission, and its successors, and I list them here:

Sir Henry N. Bate	1899-1917
Sir Henry K. Egan	1917-1920
J. B. Fraser	1920-1926
Hon. Thomas Ahearn	1927-1932
W. E. Matthews	1932-1936
Frederick E. Bronson	1936-1951
Duncan K. MacTavish	1951-1952
Major General Howard Kennedy	1952-1960
Alan K. Hay	1960-1961
Lieut. Gen. S. F. Clark	1961-

Mr. Hay, who was chairman of the National Capital Commission during the period when this history was being written, began service with the Federal District Commission in 1927, and has occupied the posts of Superintendent, Consulting Engineer, Director of Planning, Chief Engineer and General Manager. He is the first Chairman of the Commission to come out of the executive staff. This project certainly opened my own eyes to the faithful service of such officials and their colleagues, and I hope it does as much for many readers, in Canada and elsewhere.

WILFRID EGGLESTON

Ottawa, May 1961

Index

Design
and production
of this book were under
the supervision of Paul Arthur.
Jacket by Allan R. Fleming. The detail
from the portrait of Queen Victoria by Winter-
halter shown on the front end paper is reproduced by
gracious permission of Her Majesty the Queen. The book has
been printed at the National Printing Bureau, Hull, P.Q. Photographs by
the following appear: Cliff Buckman, Capital Press, Dominion Wide, Ted Grant,
Jones and Morris, Eamon Kennedy, Malak, Newton, Alexander Onoszko, Photo Fea-
tures, Rapid Grip & Batten. Maps by C. C. J. Bond, NCC Historian

SIR HERBERT HOLT